GREAT AMERICAN
SHIPS

CAR FERRY "CHIEF WAWATAM" CROSSING THE STRAITS OF MACKINAW IN WINTER

STEAMER ALGOMAH

DOCK SCENE, MACKINAC ISLAND, MICH.

A NATIONAL TRUST GUIDE

GREAT AMERICAN SHIPS

JAMES P. DELGADO
and J. CANDACE CLIFFORD

Foreword by Sen. Edward M. Kennedy

GREAT AMERICAN PLACES SERIES

John Wiley & Sons, Inc.
New York Chichester Brisbane Toronto Si

Printed in the United States of America
5   4   3   2

Library of Congress Cataloging in Publication Data

Delgado, James P.
   A national trust guide : great American ships / James P. Delgado, J. Candace Clifford ; foreword by Edward M. Kennedy.
   p.   cm. — (Great American places series)
   Includes bibliographical references and index.
   ISBN 0-471-14384-7
   1. Historic ships—United States—Guidebooks. 2. United States—Description and travel—1981-   —Guidebooks. I. Clifford, J. Candace. II. Title. III. Series.
   VM23.D45 1991
   387.2'0973—dc20   91-16933

Great American Ships has been designed and composed in Minion by Grafik Communications, Ltd., Alexandria, Virginia, based on the original design by Meadows & Wiser, Washington, D.C.

Front cover: A fishing schooner, often called a Gloucesterman, entering port in Gloucester, Massachusetts.

Back cover: Two square riggers and a steamer in San Francisco Bay, California, "when the golden gate is golden," according to the postcard. (Both, Curt Teich Postcard Archives, Lake County Museum)

■ ■ ■ ■ ■ ■ ■ ■ ■ ■ ■ ■ ■ ■ ■ ■ ■

CONTENTS

■ ■ ■ ■ ■ ■ ■   THE SHIPS   ■ ■ ■ ■ ■ ■ ■

Steamer "Thousand Islander" at Dock, Ogdensburg, N. Y.

THE MAIN DINING ROOM OF THE GREAT SHIP SEEANDBEE, C. & B. LINE, CLEVELAND, OHIO.

T WHARF, BOSTON, MASS.

■ ■ ■ ■ ■ ■ ■ ■ ■ ■ ■ ■ ■ ■ ■ ■ ■ ■

FOREWORD

I have always loved the lines from John Masefield—

> *I must go down to the seas again, to the lonely sea*
> *and the sky,*
> *And all I ask is a tall ship and a star to steer her by...*

An inescapable fact of American history, apparent even to the most casual student, is the indispensable role of ships and the sea in the development of our country. The geographical area that is now the United States was discovered, explored, and settled largely by those who came by sea. Vast quantities of our exports and imports have passed through the nation's seaports in ships of every description. So, too, have most of our ancestors, whether they originally came as immigrants seeking freedom and opportunity or as slaves in chains.

From the beginning, large numbers of our people have sought their livelihoods through fishing, and in many respects that tradition is as important today as it was when the *Mayflower* landed at Plymouth three and a half centuries ago. In every region, the rivers, lakes, canals, and coastal waterways that still serve as vital links in America's modern commerce were the principal avenues of transportation until the coming of the railroad, automobile, truck, and airplane. From the great clipper ships of the past century to the most modern vessels of the present, America's rise to international eminence and world leadership has been based in large part on our ability to project our commercial and naval power to the farthest corners and waters of the globe.

You do not need to have been raised on the seacoast to live and breathe the influence of our maritime heritage, but it helps. The sea is our very essence. As President Kennedy once said,

> *We all come from the sea. All of us have in our*
> *veins the exact percentage of salt in our blood that*
> *exists in the ocean, and, therefore, we have salt in*
> *our blood, in our sweat, in our tears. We are tied to*
> *the ocean. And when we go back to the sea—*
> *whether it is to sail or to watch—we are going back*
> *from whence we came.*

Evidence of our rich maritime past is all around us. We see it in the historic lighthouses by the hundreds that stand beside our rivers, lakes, and shores. We see it in the docks, warehouses, and other maritime structures, too many of which now lie in disarray or abandoned along backwaters that once were thriving waterfronts. We hear it in our language, in nautical expressions that have found their way into general discourse, such as "underway" or "learning the ropes." We see it in the traditions and folkways of those who continue to find employment and recreation on the water. It is vividly preserved in scores of maritime museums. But nowhere is the richness of our maritime heritage more dramatically evident than in the historic ships that are being preserved in every region of the country.

The USS *Joseph P. Kennedy Jr.* on the "launching ways" at the Fore River Shipyard, Bethlehem Steel Company, Quincy, Massachusetts, in 1945.

Caring for these cherished symbols of our history has become the concern of growing numbers of Americans in recent years, but its roots are old. One of the first vessels to be preserved was the famous and beloved frigate USS *Constitution*—"Old Ironsides." After its celebrated exploits against the Barbary pirates and its dramatic victory over the *Guerriere* in the War of 1812, Old Ironsides was almost condemned as unseaworthy in the 1830s, until a poem by Oliver Wendell Holmes aroused a national outcry and convinced the U.S. Navy to rebuild the ship and restore her to service. In a similar public campaign in the 1920s, school children raised funds to preserve her as a memorial, and she still rides majestically today at Charlestown in Boston Harbor, the oldest U.S. warship still in active service.

In this century, maritime museums such as Mystic Seaport in Connecticut, San Francisco Maritime National Historical Park, and South Street Seaport in New York City are preserving historic ships as part of their collections. Outside museum settings, other aging ships see modern service as passenger vessels, such as the breathtaking windjammer fleet on the coast of Maine or the magnificent paddlewheel steamboats, the *Delta Queen* and the *Belle of Louisville*, that still ply the Mississippi and Ohio rivers. Impressive old ships have been refurbished to train citizens in sailing or as part of other educational ventures. Still other famous vessels have been adapted as restaurants, shops, theaters, or hotels.

A vigorous federal role in historic preservation is more recent vintage. In the 1970s the National Trust for Historic Preservation established a task force that launched a national debate on issues involved in maritime preservation. In 1985 the National Park Service was directed by Congress to conduct a survey of maritime resources and develop standards and priorities for their preservation. The National Maritime Initiative was established, and the resulting inventory of preserved vessels has become the most comprehensive list of historic ships in this country.

The ships in this volume, all included in the inventory, constitute a cross section of our nation's maritime heritage, from the Revolutionary War to the nuclear age. I hope that Americans and citizens from other lands who read this book will be inspired to visit the vessels, learn about the breadth and significance of these symbols of our maritime history, and support their continued preservation for future generations.

Sen. Edward M. Kennedy

PREFACE

O nly a handful of ships remains from the period 1700 to 1900. Those two centuries were some of the greatest and most active years of maritime endeavor on this continent. Vessels crossing the Atlantic, journeying to the far Pacific to China and Oceania's many islands, trading and working in the Caribbean, crossing the five Great Lakes, and navigating the inland waterways and rivers of America made fundamental contributions to the settlement, exploration, trade and commerce, national defense, and the development of this nation.

In the 1830s American ships brought hides and tallow from California ranches to bolster the fortunes of Massachusetts's leather industry. Chinese tea, porcelain, furniture, and silks vied with whale oil, baleen, and bone as vital commodities of American maritime trade, while lumber, coal, ice, produce, and livestock were carried along the coasts and abroad, as well as from foreign ports to the United States. Canal boats linked isolated regions, bypassing unnavigable stretches of rivers to connect lakes, towns, and cities. Steamboats carried people and goods to the frontier, and sailing packets and steamships ferried the masses of people who became the founders and citizens of the United States.

Throughout history, however, ships have been more than objects of pragmatic concern. The sea and the ships that have crossed it have been the subject of passionate cultural interest that has been expressed in art, music, literature, and folklore. In the United States many great authors and poets have been inspired by maritime subjects, creating evocative stories of seafaring or, in the case of Samuel Langhorne Clemens, tales of navigating the great rivers. More than one American classic has been a nautical tale; *Billy Budd, Moby Dick, Two Years*

Few ship types survive to represent maritime history of the 18th and 19th centuries. One of the oldest, the 1797 frigate USF *Constellation*, is depicted in this 1880 engraving.

Major themes in American art, music, literature, and folklore have revolved around the sea, the ships that crossed it, and the drama of human affairs played before and around it. The U.S. brig *Somers*, here shown sinking off Veracruz in 1846, was the scene for a supression of mutiny, an event that inspired Herman Melville to write *Billy Budd.*

Before the Mast, Captains Courageous, and *The Sea Wolf* are but a few. The more modern medium of entertainment, film, also has captured and incorporated maritime themes.

In the United States are several hundred museums or historical sites that preserve and interpret the country's maritime past. Of these fewer than a hundred are large, primarily nautically oriented maritime museums. In their collections are displayed paintings, models, figureheads, engines, relics of lost ships, and in a few instances sections or major parts of historic vessels. A handful of maritime museums goes further, exhibiting floating or dry-berthed (that is, displayed on land) historic vessels. In other instances the ship is the museum or houses the museum, displaying models, artifacts, and paintings in the hold. Some historic ship museums consist of small fleets of historic ships; New York's South Street Seaport, Mystic Seaport in Connecticut, San Francisco Maritime National Historical Park in California, Charleston's Patriots Point in South Carolina, and Seattle's Northwest Seaport boast collections of several vessels. The vast majority of historic ships, however, are preserved and displayed singly by community organizations, private owners, veterans' groups, nonprofit societies, or local, county, or state park and recreation agencies. Some of these vessels are preserved as the setting for businesses, mostly restaurants but occasionally a shop, hotel, or office.

Currently fewer than 250 historic vessels in the United States are maintained in a manner that preserves their historic character and are open or accessible to the public. These few, fragile ships are all that remain of thousands built and worked. They are the largest of maritime artifacts and arguably the most important, for the ship was the basis of and the expression of maritime endeavor. Lighthouses were built to guide them; life-saving stations to rescue their crews; ports, harbors, docks, warehouses, and shipyards to service them and the cargoes they carried; and boarding houses and hiring halls to serve their crews. The past cannot be fully comprehended without a scale of reference, whether provided by a building, the undeveloped expanse of a battlefield, or the vast expanse of ruins that one finds at Mesa Verde. Similarly, the maritime past cannot be understood without reference to the ultimate artifact, the ship. No photograph, painting, model, architectural rendering, film, or description, no matter how vivid, can fully capture the sense of America's maritime heritage that comes from being aboard a ship.

During the past five years the authors have had the fortune to visit nearly every preserved historic vessel in the United States for detailed discussions with directors, curators, and staff members entrusted with the physical work of maintenance, preservation, and restoration. We have toured engine rooms, voids, and compartments, gone aloft, and on occasion sailed, steamed, and motored on the ships. These trips have provided a detailed understanding of each of them, an understanding that has been augmented by voluminous files of plans, specifications, enrollments, marine surveys, and other documents as well the thousands of photographs that we and others have taken.

The USS *Torsk* is part of the fleet of vessels at the Baltimore Maritime Museum.

A few historic ship museums in the United States host small fleets of historic vessels. New York's South Street Seaport Museum is the home port of eight vessels.

The tremendous burst of energy that the National Maritime Initiative directed toward the nation's large preserved historic vessels was the result of a 1984 congressional request that the U.S. Department of the Interior's National Park Service assess the nation's surviving maritime cultural resources—namely, its historic ships. The federal agency was to take three distinct approaches in its task—to create an inventory of the resources and to evaluate the roles of the National Register of Historic Places, a national roster of significant cultural resources, and the National Historic Landmarks program. The Park Service's initiative accomplished these goals. Also, in 1989 the Secretary of the Interior's Standards for Historic Vessel Preservation Projects, with Guidelines for Applying the Standards, were issued. The completed inventory has two parts—an "active" section, listing preserved ships, and an "archive" section, including historic vessels not currently the subject of a preservation effort—and includes more than 330 vessels. National Register listings for ships have increased, in part because of the publication of a document to assist in their nomination, "National Register Bulletin No. 20." The greatest satisfaction, however, has come from the evaluation of 145 historic ships as National Historic Landmarks (NHLs). In 1984 the number of NHL vessels stood at 30; now there are 89 NHL ships, with another 11 pending immediate review and 32 evaluated and ready for review for possible designation. Only 13 of the ships evaluated have not been designated. Until now National Historic Landmarks, representing the most significant of America's cultural properties, did not adequately represent the richness and variety of American ships and their activities.

The inventory of large preserved historic vessels along with the vital statistics for each ship—length, beam (width), tonnage (a measurement of a ship's volume rather than weight), engine types, construction materials, builder, and so forth—was published in a limited edition of 1,000 copies in early 1991. While it provides a comprehensive overview of the nation's fleet of historic ships, it does not provide a narrative text discussing their various careers, historic and architectural contexts, and fascinating tales or note how one could visit them. Therefore, the opportunity to take the materials assembled by the National Maritime Initiative and write such a compendium under the aegis of the National Trust's Great American Places Series was eagerly seized. We are particularly pleased that the royalties from the sale of this book are being directed by the National Trust, at our request, to the National Maritime Alliance, a coalition of the nation's diverse maritime preservation groups and organizations, which will use the money to further the cause of historic ship preservation.

James P. Delgado
J. Candace Clifford

■ ■ ■ ■ ■ ■ ■ ■ ■ ■ ■ ■ ■ ■ ■ ■ ■ ■ ■

ACKNOWLEDGMENTS

Foremost in our gratitude are the various vessel owners, operators, managers, curators, and historians who have over the past five years graciously provided information and photographs of their ships. The idea of a book on great American ships was first proposed by Lynn Hickerson, then with the maritime preservation office of the National Trust for Historic Preservation. Lynn's hard work and perseverance in the cause of maritime preservation cannot be emphasized enough and is gratefully acknowledged.

We wish to thank the following individuals: Richard C. Anderson, Marianne Babal, Edwin C. Bearss, Don Birkholz, Ken Black, Norman Brouwer, Robert Browning, Harry Butowsky, John Byrne, Gordon S. Chappell, Jim Cheevers, Linda Cullen, Lynn Cullivan, Nicholas Dean, Paul Ditzel, Willard Flint, Dale Floyd, Kevin Foster, David Glick, Alvin H. Grobmeier, Chuck Haberlein, Stephen A. Haller, Michael Harrington, Bill Herd, Robbyn Jackson, Karl Kortum, Robie Lang, Ben Levy, Daniel Martinez, George Mendez, Ted Miles, Kirk Mohney, Marcia Myers, Peter Neill, Dave Nettell, Mark Newton, Martin Reuss, John Reilly, Walter Rybka, Robert Scheina, Peter Stanford, the late Peter Throckmorton, and Glennie M. Wall.

We acknowledge the assistance of the following institutions and organizations: USS Arizona Memorial, Naval Historical Center, National Archives, Library of Congress, J. Porter Shaw Library of San Francisco Maritime National Historical Park, U.S. Naval Institute, The Mariners' Museum, Mystic Seaport Museum, South Street Seaport, Council of American Maritime Museums, National Maritime Historical Society, Office of the Historian of the U.S. Army Corps of Engineers, Office of the Historian of the U.S. Coast Guard, Historic Naval Ships Association of North America, Association for Great Lakes Research, National Conference of State Historic Preservation Officers, Historic American Buildings Survey and Historic American Engineering Record of the National Park Service, Steamship Historical Society, Branch of Underwater Archaeology of the North Carolina Division of Archives and History, and the state historic preservation office for the state of Maine.

The support and interest of the National Trust for Historic Preservation's Preservation Press has been much appreciated, with special thanks to Diane Maddex, former director, and Buckley Jeppson and Janet Walker. Gretchen Smith provided editorial support. Michael Naab of the National Trust's maritime office gave important technical guidance throughout the project.

A MARITIME AMERICA

From the earliest times humans have crossed the water with the assistance of floating conveyances. Logs, gourds, and inflated hides in time gave way to rafts of logs lashed together and hollowed-out canoes. From these simplest of watercraft a tremendous range of vessel types developed through the millennia. Early planked craft, essentially extensions of simple log canoes with one or more planks, eventually became wood shells that were fitted and braced with wood frames. The development of the ship in Europe and later the United States grew out of the tradition of building ships with planks over frames. In this fashion a wood skeleton is built, over which the hull planks are fastened. By the time the first European settlers reached the United States, the ship had essentially reached its basic form.

Construction of wood ships persisted in the United States through the early decades of the 20th century, and this tradition still has not completely died out. Indeed, American shipbuilders continued to launch large wood sailing ships, known as "downeasters" because they were built in Maine, well after British firms had switched to steel and iron sailing

Work bench at Lowell's Boat Shop, Amesbury, Massachusetts, which has been making dories since 1793. The tradition of building wood ships has persisted in the United States through the early decades of the 20th century and even today.

ships. The large steel-hulled, square-rigged ships preserved and displayed in the United States today are for the most part products of British and German shipyards. In the United States iron and steel shipbuilding principally focused on steam and motor vessels, although wood steamships were built in the last quarter of the 19th and early years of the 20th century.

Throughout American history hundreds of thousands of ships were built, many of specific types or classes that no longer exist except perhaps as wrecks resting on the bottom of U.S. rivers, lakes, and coasts. Although modern replicas of some of these craft and vessels have been constructed,

Opposite: Originally a cargo ship, the *Moshulu* served as a restaurant and exhibit at Penn's Landing in Philadelphia until damaged by fire in 1989. The vessel is being restored.

WHAT'S IN A NAME

Names of vessels often include a prefix identifying either the ship's source of power or its use. Sometimes a prefix may be applied by owners and used in only that one instance such as with the USF (United States Frigate) *Constellation.* These narrowly used prefixes are not included here. Following are commonly used prefixes with their meanings.

CSS	Confederate States Ship
LS	Lightship
MV	Motor Vessel
NS	Nuclear Ship
RV	Research Vessel
SS	Steamship (often generically applied to any type of mechanically propelled merchant vessel)
SV	Sailing Vessel
USCGC	United States Coast Guard Cutter
USS	United States Ship (reserved for commissioned naval vessels)
WAL, WLV	Light Vessel (reserved for lightships under the U.S. Coast Guard)

such as the bateaux, many have passed from the scene, all part of the decline of America's maritime trade and changing technologies. Currently hundreds, perhaps even thousands, of vessels in the United States are more than 50 years old, most of them unrecognized or unappreciated tugboats, fishing boats, yachts, and other craft, most probably dating to the 1920s and 1930s. Many of them have been modernized and changed so that they show little evidence of their heritage, while others, unassessed by preservationists, remain in obscurity.

To date some 250 historic ships and other vessels are recognized as historic and have been preserved or are the subject of a preservation effort. Nearly two-thirds are accessible to the public. While this group does not include every old ship in the country, it is an excellent sample of what is left, and, if these are the ships to which preservation efforts are being applied, they most likely will be the only examples of the nation's historic vessels to survive in the next century.

Ships built over the centuries in America and abroad fall into a myriad categories of types. Rather than providing a compendium of all ship types, many of which no longer exist in any case, the following examines the development and characteristics of the diverse type of vessels that played important roles in the United States and that continue to remain afloat or are ashore on display.

■ ■ ■   SCHOONERS: ALL-AMERICAN SHIPS   ■ ■ ■

If a generic American ship type were to be selected, it would undoubtedly be the schooner, particularly the two-masted schooner, the most commonly and extensively built American sailing vessel of the 18th, 19th, and early 20th centuries. Tens of thousands of these vessels were built on the Pacific, East, and Gulf coasts and on the Great Lakes. The schooners dominated maritime commerce such as the North American fishing and lumber trades, much of the South American and African trades, including slaving and sealing, and considerable European trade. Schooners were also used as naval vessels, as revenue cutters, and by pirates and illicit traders.

The number of schooners rapidly increased at a time when other types of sailing craft were quickly disappearing. The spread of the schooner's popularity was remarkable. Beginning as an almost local type and rig, the schooner gradually became popular along the Atlantic seaboard to Canada, then in Europe and in Central and South America, and finally in the Pacific and Far East. By 1790, if not earlier, the schooner was the most ubiquitous rig in both the United States and Canada. It remained the most common U.S. sailing rig through the death of commercial sailing in the 1930s, having survived the death of other rigs in the 1880s, 1890s, and early 1900s.

A small number of three-, four-, five-, and six-masted schooners were built for more cargo-carrying capacity and were used until the 1930s. Only three of the three-masted schooners survive—the *C. A. Thayer*, the *Wawona*, and the *Victory Chimes.* The rotting, collapsing hulks of three four-masters—the *Hesper*, *Luther Little*, and *La Merced*—and one five-master, the *Cora F. Cressey*, rest ashore in Washington and Maine; however, none has been preserved.

Left: The three-masted schooner *C. A. Thayer,* moored at the San Francisco Maritime National Historical Park, is undergoing a mast change. Some 250 historic ships and other vessels such as this are recognized as historic and have been preserved or are the subject of an ongoing preservation effort. Below: The *Victory Chimes* is one of three remaining three-masted schooners afloat in the United States.

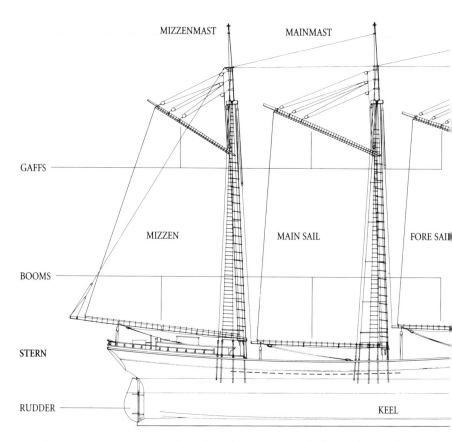

MIZZENMAST   MAINMAST

GAFFS

MIZZEN   MAIN SAIL   FORE SAIL

BOOMS

STERN

RUDDER   KEEL

The schooner *Wawona*, built in 1897 and now on view at the Maritime Heritage Center, Seattle.

Throughout the centuries in which the schooner dominated American maritime trade and commerce, it incorporated a variety of hull forms. These variations of the vessel's underwater body and the deck configuration were well documented after 1860, and many of these variations derived from the requirements of specific trades, such as oystering, fishing, or general coasting. The growing science of naval architecture introduced hydrodynamic theory and design.

COASTERS

The two-masted schooner was used for coasting, the transport of cargo from one coastal port to another from the early 19th century to around the outbreak of World War II. Designed to run fairly close to shore, the coaster lacked the fishing schooner's ability to ride out a gale offshore on the fishing grounds. The coaster never approached the scale of the great four-, five-, and six-masted coal schooners that came into use late in the 19th century to transport coal from southern to northern ports. Deep-water sailors who occasionally took a large schooner across the Atlantic scorned the useful and ubiquitous little coasters, sometimes accusing their skippers of "setting their course by the bark of a dog."

Early coasting trade was carried out in vessels of all types, but the schooner gradually monopolized the trade. Although the straight fore-and-aft-rigged schooner is primarily a coasting vessel, coasters occasionally ventured as far as the Caribbean. The schooner supplanted the square-riggers in the coasting trade for practical reasons. The fore-and-aft rig required fewer sailors to handle the vessel and allowed it to be

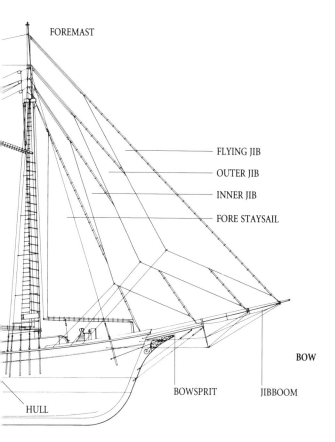

FOREMAST

FLYING JIB

OUTER JIB

INNER JIB

FORE STAYSAIL

BOW

BOWSPRIT   JIBBOOM

HULL

The two-masted schooner, the most common American ship type of the 18th, 19th, and early 20th centuries, served a variety of functions. Shown here during a 1989 restoration in Gloucester, Massachusetts, the *Pilot* was used to guide ships in and out of Boston's harbor.

The *Alma* is the sole remaining floating example of a schooner with a scow-formed hull.

maneuvered into and out of harbors and rivers more easily than any square-rigged craft. The schooner could also, as a rule, travel more quickly, because it could sail closer into the wind; for example, it did not need to sail from Maine to New York by way of the Bermudas, as some square-rigged vessels had done during baffling winds. Also, schooners were easily built of readily accessible materials.

These unromantic little vessels, described by a man who spent his youth on them as "no more than seagoing tipcarts, hauling their prosaic cargoes from one coastal port to another," were nonetheless important. They were the long-haul trucks of the coasts in an era before the advent of good, all-weather highways. A few dozen wood two-masted schooners are preserved in the United States. These include cargo carriers, such as the *Grace Bailey*, the *Mercantile*, the *Equator*, the *Stephen Taber*, the *Governor Stone*, the *Lewis R. French*, and the *Alma* (the sole example of a scow-formed hull); pilot boats, such as the *Pilot*, the *Roseway*, the *Alabama*, the *Timberwind*, and the *Adventuress*; the Arctic exploration schooner *Bowdoin*; the yachts *Surprise* and *Wendameen*; and the iron-hulled two-master *Pioneer*.

FISHING SCHOONERS

The next largest group of two-masted schooners was those built for fishing. The fishing industry of the United States, while spread throughout the nation and found on every waterway and coast, was born in New England waters some 300 years ago. From the fishing ports of Massachusetts, particularly Gloucester, hailed the nation's largest fleet of fishing schooners. Gloucester thrived as a fishing port and shipbuilding center from colonial times through the 1920s and today continues to be an important center of the American fishing industry. From Gloucester and other small towns fishing fleets sailed to work the Grand Banks of Newfoundland and other fishing grounds off the eastern seaboard where shoal waters hosted tremendous numbers of cod, haddock, hake, halibut, pollock, cusk, skate, catfish, whiting, monk fish, wolf fish, and lump fish. To meet the conditions of the trade, shipyards in Gloucester and nearby towns, notably Essex, designed and built thousands of American fishing schooners in the 19th and early 20th centuries.

Hundreds of fishing schooners were built in and around Gloucester, many of them in the town itself. In the 1880 census assessment of U.S. maritime activity and industry, Henry Hall counted 475 vessels in the Gloucester district, 133 of which had been built in Gloucester, 215 in nearby Essex, and the rest principally in Maine. The Gloucester fishing schooners, known as "Gloucestermen," took many forms during the century they dominated America's fisheries. Various types were predominate in certain years; clipper schooners, *Fredonia*-type inshore and offshore schooners, "Indian headers," and "knockabout" schooners were among the better-known types.

The introduction of steam engines led to a short-lived adoption of this form of power to fishing vessels in the 1880s and 1890s. Bulky and expensive, steam engines were not

A catch aboard the Grand Banks fishing schooner *Effie M. Morrissey*, now the *Ernestina*, in 1913.

economically suitable for the New England fisheries, however. The development of the internal combustion engine led to the rise of the auxiliary schooner in the 1890s. After 1901 the number of gasoline engines installed in schooners then under construction and the modification of older, sailing schooners increased. By 1925 the bulk of the fishing schooners had been converted to auxiliaries, and sail propulsion had been replaced by the engine. Diesel trawlers and seiners with oil engines became the most prevalent fishing vessel type after 1930. Flush-decked trawlers, with their steel and wood hulls, were a vastly different type, using nets instead of dories for fishing. The last sailing fishing schooner constructed in Gloucester was the *Gertrude L. Thebaud*, built in 1930, even then almost an anachronism.

One of two remaining examples of the *Fredonia*-model schooner, the *Lettie G. Howard* fished the Gulf of Mexico as the *Mystic C.* from 1923 to 1966.

Two-masted fishing hulls preserved in the United States include the *American* and the *Sherman Zwicker*, both foreign built, and the *American Eagle*, the *Adventure*, the *Evelina M. Goulart*, the *Lettie G. Howard*, the *Ernestina*, and the *L. A. Dunton*, all American built. Preserved nonsailing fishing vessels are fewer in number but include three wood-hulled motor-powered fishing tugboats from Lake Michigan, the *Buddy O.*, the *Aloha*, and the *Evelyn S.*; the dragger *Florence*; and the sponge boat *St. Nicholas III.* This does not, however, include the fore- and aft-rigged skipjacks or other schooner-rigged oyster vessels.

OYSTER SCHOONERS, SLOOPS, AND SKIPJACKS

Oyster harvesting was one of the earliest fishery industries in North America. Native Americans harvested the rich oyster beds that proliferated along the coast from Texas to the Gulf of St. Lawrence as well as in San Francisco Bay. Colonial interest in oystering led to widespread and intensive harvesting and ultimately, by the 18th century, to government efforts to regulate the industry and conserve and nurture oyster beds. In fact, in the 1820s the demand for oysters was so high that oyster cultivation was pursued to gradually reinvigorate the flagging industry. Millions of acres of seabed were cultivated and harvested; in New York's Great South Bay alone, for example, 50,000 acres were under cultivation in 1916. Fleets of hundreds of schooners, sloops, and oyster boats worked the beds, and thousands of men and women were employed afloat or ashore, tonging, dredging, shucking, canning, and serving oysters.

The vessels used to harvest and bring oysters to market generally fit into three categories: (1) the oyster-tonging boats, usually canoes, skiffs, or sharpies in which one person used wood tongs to pluck the oysters from the seabed; (2) the oyster sloops, round-bottomed, gaff-rigged, centerboard one-masted vessels that pulled oyster dredges or served as platforms for tonging; and (3) the sailing oyster freighters, which were two-masted centerboard schooners. These schooners, which were developed in the mid-19th century, were stout and rugged. Their shallow draft and long straight keel allowed them to rest on a beach between tides while loading cargoes or making repairs. Moreover, their light draft had the added advantage of permitting them to sail in shallow inlets and bays.

One advantage of the two-masted schooner in the oyster trades was its wide decks, which provided stability and space to stow large numbers of oysters on deck instead of in the hold. Although some larger sloops worked as freighters, their large rigs made them difficult to maneuver. In the early 20th century principles of naval architecture led to more streamlined vessels with an emphasis on better hydrodynamic characteristics. These late, or final form, oyster schooners were distinguished from their older, slower predecessors, many of which remained in service, although their ability to dredge efficiently and rapidly under sail decreased. Many of these later oyster schooners actively raced each other, and their competition culminated in an organized Great Schooner Race on Delaware Bay in August 1929.

Oystering with sailing boats continued along the eastern seaboard until 1946, when a change in New Jersey laws allowed oyster dredging by motorized boats. That year many oyster sloops and freighters were converted to motor vessels. Oystering under sail persisted only on the Chesapeake Bay. The decline of oystering was marked by the destruction of much of the fleet in the great hurricane of 1938 and during World War II. After 1950 the introduction of boom and later hydraulic dredges decreased the need for the older style of sail-propelled boats, and despite periodic activity oystering declined because of pollution and decreased consumption. By the early 1970s the New England oyster fleet was described as consisting of a "small varied assortment of ancient and near ancient craft." No known conventional-style oyster boat continued to be built. Conventional-style boats remaining in service had all been converted to motor vessels, except for the small sailing skipjacks of the Chesapeake Bay, which remain in use today. Only six oyster schooners are known to survive in the United States, all of which sailed on Delaware Bay—the *Isaac H. Evans* (1886), the *Priscilla* (1888), the *Nellie and Mary* (1891), the *Richard Robbins, Sr.* (1902), the *Clyde A. Phillips* (1928); and the *J. & E. Riggin* (1929).

As shallow-water oyster beds were depleted, tonging for oysters became difficult, if not impractical, for beds at depths greater than 12 feet. The solution was the dredge, described as "essentially a kind of rake with a bag attached and long rope, cable, or chain replacing the wooden handle...A sailboat pulled the dredge along the bottom...when full, the dredge

One of the few remaining oyster schooners, the *Nellie and Mary* awaits restoration in Bridgeton, New Jersey.

Above: Many skipjacks participate in educational or public awareness programs during their off-season months. The *Thomas Clyde* was moored at Evelynton Plantation in Charles City County, Virginia, as part of a public awareness program during the summer of 1990. Right: Dwindling oyster reserves have reduced the Chesapeake Bay skipjack fleet to a dozen or so operating vessels. The *Kathryn* continues to operate out of Tilghman Island off Maryland's Eastern Shore.

was hauled aboard by hand, dumped, and then thrown overboard again." The vessel type developed for dredging was the single-masted oyster sloop, which operated under sail until the development of powered dredge boats after the turn of the century.

The oyster sloop was developed in the 1830s and was, throughout its long use, simple. The rig consistently consisted of the jib-and-gaff mainsail sloop until after 1900, when auxiliary power was introduced and the useful main gaff topsail was eliminated, leaving a very simple, efficient rig. The hull form basically remained the same, with subtle regional variations. The New York oyster sloops were developed after the adoption of the centerboard in the New York area sometime in the 1830s, and by the end of Civil War the shoal centerboard sloop of the New York style appeared all along the shores of western Long Island Sound, in northern New Jersey, and southward into Delaware and Chesapeake waters. Thus, the sloop became the generic type for the nation's principal oyster fisheries. Its form was distinctive; it was a wide, shoal centerboarder with a rather wide, square stern and a V bottom with stocky proportions and clipper bows, the cabin aft and hold forward.

Oyster sloops remained in use well into the 20th century, some continuing to dredge under sail but most using auxiliary power. The number of vessels sharply declined, however. Modern, motor-powered vessels, different in form and use from the old sloops, took their place in a dwindling market, the result of decreased demand and pollution. From the 1880s, when more than 300 boats fished the Connecticut beds alone, the fleet dwindled to only two dozen sailing boats in the 1930s. By 1958 no sailboat dredged for oysters north of the Chesapeake. Today only three oyster sloops are preserved outside the Chesapeake Bay—the *Christeen* (1883), the *Modesty* (1923); and the *Hope* (1948).

Developed in the 1890s to dredge oysters, the Chesapeake Bay skipjacks are characterized by cross-planked construction with a shallow draft, a hard chine, and a deadrise, or V, bottom. They are short (39 to 56 feet long) and beamy, their width generally a third of their length. When fitted out for oystering, they have rollers amidships on the rails, power winders amidships, two iron dredges, and pipe davits over the stern from which a motorized pushboat is suspended. The skipjack's traditional rig uses a jib-headed mainsail laced to the boom and a single large jib with a club on its foot. Painted white, most skipjacks, despite their utilitarian, hardworked existence, carry decorative trail boards on their longhead bows.

Maryland's conservation laws, which allow oyster dredging only by sail-powered vessels, is responsible for the fleet's survival. However, dwindling oyster resources have reduced the number of active vessels from approximately one thousand at the turn of the century to the dozen or so that operated during the 1990 season. Most operating skipjacks can be found on the Eastern Shore of Maryland in Tilghman, Rock Hall, and Wewona, where they can be seen at their docks during the offseason months. Some are used as educational vessels during the summer and fall months. The *Thomas W. Clyde*, for example, left its home port in Wewona, Maryland, to spend the summer of 1990 at Evelynton Plantation in Charles City County, Virginia, as part of a public education program on skipjacks. Many of the preserved skipjacks are used as exhibits or are being restored for use as sailing ambassadors, including the *City of Norfolk*, the *E. C. Collier*, the *Mary W. Somers*, the *Minnie V.*, the *Rosie Parks*, and the *Stanley Norman*. Other skipjacks are warehoused, some are abandoned, and others are for sale. In 1990 three skipjacks were restored for continued operation as dredges. Other preserved vessels from the Chesapeake Bay oyster fleet include three bugeyes (ketches with two raked masts) and a brogan (a small type of bugeye): the *Wm. B. Tennison*, the *Edna E. Lockwood*, the *Little Jennie*, and the *Mustang*—all excellent examples of vernacular Chesapeake oystering craft that evolved from log canoes. The *Wm. B. Tennison* is also termed a "buyboat," a boat from which oysters or other seafood might be sold.

■ ■ ■ ■ ■ THE LARGE SAILING SHIPS ■ ■ ■ ■ ■

A variety of square-rigged vessel types was developed and built in Europe and the United States for deep-water voyages. Universally referred to as sailing ships, they were large, having a greater carrying capacity than the schooner. The sailing ship was America's link to Europe, Asia, and South America. The whaling ships, those carrying the ice trade, the China trade, the hide-and-tallow trade to California, and the packets that linked European ports to the United States, carrying passengers and freight, were all square-riggers. The hull forms changed over time, from bluff-bowed, "apple-cheeked" merchant ships to sleeker, faster vessels culminating in the 1840s, 1850s, and 1860s in the United States with the wood clippers, the "greyhounds of the sea." After the Civil War stouter vessels, with greater carrying capacities but with some evidence of clipper form in their bows and sterns, were built. These wood giants, the epitome of American wood sailing ships, were first advertised as "medium clippers" but in time gained greater fame as "downeasters," because most were built in Maine.

The square-rigged ship carries sails on spars that cross its masts. From the two-masted brigs and brigantines to the three-masted, full-rigged ships, barks, and barkentines, these ships eventually grew to four-, five-, and six-masted behemoths, although few of these giants were products of American shipyards. The multimasted vessels that were built in America were late 19th- and early 20th-century schooners and barkentines.

Britain, faced with the decline of its forests, first used iron in shipbuilding. Beginning in the late 18th century, iron knees, braces, and breasthooks supported the heavy gundecks of British warships. Iron was introduced to merchant construction in the 19th century, and by midcentury the composite ship was born. Many vessels, such as the tea clipper *Cutty Sark*, had graceful iron frames over which teak or other hardwood planks were laid. Composite construction gave way to iron and then to steel ships. In the United States very few composite or metal-hulled sailing ships were built; rather, steamships became the major American beneficiaries of the Bessemer steel-making process. However, British yards launched scores of deep-water ships of iron and steel in the last quarter

of the 19th century. In the early 20th century large four-masted ships, representing the apex of the sailing ship, were built, many in German and French shipyards. Some remained in service beyond the climax of the sailing era, as the clouds of World War II gathered.

Not counting naval vessels, only one American wood sailing ship, the whaler *Charles W. Morgan*, survives. The others, as previously noted, were constructed in British or German yards, starting with an iron-hulled vessel, the *Star of India* (1864), through the early years of steel ships, as represented by the *Elissa* (1877), the *Falls of Clyde* (1878), the *Wavertree* (1885), and the *Balclutha* (1886), and finally the large German-built steel sailers of the early 20th century, the *Moshulu* (1904) and the *Peking* (1911), all large vessels built to compete with the tramp steamers then dominating ocean trade.

Few large wood sailing ships survive. Steel-hulled ships, such as the *Balclutha*, have proved more durable. As the *Star of Alaska* the *Balclutha* spent three decades in the Alaskan salmon trade.

■ ■ ■   WESTERN RIVERS STEAMBOATS   ■ ■ ■

The western rivers system, composed of the Mississippi, Ohio, Missouri, and other tributary rivers, carried most of the immigrants and freight that settled the Midwest. Starting in the late 1700s, most settlers traveled from the East Coast overland to points along the Ohio River such as Pittsburgh and Wheeling, West Virginia, and then down the river to points west.

Until Robert Fulton built the steamboat *New Orleans* with its revolutionary reciprocating steam engine in 1811, river traffic was chiefly dependent on favorable currents, wind, and human strength. Along the Mississippi River, for instance, boats with cargo and passengers would follow the current downstream to embarkation points along the river, then, at journey's end, be dismantled. Those in charge of this type of commerce would travel by land upstream to build another boat following the same pattern as the first. Robert Fulton's invention revolutionized river transportation and commerce: for the first time boats carried with them their own power source. Schedules could be met, deliveries made, and passengers guaranteed arrival. Built in Pittsburgh, the *New Orleans* proceeded down the Ohio and Mississippi rivers to its namesake city, attracting publicity and attention along the way. Steamboats hereafter would provide convenient, inexpensive transportation and greatly facilitate the opening of the continent to settlement.

The *New Orleans* and the boats patterned on it were powered versions of canal boats. Their long, narrow, deep hulls were better suited to deep eastern rivers than the shallow Mississippi but were needed to support heavy steam machinery. These and other design problems had to be overcome before steamboats could be a real success on the western rivers.

To navigate the shallow western rivers, steamboat hulls and machinery had to be made as light as possible. Machinery weight problems were solved first. In 1813 a lightweight, high-pressure engine was built to propel a small boat called the *Comet*. The power system was further refined in 1816 by Henry Shreve, who put the boilers on deck and designed a new type of engine to distribute machinery weights over a large area of hull. Shreve's new engine design used a direct-acting, horizontal, high-pressure engine to drive the paddle-wheel propeller. The second design problem was solved gradually over the years. Eventually, lightweight hull construction replaced earlier, robust canal boat construction. A broad, shallow-draft, hull form, using a truss-rod system rather than heavy wood beams, was developed over time. To turn a profit these lightly built boats had to carry a large amount of freight and many passengers. In response to this requirement, sponsons, strongly bracketed platforms overhanging each side of the hull, were built to extend the deck area, and the super-structure was raised several decks above the boiler deck to support passenger cabins.

The essential design elements of the western rivers steamboat had been incorporated by 1825. Broad, shallow-draft vessels having boilers and engines on deck, side wheels or stern wheels for propulsion, and cabins built on lightweight decks above the freight and machinery-laden main deck soon appeared on every tributary of the Mississippi. The ease and economy of this service caused the quantity of goods reaching New Orleans to double every 10 years from 1820 to 1860.

While western river steamboats offered improvements in the way of transporting goods and people throughout America's heartland, their light construction and unreliable machinery sometimes made them dangerous modes of transportation. Early boats were particularly susceptible to boiler explosions, fires, and sinkings caused when they grounded or hit snags. Other threats included floods, tornadoes, and ice gorges. The lifetime of a steamboat in the 1840s and 1850s was estimated at less than five years. But these hazards did not deter the steamboat business, and, in fact, substantial salvage operations developed. As old boats were lost to various causes, new boats replaced them, often incorporating parts salvaged from those destroyed.

Public concerns about safety persisted, but progress toward lessening the hazards was slow. In 1838, the federal government forced builders and operators of steamboats to become more conscious of safety by passing an act that required steamboat inspections. This law was strengthened in 1852 after more than 700 lives were lost the previous year in six steamboat disasters. The Steamboat Inspection Act of 1852 set standards for both boats and operators and created a system of federal inspection to oversee them.

As time progressed steamboat designs diversified to meet the needs of various trades and routes. Passenger vessels required high speed and high-class accommodations. Ferries called for wide stable hulls. Package freight boats, which carried heavy cargo on deck or in barges alongside, required dependable engines and sturdy construction. In some services speed became paramount, even surpassing safety concerns. Faster vessels required streamlined design, powerful engines, and multiple boilers to supply plenty of steam. Shallow tributary rivers such as the Missouri and the upper regions of other rivers required boats with exceptionally shallow draft. The *Bertrand*, sunk in 1865 on the Missouri River, drew only 18 inches when lightly loaded. To operate in such shallow water steamboats had to sacrifice all unnecessary weight and be satisfied with minimal superstructures. By 1880, although a depression in river trade had hurt steamboat companies, riverboat technology continued to advance. Several distinct types of steamboats had been developed for work on the western rivers. Passengers were carried on riverboats of any kind from time to time, but several types were particularly adapted for passenger service. The most elaborate of these were saloon or palace steamers providing luxury passenger transportation in elegant cabins. Such boats usually ran on a schedule and often carried mail to designated ports. These services duplicated those of ocean-going packet companies; hence, these boats were aptly termed packets.

Other passenger vessels were adapted for carrying groups and charters for short day excursions to nearby scenic areas and for longer cruises. These excursion boats were usually large side-wheelers operating from large port towns. Smaller boats also made occasional trips on the rivers, lakes, and sounds, "tramping" for charters.

■ ■ ■ ■ ■ ■   STEAMSHIPS   ■ ■ ■ ■ ■ ■

The steamship grew out of the steamboat, which as previously noted was a product of the late 18th century and the first decade of the 19th century. While small steamers were built to serve on the rivers as ferries, crossing small bodies of water or harbors, the concept of steamships actually crossing the ocean was slow to catch on because of the problems of carrying enough fuel and water for the boilers. Early ocean steamers were built with a steam engine in a sailing hull, as was the *Savannah*, built in 1818 with folding paddle wheels as well, the first American steamer to cross the Atlantic. The utility of the arrangement was limited, and on its eight-day maiden voyage from New York to Savannah the engines worked for only four and a half hours. The *Savannah*'s voyage to Britain was marked by similar difficulties. For the next few decades American steam endeavors on the sea focused on coastal passages, and steam packets linking New York with ports south proved successful.

The spread of deep-water steam technology in the United States was slow until the 1840s. Until then, few foundries were skilled in the manufacture of engines and boilers, builders of wood ships were inexperienced in the construction of steamers, owners were loath to invest in the expensive technology, masters who operated the ships disdained the "stinking smokepots," and competent marine engineers were few and far between. This situation changed after 1846, when Congress subsidized the construction of ocean-going steamers to carry the mail and serve as auxiliary steam warships in time of war. Three significant companies were established— the Collins Line, whose ships crossed the Atlantic, and the U.S. Mail Steamship and the Pacific Mail Steamship companies, two New York–based lines that linked the eastern seaboard with the United States' newly acquired possessions in the Pacific.

Linking up on the Isthmus of Panama, the U.S. Mail and Pacific Mail companies' fortunes increased with the discovery of gold in California in 1848, and by 1850 tens of thousands of people crossed the isthmus and sought any available means of passage to San Francisco, including Pacific Mail's overcrowded and overtaxed steamers. The result was a boom in steamship construction that introduced steamers to the Pacific in record numbers. Most were side-wheel steamers, but a few were screw, or propeller, steamers. A handful of iron-hulled steamers were built at this time, mostly in Britain, although the U.S. Revenue Marine (now the U.S. Coast Guard) and the navy experimented with them. From California the use of steamers spread to the Northwest and then across the Pacific. The first steamship to cross the Pacific, the *Monumental City*, was a veteran of the California gold rush and made a voyage to Australia in 1853. Successful wood steamers, primarily side-wheelers, followed, as larger hulls with more powerful engines and boilers were built to link the United States to Europe and after 1867 to the Orient. At this time, too, steamships began to break completely away from their sailing-ship ancestors in appearance and design. The 380-foot-long behemoths that linked the Orient with America were among the largest wood ships ever built. Operated by the Pacific Mail Steamship Company, the steamers to Japan, China, and the Philippines made the former gold rush coastal company the most important American steamship line of the 19th and early 20th century.

The steady supply of wood, the United States' 200-year tradition of building wood ships, and the skill of American shipbuilders induced U.S. yards to continue building wood steamers and sailing ships long after European yards had shifted to metal. The weakness of large wood hulls carrying engines was remedied with the introduction in the 1830s of diagonal iron strapping, a British invention, and wood trusses. The U.S. Navy, following the new technology, had also added steam engines to the battle line. After experimenting in the 1840s it built several steam warships before the Civil War. That conflict firmly pushed the navy into the steam age, as well as the age of iron, with the development of ironclad steamers and the monitors.

After the Civil War, American merchant steamers gradually shifted to the use of iron and then steel. Britain had led the way in metal steamer construction, and one British Cunard Line steamship, the *Unicorn*, was actually chartered and then bought for service during the California gold rush. The introduction of metal hulls solved several problems of shaft alignment and vibration that had plagued wood screw steamers, and the need for fast, efficient screw steamers to run the Union blockade of southern ports during the Civil War demonstrated the superiority of twin-screw steel steamers.

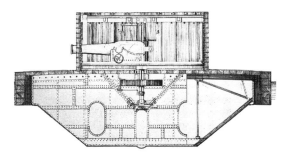

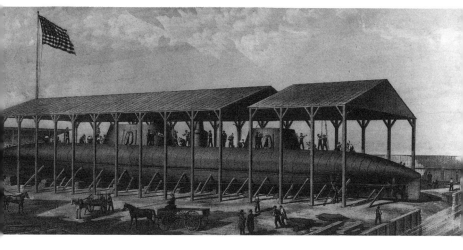

The heart of the United States' industry for iron and steel ships was the Delaware River. After the Civil War, yards such as Harlan and Hollingsworth and Pusey and Jones, in Wilmington, Delaware, Neafie and Levy in Philadelphia, and John Roach's Delaware Iron Shipbuilding and Iron Works in Chester, Pennsylvania, the most famous in the 1870s, surpassed the previous center of deep-water wood shipbuilding—New York. Many New York yards, even those building steamers, closed, and the iron and steel steamers launched into the waters of the Delaware River dominated America's maritime industry. The introduction of the compound steam engine, with its efficient condensers and boilers, revolutionized deep-water steamships, and in the 1870s and 1880s many steamship lines, including Pacific Mail, began replacing

Top: Following the development of the steam engine, the U.S. Navy introduced ironclad steamers and monitors for military uses during the Civil War. One of the more famous was the USS *Monitor*. Above: The *Keokuk*, another steam-propelled ironclad, was launched in 1862.

By the end of the 19th century iron and steel steamers dominated nearly every American maritime trade. Large passenger liners, such as the Pacific Mail's *City of Rio de Janeiro*, were a common type.

their older wood steamships with new, more efficient iron-hulled vessels. Steel-hulled construction was introduced in 1883 by John Roach when he produced four steel vessels for the U.S. Navy. By the end of the century iron and steel steamers dominated nearly every American maritime trade, even the coastal steamship trade, with a few wood hold-outs, such as the cheaply built, short-lived steam schooners of the Pacific Coast lumber trade, left to continue the legacy of wood steamers. More common were large passenger liners, such as Pacific Mail's *City of Rio de Janeiro* of the 1880s or the transatlantic liners, such as Roach's *St. Louis*. The *St. Louis*, built in 1893, was 535 feet long and powered by two quadruple-expansion marine steam engines that produced 20,500 horsepower.

Cargo steamers, tankers, and smaller steamers were built in the 1890s and the early 20th century. The same period saw the rise of massive steel battleships and cruisers and the creation of a diverse, powerful navy that included submarines and destroyers, which within a century would become the naval ships built in the largest numbers. The first decade of the new century introduced yet another revolution in steamships—the steam turbine—which proved as significant as the introduction of the compound steam engine in the 1870s. The first turbine-powered American steamer, the *Creole*, was launched in 1906. Other turbine steamers slowly followed, but the traditional compound-, triple-, and quadruple-expansion marine steam engines remained in use well into the 1940s, in part because of their simplicity, which served well during the mass production of steamers during the two world wars. World War I saw the reintroduction of wood steamers and concrete ships to meet the demand for hulls.

During World War II construction of an emergency fleet built of steel introduced a number of identical ships, including the well-known Liberty and Victory ships. The World War II shipbuilding programs in particular pushed the nation's shipbuilders fully into welding, which replaced riveting as the method of hull construction. After World War II oil-fired steamers with geared turbines and diesel-powered motorships began to dominate the maritime industry. In the 1950s and 1960s, as American shipbuilding declined, motor vessels were built, along with some turbine steamers, including the NS *Savannah*, which used nuclear power to produce steam to drive the turbine. Nonetheless, a number of steamers—some with wood hulls, others with iron and steel, and having a variety of engines, some of which dated to the last half of the 19th century—continued in service, a few even firing their boilers by hand with coal, as was done at the beginning of the age of marine steam.

While a number of steel passenger and cargo-carrying vessels and a few examples of private, steam-powered craft for recreation survive in the United States, only a few wood-hulled steamers still exist—the *Lone Star* (1868), the *Eureka* (1890), the *Ticonderoga* (1906), the *Sabino* (1908), the *Wapama* (1915), and the *Virginia V* (1922). Passenger vessels in-

Top: The *Ticonderoga*, one of the few surviving wooden-hulled steamers, is now a dry-berth exhibit on the grounds of the Shelburne Museum, Shelburne, Vermont. Left: The steam yacht *Cangarda*'s main steam engine.

clude steamboats for service on shallow rivers—overnight and day excursion boats and packets; steamboats for service on protected waters, usually bays, sounds, or lakes; and ferries. A few steam freighters or cargo vessels have been preserved; one is a wood-hulled vessel, the steam schooner *Wapama*, and three are examples of wartime emergency fleet ships—namely two Liberty ships, the *Jeremiah O'Brien* and the *John W. Brown*, and one Victory ship, the *Lane Victory*. The others are "lakers," steamers built for service on the Great Lakes, including the sole surviving example of a whale-back, the *Meteor*, and a handful of Great Lakes bulk and ore freighters. There are also three steam yachts—the *Medea*, the *Kestrel*, and the *Cangarda*. The majority of the other surviving steamers, such as the *Geo. M. Verity* and the *W. P. Snyder, Jr.*, worked the western rivers.

■ ■ ■ ■ ■ ■   FERRIES   ■ ■ ■ ■ ■ ■

Ferries have been used to carry people, horses and other animals, and vehicles across narrow bodies of water since antiquity. In addition to a variety of hull designs, ferries used a succession of means of propulsion, ranging from pulling and sailing to oars and paddles. The first ferry known to have operated in America plied the Charles River between Chelsea and Charlestown, Massachusetts, in 1631. Ferries remained little more than nominally powered barges until the late 18th century, when two technological developments were introduced in the United States to produce the direct ancestor of the modern ferries. The first was the adoption on American rivers of a broad, shallow-draft, scow-formed hull with loading ramps. These hulls, developed in the Netherlands, proved capacious and, because of the ramps at each end, easy to load and unload. Along with the development of these "double-ended" ferries, Americans experimented with mechanical propulsion, including "horse ferries," vessels having horses below decks that turned gears to power paddle wheels. The development of marine steam technology provided the final design element for the standard American ferry.

In 1809 Robert Fulton patented the double-ended steam ferry and built several for service across New York's Hudson and East rivers. A grateful New York named the Manhattan boulevard joining the two ferry landings Fulton Street in his honor, a harbinger of the approbation accorded the new vessels, whose design was adopted throughout the country. In time four basic ferry types were developed in the United States: (1) the double-ended ferry; (2) the western river, stern-wheel and side-wheel shoal-draft ferry; (3) the car-transfer ferry; and (4) the Great Lakes car ferry. The double-ender, the most common type, was used on most harbor routes, but its evolution took place in New York and San Francisco. Its de-sign and development addressed the problems of the rapid transport of people and vehicles between congested areas separated by water. The double-ended ferry permitted efficient unloading and loading without any preparations other than the reversal of the main engines. Essentially the double-ended ferry was a floating bridge. Not surprisingly, most of the ferries older than 50 years left in the United States are double-ended ferries from New York or San

Francisco. These include the *San Mateo*, the *Berkeley*, the *Eureka*, the *Klamath*, the *River Queen*, the *Binghamton*, and the *Maj. Gen. Wm. H. Hart.* Another survivor is the Great Lakes car ferry *City of Milwaukee*, a screw-propelled ship with a flat stern for loading; it was entirely enclosed because of the ice and cold of winter and the vast expanses of open water on the inland seas in summer.

The double-ended ferries, while conforming to a general design, did incorporate regional variations. New York ferries provided seating accommodations and lavatories. Norfolk ferries in some cases provided restaurant facilities. Ferries on the Chesapeake had restaurants and staterooms on three passenger decks to accommodate very long runs. Some San Francisco ferries had restaurants and well-furnished bathrooms. West Coast ferries, particularly those operating in Puget Sound, had a greater height between decks and a more square superstructure than the eastern ferries.

The majority of the ferries, regardless of where they served, were side-wheelers until the late 19th century. The screw propeller was developed by a number of inventors during the 1840s, but debate over its merits continued until the 1880s, when propeller-driven ferries began to appear. Particularly on the East Coast propellers were increasingly used, replacing the paddle-wheel ferry. Later ferry variations included the adoption of diesel-electric and direct diesel drive, the introduction of more commodious, lighter superstructures over the vehicle decks, and all-steel construction in conformity with U.S. Coast Guard regulations regarding fire safety. A declining number of ferries continue to be built in the United States. The development of bridges and subterranean tubes, as well as mass transit systems, ended the heyday of ferries on many waterways.

The double-ended ferry permitted efficient unloading and loading without any preparations other than the reversal of the main engines. The *Eureka* served the ferry route connecting San Francisco with the Southern Pacific passenger trains in Oakland, California.

■ ■ ■ ■   TUGBOATS AND TOWBOATS   ■ ■ ■ ■

Above: Still in service to the marine division of New York City's fire department, the *John J. Harvey* was the largest and most powerful gasoline-operated American fireboat when built in 1931. Below: The *Hercules* is the last remaining largely unaltered example of an early 20th-century ocean-going steam tugboat.

Among the most ubiquitous ships on any waterfront or riverfront are the tugboats and towboats, the latter being used on rivers. Included in these types are fire-fighting vessels. The nation has a small fleet of historic fireboats—the oldest is the *Edward M. Cotter* (1900)—that includes the *Fire Fighter*, the *Ralph J. Scott*, the *Alki*, the *David S. Campbell*, the *Deluge*, the *Fireboat No. 1*, the *Duwamish*, and the *John J. Harvey*. A handful of historic tugboats has survived as display or historic vessels. All but three, the *W. O. Decker*, the *Arthur Foss*, and the *John Taxis*, are iron- or steel-hulled; these include the *Baltimore*, the *Reiss*, the *Hercules*, the *Edna G.*, the *Jupiter*, the *New York Central No. 16*, the *Mathilda*, and the *Dorothy*.

The first steam-powered tugboat was the British *Charlotte Dundas*, built in 1802 for use on the Forth and Clyde Canal in Scotland. The side-wheel–propelled tugboat proved successful, and by the 1830s scores of steam tugboats had liberated sailing ships from dependence on the wind and tides when entering or leaving port. The introduction of screw propulsion in the 1840s revolutionized tugboats, as did the subsequent development of more powerful marine steam

engines, such as compound- and triple-expansion steam engines in the 1860s. After 1860 first iron and later steel hulls were introduced, making tugboats stronger and more capable workhorses of ports and harbors. Around this time tugboat design was standardized. Tugboats had a high bow, plumb stem, and a graceful sheer that curved back to a counter stern and prominent rub rails lining the beam. The pilothouse was usually at the forward end of a single deck house. A single smokestack typically rose with a rake from behind the pilothouse.

Tugboats have been grouped by their trades into three general groups, and their hull designs reflected the requirements of these trades. The various types were developed early, and most of the designs are little changed from the early days. Transfer and harbor tugboats were and are the most common and the smallest of the three types. Designed to operate in protected waters close to home, they have small deckhouses and are usually propelled by a single propeller. The next larger type is generally more than 120 feet long and designed for offshore, long-distance towing. These ocean-going tugboats have more freeboard and often are equipped

with particularly high bows to turn aside high seas. The final and largest type of tugboats was designed to save ships in distress. These salvage and rescue tugboats are generally about 200 feet long and equipped with twin screws for greater power and maneuverability.

The compression-ignition engine patented by Rudolph Diesel in 1892 offered even more advantages than earlier advances in marine engineering. Diesel engines are more efficient and require smaller crews to operate. Unlike steam engines, diesel engines give a constant pull and can be started in minutes. The biggest drawback to using diesel engines for marine propulsion is that the large, heavy-pitch propellers used by tugboats are more efficient at slow speeds, while

The tugboat *Major Elisha F. Henson*, now called the *Nash*, was built for the U.S. Army to participate in the large United States sealift to Europe before the D-Day invasion in World War II.

The steam-powered *Geo. M. Verity* pushed barges loaded with coal and scrap iron on the Ohio and Mississippi rivers.

diesels are more efficient at higher speeds. In a regular diesel-powered vessel, operating the propeller and engine at the most advantageous speed requires a compromise among the various operating speeds. This can be done by installing expensive gearing between the engine and propeller or by using the engine to turn an electrical generator and supply power to an electric motor, which turns the propeller. The U.S. Navy adopted electric propulsion for some submarines before World War I, but not until 1926 was diesel-electric propulsion applied successfully to a surface vessel. Three diesel-electric tugboats were built in that year, and from that time the system spread steadily.

All tugboats are designed to serve as additional power for other ships, but the form of that assistance varies. The earliest tugboats towed other vessels only on the end of a hawser; this is still the most common method of towing in open water. Later, tugboat captains learned how to nudge large vessels directly to assist them into a berth. Tugboats can also be lashed to a barge or other vessel thus becoming, in effect, a strap-on engine. On American rivers this was found to be the best method of dealing with strong, confused currents.

On the rivers vessels specially built to move unpowered barges or log rafts came to be called towboats. They replaced their more mundane sisters, the western river steam packets, which carried cargo wherever it could be found. Such nonscheduled steamboats often pushed one or more barges to increase cargo capacity or to decrease draft in periods of low water. Coal was carried in barges alongside packets from the 1840s, and later salt, hay, iron ore, and grain were carried. A few boats specialized in pushing huge log rafts downstream to lumber mills. By 1850 a system of moving barges and log rafts lashed alongside and ahead of the towboat was developed, thus allowing greater control than towing with a hawser. This type of service favored stern wheel–propelled boats over side-wheelers and promoted other improvements as well. River towboats became a distinct type by 1860.

Barges also developed in size and construction and soon were built in standard sizes. Early barges were of two general types. The more common type was a long narrow scow hull, built of planks and used on one-way trips downriver carrying coal. It developed from the flatboat and like it was broken up and sold for lumber when the cargo was disposed of. The other type of barge was used for voyages both up- and downstream. These vessels, called model barges because of their finely modeled ends, were usually greatly enlarged versions of the barges of the 1820s. By 1889 barges of all kinds were carrying more than 19 million tons of freight per year.

Towboats are designed as floating engines to propel barges. Only the barge, not the expensive towboat, need be detained while loading or unloading cargo. Barges towed with a hawser are hard to control in narrow river channels, while those lashed alongside and ahead of a towboat are easier to control. On the lower Mississippi strings of up to 60 barges occasionally are pushed. Fifteen barges is the more usual number on the upper rivers, because the limited size of river locks requires breaking tows into several pieces. On smaller rivers towboats can handle only one or two barges.

New propulsion methods and new engines were introduced on the rivers as they were in other parts of the country. Compression ignition (that is, diesel) engines were first used about 1910 for smaller stern-wheel towboats but did not gain ascendancy until the late 1930s, when diesel-powered propeller boats appeared. The introduction of screw propellers to the rivers came late because of their vulnerability to damage and the greater depth of water required for efficient operation. Competition from newer diesel-powered screw-propelled towboats, with smaller crew requirements, made continued operation of steam towboats uneconomical during the late 1940s. Some steam-powered, screw-propeller towboats were built but were either later converted to diesel power or retired. Stern-wheel boats were considered to be more efficient than screw-propeller boats for smaller horsepower engines and shallow water, and a few diesel stern-wheelers stayed on the rivers after steam stern-wheelers had disappeared.

In recent years, advances in technology have been met by improvements in operating methods. Powerful modern towboats push large tows of barges bound for various destinations. Towboats are kept underway while various services are performed to make the operation as efficient as possible. Fuel, groceries, and other boat supplies are carried out to towboats by fast launches. Small "shifting service" towboats meet large towboats underway, bringing barges to add to the towboat and removing barges bound for separate destinations. The shifting service often is performed in conjunction with "fleeting" services. Barges are kept in holding areas, similar to railroad yards or parking lots, called fleets. Another towboat will tow the dropped barges on to their destination. Underway services substantially reduce the costly in-port time of large towboats. Other advances in operating techniques include radio dispatching and communications, computerized records, and fully integrated tows of matched barges to reduce water resistance.

■ ■ ■   NAVAL AND GOVERNMENT SHIPS   ■ ■ ■

The greatest number of preserved historic ships are naval and
other former government vessels. These encompass aircraft
carriers, battleships, cruisers, a sailing frigate and a sailing
sloop, a gunboat, a brig of war, destroyers, fleet submarines,
minesweepers, patrol torpedo (PT) boats, naval auxiliaries,
including two former presidential yachts, and prizes of war,
including a German U-boat, two Japanese midget submarines, and two manned torpedoes. There are also a number of
experimental craft, including Confederate submarines and
the first true submarine hull, the USS *Albacore*. The largest
group of any specific type of preserved naval ships is a collection of 23 submarines of various classes, followed by a collection of eight destroyers. Throughout this book naval vessels
will be referred to by type and class. When changes occur in a
ship type, whether a destroyer or an aircraft carrier, they are
embodied for the first time in a newly built and designated vessel. The name of that vessel, as the lead ship of the class, then is
used to describe all other ships built to that design. Thus, the

The *Mayor Andrew Broaddus* is
the only remaining floating lifesaving station in the United States.

USS *Balao* was the first of many *Balao*-class submarines, just as the USS *Essex* was the first of the *Essex*-class aircraft carriers, and the USS *Iowa* was the first of the *Iowa*-class battleships.

A few cutters, a lighthouse tender, a buoy tender, lightships, and the only remaining floating lifesaving station represent the maritime heritage of the U.S. Coast Guard. The U.S. Army Corps of Engineers also is represented by a large group of preserved ships, including dredges, snagboats, inspection craft, and tugboats. These preserved naval and government ships will be discussed in more detail in the individual entries.

By the first decades of the 20th century, American ships had for the most part shifted from wood-hulled, sail- and steam-powered vessels to metal-hulled ships powered by steam, diesel, and diesel-electric engines. The principal American ship types after the 1920s were intercoastal freight and passenger steamers (coasters), operating on the nation's sounds and bays, on the Great Lakes and inland waterways, and in the harbors. These included coastal passenger, mail, and freight steamers and motor ships, fishing vessels, tankers, night- and day-service passenger, mail, and freight carriers on the sounds and bays, and the ubiquitous and numerous harbor craft—towboats, tugboats, fireboats, barges, dredges, derrick boats, workboats, scows, ferries, car floats, and lighthouse tenders and lightships. The inland rivers, lakes, and canals all had specialized ship types—excursion steamers, snagboats, barges, pushboats, train and car ferries, bulk and package freighters, passenger vessels, and lakers, canallers, and self-unloaders of the Great Lakes.

These ship types and their survivors represent a tremendous sweep of maritime and naval history, naval architecture, and marine engineering. They do not cover all aspects of the maritime heritage of the United States or of the world, however, for far too many vessels, particularly those dating before 1875, simply no longer exist.

The steam-propelled dredge *William M. Black*, launched in 1934, incorporated features of many earlier U.S. Army Corps of Engineers vessels that deepened and redirected the western rivers, allowing the spread of navigation to regions previously inaccessible.

PRESERVING SHIPS

The concept of preserving significant artifacts from the maritime past dates to antiquity. Following his stunning naval victory over Antony and Cleopatra's forces at Actium in 31 B.C., Octavian removed the bronze rams from the bows of the captured warships and placed 35 of them on a marble wall inside a temple on a hill overlooking the site of the battle. After its epic voyage of circumnavigation and piracy in the 16th century, Francis Drake's *Golden Hinde* was moored on the Thames and kept as an exhibit until its rotten timbers gave way and it sank. A chair made from the *Golden Hinde*'s remains is now a prominent display at Woburn Abbey.

In the United States the idea of saving the records and artifacts of maritime endeavor began, if a place and time can be ascribed to a principle, with the establishment of the East India Marine Society. The society had its origins in a meeting held at Salem, Massachusetts, then the maritime center of the United States, on August 31, 1799. On that date 22 ship captains agreed to organize the society to assist the families of deceased members, collect navigational information, and create a museum. The society was incorporated on March 2, 1801, and by 1821 it had accepted 4,299 accessions, including models of ships and artifacts gathered on voyages to the South Seas, India, and the Orient. In 1824 the society laid the cornerstone of a building to house it and its collections at the corner of Essex and Washington streets. On October 14, 1825, the East India Marine Hall was dedicated. Thus was created an institution that in time became the Peabody Museum of Salem.

The idea of preserving entire ships, however, did not receive much attention. Public outcry against the idea of breaking up the USS *Constitution*, "Old Ironsides," induced the navy to save the venerable warship. A poem written by Oliver Wendell Holmes in 1830 bewailed the fact that "the harpies of the shore shall pluck the eagle of the sea!" If the ship could not be saved, opined Holmes, then

> Oh, better that her shattered hulk
> Should sink beneath the wave;
> Her thunders shook the mighty deep,
> And there should be her grave;
> Nail to the mast her holy flag,
> Set every threadbare sail,
> And give her to the god of storms,
> The lightning and the gale!

Rebuilt and restored to duty in 1835, the *Constitution* was from that day forward a special if not sacred ship, more a relic than a man-of-war. Rebuilt in 1871 and again for its centennial in 1897, it was restored in 1907. In 1927, after a nationwide campaign that included donations of pennies, nickels, and dimes from schoolchildren and by 1930 had raised $154,500, "Old Ironsides" underwent a reconstruction that ended in 1931. The frigate then toured the nation on a 22,000-mile trip to 33 ports before returning to Boston in May 1934. Additional work was done to the ship during the American

The idea of preserving entire ships was introduced when the USS *Constitution* was rebuilt and restored for duty in 1835.

Through the 1960s historic vessels often were raised from their resting places in lakes and rivers, a practice now rarely advocated because of the harm caused by removing these historic resources and the investment needed to conserve them. The schooner *Alvin Clark* was raised from Lake Michigan in 1969 fully intact, but because no effort was made to conserve it, it has since badly deteriorated.

Revolution bicentennial, and yet another rebuilding is scheduled for the ship's own bicentennial in 1997.

Other ships were preserved in the 19th century, among them the tiny *Sparrowhawk,* a pilgrim craft that had wrecked on Cape Cod and was later exposed on the beach after a winter storm in 1863. The 40-foot-long vessel's timbers were excavated, displayed on the Boston Common, and then taken on tour by P. T. Barnum before ending up as a permanent exhibit in Pilgrim Hall at Plymouth, Massachusetts. The recovery of this tiny merchant craft was an anomaly in a period that otherwise confined its attention to the preservation of naval vessels. In the early 20th century, efforts to save historic ships included raising wrecks from the cold, fresh waters of inland lakes, notably the brig *Niagara,* recovered from Presque Isle

Bay in Lake Erie in 1913 and rebuilt, and the Revolutionary War gundelo *Philadelphia*, sunk during the Battle of Valcour Bay on Lake Champlain on October 11, 1776, and raised from the lake in 1935. This tradition of raising historic vessels, most of them naval craft, persisted through the 1960s with the recovery of the Confederate river warships *Chattahoochee* and *Jackson* from the Chattahoochee River in Georgia, the salvage of the Union gunboat *Cairo* from the Yazoo River in Mississippi, the Confederate ironclad *Neuse* from its namesake river in North Carolina, the schooner *Alvin Clark* from Lake Michigan, and the War of 1812 schooner *Ticonderoga* from the Poultney River in Vermont, to name a few.

Early preservation efforts focused on saving retired naval vessels from being scrapped or sunk. The USS *Hartford*, David

Glasgow Farragut's flagship during the Battle of Mobile Bay, was kept afloat and like the *Constitution* survived into the 20th century as a result of rebuildings. In October 1945 the aging steam warship was declared a naval relic and moored for display at the Norfolk Navy Yard, in Norfolk, Virginia. The *Hartford* remained there until it sank at its berth in November 1956. It was broken up, and pieces and artifacts were sent to museums and navy facilities around the nation. Another naval vessel, the battleship *Oregon*, built in 1893 and a veteran of the Spanish-American War, was saved from use as a target hulk in 1920 when Oregon citizens and Spanish-American War veterans waged a campaign to save the battleship. Towed up the Columbia River to Portland in 1925, the *Oregon* remained on display until a misguided scrap drive during World War II, when it was partially scrapped and sent into the Pacific as an ammunition hulk. A postwar drive to restore the hulk failed, and in 1956 the *Oregon* was scrapped in Japan.

Another endeavor proved successful, however, when the U.S. Navy deeded the dreadnought USS *Texas* to its namesake state in 1948. At the end of World War II many states and cities had begun campaigns to acquire some of the numerous newly decommissioned warships. The *Texas* alone was saved at this time, although it paved the way for other naval vessels to be saved. Private and in some cases local or state-funded enterprises managed to acquire, restore, and open four other

Deeded to its namesake state in 1948, the USS *Texas* underwent restoration as a floating exhibit at Todd Shipyard in Galveston, Texas, in 1989.

Mystic Seaport Museum, Mystic, Connecticut, served as the center for the nation's first successful merchant ship preservation project when it acquired the last American whaler, the *Charles W. Morgan.*

warships to the public by 1965. Adm. George Dewey's flagship from the Battle of Manila Bay, the USS *Olympia*, opened in Philadelphia in 1958, followed by the battleships *Alabama*, *North Carolina*, and *Massachusetts* in their respective states. These pioneers formed the core of the Historic Naval Ships of North America (HINAS), an organization of 70 ships founded in 1966 by 11 organizations with historic naval vessels. HINAS's ranks now include other battleships, such as aircraft carriers, and smaller but equally important destroyers, submarines, minesweepers, PT boats, and the restored brig *Niagara*.

The preservation of merchant vessels that began with the establishment of the East India Marine Society continued with the creation of other maritime museums. Notable additions were the Mariners Museum, which opened in Newport News, Virginia, in 1930, the result of the largesse of the shipping magnate and philanthropist Archer Huntington. A year earlier the Mystic Seaport Museum opened at Mystic, Connecticut. In time its collection grew to include several historic vessels and more than 60 buildings depicting a typical New England seafaring community of the 19th century, including industrial and commercial facilities such as a sail loft and a ship chandler's shop. Mystic Seaport also served as the center for the nation's first successful merchant ship preservation project when it acquired the last American whaler, the *Charles W. Morgan.* Symbolic of a romantic view of whaling entertained by most Americans and reinforced by *Moby Dick*, the *Morgan* ended its whaling career in the 1920s at New Bedford. Saved from burning or scuttling, it was placed in a cofferdam surrounded by sand and exhibited at South Dartmouth until acquired by Mystic Seaport in 1941. Completely restored and once again afloat, the ship was one of the first vessels declared a National Historic Landmark; thus its status as a sole survivor of an important American trade was confirmed.

The 1950s saw the birth of a significant maritime museum and the genesis of what in time would be the nation's largest collection of merchant vessels when the San Francisco Maritime Museum was established in 1951. Growing out of the interest of Karl Kortum, a young sailor and ardent preservationist, and those he enlisted in the cause, the museum saved the square-rigger *Balclutha* in 1954 and opened it to the public on July 19, 1955. The event was a triumph for maritime preservation and heralded a period in which large ships, particularly square-riggers, were sought out for salvation. Many were not saved, but in the 1960s and 1970s the *Balclutha*

Caretakers of the largest fleet of merchant vessels, including here the *Balclutha*, the *Eureka*, and the *C. A. Thayer*, the San Francisco Maritime National Historical Park was established as the San Francisco Maritime Museum in 1951.

was joined by the barks *Star of India, Peking, Elissa,* and *Moshulu* and the ships *Wavertree* and *Falls of Clyde*. These vessels were displayed at ports around the nation. The *Balclutha*'s success led the state of California to purchase a number of historic vessels for a new state maritime historical park on the city's waterfront: the three-masted schooner *C. A. Thayer*, the steam schooner *Wapama*, the scow schooner *Alma*, the ferry *Eureka*, and the tugboat *Hercules*. Meanwhile the San Francisco Maritime Museum rescued and restored the British tugboat *Eppleton Hall*. (The San Francisco Maritime Museum and the state historical park were later merged under the National Park Service, becoming the San Francisco Maritime National Historical Park.)

Other museums dedicated to preserving individual ships were founded at this time, including South Street Seaport in New York in the 1960s and the San Diego Maritime Museum in the 1970s. These included museums with local and regional collections that saved smaller generic and significant craft, such as Chesapeake Bay skipjacks, and existing museums without a major maritime thrust that saved ships, such as

Many small maritime museums, such as the Calvert Marine Museum, have developed collections focusing on local and regional resources.

Vermont's Shelburne Museum, which rescued the Lake Champlain excursion steamer *Ticonderoga* and brought it ashore as its centerpiece. Across the country like-minded people pursued the goal of saving as much of America's maritime past as they could. The majority of this effort focused on the major artifact of that past—the ship.

Another form of ship preservation that occurred outside the museum setting began during the Depression, when the artist Frank Swift, then living at Bucksport, Maine, conceived an idea for saving the rapidly vanishing schooners. While watching a coaster unloading pulpwood at a mill on the Penobscot River near his home, Swift thought of chartering a schooner for extended passenger cruises. Although several vessels, including the schooner *Stephen Taber*, were available for day-long sails, a prolonged cruise, offering an experience similar to that of the "dude" ranch in the West, was a new

The restoration of schooners for Maine's windjammer fleet preserves the vanishing trades of shipwrightery and much of the historic fabric of the vessels. Here one worker is fastening gudgeons, hardware used to mount the ship's rudder (above right), on the *Mattie*, recently renamed *Grace Bailey*, while another drives fasteners into hull planking.

concept. It was also the first time that the concept of adaptive use of a historic vessel was applied to maritime preservation. Swift's first vessel, the 1881 schooner *Mabel*, was chartered in 1936, with a Deer Island skipper as captain and his wife as ship's cook.

The concept was slow to catch on, but by 1939 Swift was able to purchase the schooner *Annie F. Kimball* and began operating it out of Camden, Maine, on six-day cruises at $32 a head. Around that time Swift advertised in a promotional pamphlet one- or two-week cruises:

> *These schooners are not yachts—just picturesque down-east sailing vessels, clipper-bowed and able, with billowing sails and hempen rigging. Each Monday, from July 4th until September 10th, the* Annie Kimball *and the* Lydia Webster *will sail from Camden, Maine, for a week's cruise—not to follow an exact itinerary but to use the winds and tides to make the cruise most interesting.*

Other entrepreneurs followed Swift's lead, and by the late 1940s several schooners, saved from oblivion, were part of the Maine windjammer fleet.

In the early days of these windjammer cruises, scores of old vessels still were put out of service and left to rot in every cove and mudflat along the coast. Having an overabundance of schooners, Swift and other owners usually ran a ship hard, stripped and sank it, and bought another. But by the 1970s, demand had increased for the windjammer experience in an age of few surviving historic schooners, and young entrepreneurs turned to building new schooners along the lines of the old vessels, with a few modern improvements, and rescuing unused or soon-to-languish schooners, some of them former fishing vessels, for the trade. In 1971 the 1886 oyster schooner *Isaac H. Evans* was rescued by Doug and Linda Lee and restored. The success of the *Evans* inspired John Foss, who bought and restored the *Lewis R. French* between 1973 and 1976. To do the work, Foss and the Lees purchased an old shipyard at the north end of Rockland, Maine. Joined by the dragger *J. & E. Riggin*, a 1927 schooner owned by David and Sue Allen, the fleet, collectively run out of the North End Shipyard as the Maine Windjammer Cruises, was augmented by the arrival of the Gloucesterman *American Eagle*, bought and restored by John Foss in 1986.

The windjammers operating along the Maine coast no longer carry loads of wood or granite but, as owner-captain Doug Lee remarks, "carry the only cargo that loads and unloads itself." The windjammers are unique in the nation in offering marine recreation. They do not provide sail training but instead instill a relaxed sense of the sea and travel under sail, in which the passengers are encouraged but not required to lend a hand as needed. The North End Shipyard continues to maintain and restore the schooners as needed and offers its services to other historic vessels on the coast. Thus, along with the historic fabric of the vessels themselves, skills are preserved—the vanishing trades of shipwrightery and, in the operation of the schooners, the skills of seamanship.

The success of maritime preservation was evidenced also by the creation of the National Maritime Historical Society

(NMHS) in 1963. Headed by Peter Stanford, the driving force behind the creation of New York's South Street Seaport, NMHS has been an active force in American maritime preservation. The society publishes a magazine, *Sea History*, and for the past several years has offered an invaluable newsletter, the *Sea History Gazette*. The NMHS has successfully lobbied for many maritime projects, including saving historic ships, and promoted greater public appreciation and support for preserving the nation's seafaring past. Extending its work abroad, it champions the cause of preserving significant American ships abroad and foreign-built ships of paramount importance to the nautical past, such as Brunel's *Great Britain* and the bark *Vicar of Bray*, which was used during the California gold rush.

The *Jeremiah O'Brien*, the last unaltered World War II Liberty ship, was restored partially through a major grant from the National Trust for Historic Preservation. Restoration involved contributions from maritime unions, trades, and industries including voluntary labor.

Public interest in maritime preservation at this time was greatly aided by the first Operation Sail (OpSail). On July 4, 1964, a parade of 24 tall ships in New York Harbor, accompanied by naval vessels, yachts, and other craft, revived an interest in the days of sail. During the nation's bicentennial celebration, OpSail '76, televised and seen by millions, spurred the movement forward. A third and equally successful event, OpSail '86, heralded the restoration of the Statue of Liberty. Fourteen million people in New York witnessed the spectacle of canvas spread to the wind and vessels of all types—battleships, square-riggers, and lovingly restored schooners and skipjacks—passing in review before Bedloe's Island. A more pragmatic result of the 1976 celebration was a five-year maritime heritage grants program (1978–82) at the National Trust for Historic Preservation, which distributed $5.5 million to 155 maritime projects in 33 states. Key successes of the maritime grants program included rescuing the *Jeremiah O'Brien*, the last unaltered World War II Liberty ship; the bark *Elissa*, built in 1877; and many other less well-known but important vessels. The program could not fulfill all expectations in the maritime community, however, and in 1982 the National Trust established the Maritime Heritage Task Force to address the larger concerns of maritime preservationists. In 1984 a series of recommendations agreed upon by the task force was taken to the U.S. Congress.

■ ■ ■   NATIONAL MARITIME INITIATIVE   ■ ■ ■

In 1984 maritime preservation faced a fundamental crisis. Despite the funding programs of 1978–82, maritime preservation for the most part did not enjoy the basic achievements that many other areas of historic preservation did. There was no inventory of maritime resources or, for that matter, consensus on exactly what constituted a "maritime resource." Ships, shipwrecks, lighthouses, and other maritime sites were underrepresented in both the National Historic Landmarks program and the National Register of Historic Places. No basic standards or guidelines for the preservation of ships existed, nor did agreement on priorities for preservation. The benefits of historic preservation practice resulting from the passage of the National Historic Preservation Act in 1966 had little impact on maritime resources. Maritime preservation lagged behind land-based preservation efforts, or, as one preservation advocate remarked in 1985, "Maritime preservation is 20 years behind the times."

Despite the significance of maritime culture in American history, maritime resources languished, partly because of the harsh environment that hosts most maritime resources and partly because maritime preservation was not in the mainstream of general historic preservation. Historic ships lay rotting, even under government stewardship. Historic lighthouses were vandalized or were in danger of toppling into the ocean. Historic shipwrecks were being plundered and looted for "treasure" and souvenirs—actions that would not have been tolerated for land-based archeological sites.

These and other problems were addressed by the National Trust's Maritime Heritage Task Force, whose findings were

Maryland leads the states in the number of vessels listed in the National Register of Historic Places, largely because of its listing of the Chesapeake Bay skipjack fleet in 1985. The *Mary W. Somers* was one of 23 skipjacks listed that year.

reflected in language added to the 1985 fiscal year appropriation by the U.S. Congress for the National Park Service. The legislation required the National Park Service, "in cooperation with the National Trust for Historic Preservation and the maritime preservation community…[to] conduct a survey of historic maritime resources, including those of the Service; recommend standards and priorities for the preservation of those resources; and recommend the appropriate Federal and private sector roles in addressing these priorities." Thus several basic tasks for maritime preservation were defined: (1) find out what maritime resources existed; (2) rank the needs of these resources; and (3) meet the needs in a systematic manner that applys a consistent, professionally sound approach. The mandate led to a cooperative initiative called the National Maritime Initiative, based at the National Park Service.

CREATING A NATIONAL INVENTORY

In 1986 the National Park Service created a computerized inventory of large preserved historic vessels. The figure for defining "large" vessels—40 feet long and measuring 20 tons (one ton equals 100 cubic feet)—was taken from the definition of a large vessel used by Norman Brouwer of New York's South Street Seaport Museum, who, under the auspices of the World Ship Trust, published the *International Register of Historic Ships* in 1985. For the purposes of this inventory, vessels to be considered historic had to be listed or determined eligible or likely to be considered eligible for listing in the National Register of Historic Places. Later this definition was refined to include only those vessels that were the focus of a preservation effort.

One important product of the computerized inventory is a compilation of statistical data that provides a nationwide analysis of the status of the country's preserved historic ships, their condition, uses, and preservation needs. In 1987, when the inventory stood at nearly 250 ships, statistics for condition, preservation objective, estimated preservation cost, type, age, present use, geographic distribution, and National Register and National Historic Landmark status were prepared, providing the first fairly comprehensive look at the nation's historic ships. The results dispelled some commonly held assumptions about the ships—that most dated to World War II, that most were in New England, and that most were in poor condition and required large sums of money to maintain and restore.

As a follow-up to the large ships inventory, in 1987 the NPS developed formats for computerized inventories of aids to navigation (lighthouses, lightships, and so forth), shipwrecks and hulks, small craft collections, document collec-

Since the creation of the National Park Service's National Maritime Initiative, 59 vessels have been designated National Historic Landmarks, bringing the total to 89 in May 1991. The Lightship *WAL-604* ("Columbia") was designated a National Historic Landmark on December 20, 1989.

tions, artifact collections, and maritime sites and structures on land. The only two inventories currently maintained by the National Maritime Initiative, in addition to that of large ships, are the aids to navigation and shipwreck inventories. These data reflect the initiative's decision to focus its effort on specific cultural resources that usually do not enjoy protection in museum collections. The small craft inventory was provided to the Museum Small Craft Association (MSCA), a cooperative venture of various museum small craft curators who are preparing a "union list" of historic small craft.

Eight ships were listed in the National Register of Historic Places during its first year in 1966. The *Olympia*, the oldest steel-hulled American warship afloat, was among those eight National Historic Landmark vessels listed.

NATIONAL REGISTER AND HISTORIC SHIPS

Currently 177 large (that is, more than 40 feet long) historic vessels in the United States are individually listed in the National Register of Historic Places. In addition, five large historic vessels are listed as contributing elements to a National Register historic district. Those listed represent only a little more than half of the candidates presumably eligible for listing. The fact that these vessels are listed is due primarily to two factors—the preparation of multiple property listings by the states of Maryland and Florida, for skipjacks and spongeboats respectively, and the National Historic Landmarks (NHL) Program, which in 1985–86 studied World War II warships associated with the Pacific war and, in cooperation with the National Maritime Initiative, has studied large preserved historic vessels as part of a larger "Maritime Heritage of the United States" theme since 1988.

PRESERVATION STANDARDS

The preservation, rehabilitation, and restoration of historic structures greatly benefitted from the preparation of the Secretary of the Interior's Standards for Rehabilitation and Guidelines for Rehabilitating Historic Buildings published by the National Park Service in 1976. A significant need existed, however, for separate standards and guidelines for a unique class of structures—historic ships. The need for standards for maritime preservation, identified by the National Trust's task force, was again raised at a conference on maritime preservation held in San Francisco is September 1985. Throughout the conference considerable discussion after each session focused on defining the issues and developing a policy statement concerning maritime preservation. An ad hoc committee worked to draft and present suggested standards for the management of historic vessels. These standards were modified in discussion with the participants, and at the close of the conference a resolution supporting the suggested standards was enthusiastically adopted.

The creation of the National Maritime Initiative provided the first opportunity for the National Park Service to develop formal standards for ships to supplement the existing Secretary of the Interior's Standards for Historic Preservation. A draft of the standards, developed with guidance from a committee of maritime preservation professionals representing a wide range of organizations and experience across the country, followed the format of the Secretary of the Interior's Standards for Historic Preservation Projects with Guidelines for Applying the Standards. After an extensive review process, the final product was prepared and published in 1990.

The schooner *Lettie G. Howard*, shown here in 1989 at South Street Seaport, is a National Historic Landmark. Restoration of the vessel has been based on the National Maritime Initiative's standards issued in 1990.

The new Secretary of the Interior's Standards for Historic Vessel Preservation Projects with Guidelines for Applying the Standards are now available from the National Park Service and meet a longstanding need in maritime preservation for uniform standards for historic ship projects. Guidelines for eight historic preservation treatments and definitions for key maritime preservation terms form a major part of the document. The need for such a document was demonstrated throughout the five-year period of its preparation by requests for draft versions of the standards for use in several projects.

■ ■ ■   NATIONAL MARITIME ALLIANCE   ■ ■ ■

One of the more successful aspects of maritime preservation in recent years has been the creation of the National Maritime Alliance. A loose-knit confederation of various maritime preservation organizations, the Maritime Alliance was founded at the suggestion of Henry H. Anderson, Jr., a trustee of the National Maritime Historical Society. The National Maritime Alliance seeks to build a nationwide coalition among the diverse interest groups in maritime preservation. These include those interested or involved in saving ships, lighthouses, shipwrecks, canals, and traditional maritime folkways and other historic preservationists. The group has launched a campaign entitled "Save Our Ships," a time-honored battle cry of the movement, and is now working on a variety of programs and concepts to ensure that the maritime preservation movement speaks with one voice as it seeks legislative and financial support.

████████████████████

GUIDE TO THE GUIDE

The ships included in this volume were selected primarily from the National Maritime Initiative's Inventory of Large Preserved Historic Vessels. These ships are for the most part at least 50 years old, 40 feet or more in length, and registered at 20 tons or more. They are also, with a few exceptions, accessible to the public as museum exhibits, memorials, sail training or education vessels, operating passenger vessels, sailing ambassadors, or restaurants, theaters, and hotels. Historic vessels that are privately owned and used for private recreation, such as yachts, are not included, nor are historic vessels currently used in commercial operations that do not involve passengers, such as many of the Maryland skipjacks and Florida spongeboats.

All National Historic Landmark vessels, regardless of their accessibility, are included. These have been recognized to be of exceptional significance in the United States' maritime heritage. Also included are museum-displayed remains of entire vessels, such as the USS *Cairo* or the *Sparrowhawk*, and the three viewable hulks of the last four-masted schooners in the nation.

Generally the ships listed in this volume have been or are currently the focus of some type of preservation effort. For some, restoration was still in process at the time of publication; most should open to the public in the near future. In addition, a location is noted for each entry. Many historic vessels still operate, so they may not be moored at their berths for perhaps days, weeks, or months at a time. Unfortunately, some vessels will change their berths permanently; perhaps they will leave a trail of their whereabouts. At the end of each entry the bracketed information notes the owner or manager of each vessel. In most cases, these persons or organizations would be happy to supply more information about their vessels.

The entries are organized geographically by region and alphabetically by state. Because some states may fall into more than one region (for instance, New York is included in the Mid-Atlantic and the Great Lakes regions), states may be listed more than once. Within states the vessels are listed alphabetically according to the nearest city or town. In entries describing a military vessel, a hull number follows the vessel's name in parentheses; this unique number identifies the vessel type and number assigned to the individual vessel. At the end of an entry "NR" indicates that the vessel is listed in the National Register of Historic Places. "NHL" indicates that the vessel has been designated a National Historic Landmark. The letters "ASME" refer to a National Historic Civil Engineering Landmark of the American Society of Mechanical Engineers.

NEW ENGLAND

The *Brilliant*, Mystic, Connecticut,
a schooner-yacht of the 1930s.

■ ■ ■ ■ ■ ■ ■ CONNECTICUT ■ ■ ■ ■ ■ ■ ■

ESSEX

■ **Christeen**
Connecticut River Museum
End of Main Street
1883

From the 1880s through the 1930s oystering was a national industry with thriving centers on the Narragansett, Delaware, Chesapeake, Mobile, San Francisco, and Great Sound bays, as well as on Long Island Sound. At the turn of the century oysters were the chief fishery product of the United States. The most common large vessel built to harvest oysters was the oyster sloop, a universal craft with some regional variation. Only three oyster sloops are known to survive in the United States—the *Christeen* (1883), the *Modesty* (1923), and the *Hope* (1948). The *Christeen* is the oldest surviving working example of an oyster sloop in the United States and an outstanding representative of the early form of oyster sloop, a type that dates to the 1830s. Of all these vessels the *Christeen* best exemplifies the type and its employment. In its career it fished, clammed, scalloped, freighted potatoes and furniture, and was a chartered excursion and sightseeing vessel; in short, "she did almost everything these ubiquitous sloops had done" in their long history.

The *Christeen* was built in 1883 at Glenwood Landing on Long Island for oysterman William W. Smith of Oyster Bay, New York. The vessel was licensed to work the offshore oyster beds of Long Island and participate in the coasting trade in 1884. The sloop worked the oyster beds and carried occasional bulk cargoes, as did others of its type, through the 19th century. In 1894, then owned by Henry W. Schmeelk, Jr., of Greenwich, the *Christeen* was licensed to work the Connecticut oyster beds. The sloop continued to oyster and carry cargoes under sail until 1914, when a small engine was added and it was converted to an auxiliary powered motor vessel. The vessel retained its rig but worked primarily under power, occasionally dredging oysters and carrying cargoes between Connecticut and Long Island for William Bond of Southold, New York.

In 1936, on Bond's death, the *Christeen* was sold. The sloop worked in the New Jersey fisheries, sometimes serving as a "liveaboard" when laid up for periods of time. After a brief service as an excursion and sightseeing charter boat in the 1970s, the *Christeen* was sold again and became a liveaboard at New London, Connecticut, when it was discovered and purchased by its present owners, who have restored the vessel's 1914 appearance and are now rehabilitating it to return to sailing and occasionally dredging for oysters. [Tradewinds Education Network]

GROTON

■ **HA-8**
Nautilus Memorial and
Submarine Force Library
and Museum
Naval Submarine Base
1938

The development of submersible craft as weapons for naval warfare began with the construction of small vessels. From Bushnell's "Turtle" and Horace Lawson Hunley's Confederate *David* through John Holland's *Fenian Ram* and *Holland I*, submersible craft grew larger, achieving greater size and effective use by World War I. The success of the "submarine" during the war led to increased programs of development and construction by various nations. In Japan subma-

The *HA-8*, an early example of the midget submarine used by the Imperial Japanese Navy during World War II.

rine development included "midget" submarines. In 1933 Capt. Kishimoto Kaneji of the Imperial Japanese Navy designed two torpedo-shaped midgets as auxiliary weapons to be carried by fast surface vessels. Built in 1934 at Kure Navy Yard and known as "A-Hyoteki," or "A-Target," these vessels, which had conning towers fitted as a result of experimentation, led to a later version, "A-Hyotelei"; two submarines of this version, the *HA-1* and the *HA-2*, were built in 1936. In 1938 the midget program, operating under stringent security, commenced in earnest on 49 of the Type A vessels, the *HA-3* through the *HA-52*. Among the vessels built during this initial burst of construction was the *HA-8*, a "sister" of the *HA-19*, which would later participate in the attack on Pearl Harbor and be captured. The two midgets are the only examples of the type displayed in the United States as prizes of war. The *HA-8*'s history and capture are unknown. The midget is displayed along with a German and an Italian midget submarine in front of the Submarine Force Library and Museum, adjacent to the USS *Nautilus*. [Nautilus Memorial and Submarine Force Library and Museum]

The brainchild of Adm. Hyman G. Rickover, the "father of the nuclear navy," the USS *Nautilus* was the world's first nuclear-powered submarine. Its propulsion system is a landmark in the history of naval engineering and submersible craft. All vessels previously known as submarines were in fact only submersible craft. The *Nautilus*'s nuclear power system enabled the boat to remain submerged for weeks, even months. Thus, it was the world's first true submarine. Scores of nuclear submarines followed the *Nautilus*, replacing the United States' diesel boat fleet.

On its maiden voyage to Puerto Rico in 1955 the *Nautilus* remained submerged for 1,381 miles and 89.9 hours, the longest submerged cruise to that date. Another first was accomplished in 1958, when the vessel left Pearl Harbor,

■ **USS Nautilus (SSN-571)**
Nautilus Memorial and
Submarine Force Library
and Museum
Naval Submarine Base
1954

Hawaii, under classified orders to conduct Operation Sunshine, the first crossing of the North Pole by a ship. With 116 men aboard the *Nautilus* sailed beneath the Arctic icepack to the North Pole to broadcast the famous message: "*Nautilus* 90 North." Deployed to the Mediterranean Sea in 1960, the *Nautilus* was the first submarine assigned to the U.S. Sixth Fleet. Over the next six years the *Nautilus* participated in several fleet exercises while steaming more than 200,000 miles. Later the *Nautilus* was involved in a variety of developmental testing programs while continuing to serve alongside many of the more modern nuclear-powered submarines. The *Nautilus* cruised 62,562 miles on its reactor's first core, 91,324 miles on the second, and 150,000 miles on the third. Decommissioned in 1980 after a career spanning 25 years and almost a half million miles, the *Nautilus* was towed back to its place of construction in 1985. The ship is now open to the public at the Nautilus Memorial and Submarine Force Library and Museum in Groton, Connecticut, where many of America's submarines in addition to the *Nautilus* have been built since 1940. NR. NHL. [Nautilus Memorial and Submarine Force Library and Museum]

The *Nautilus*, shown here in New York Harbor in 1958, could remain submerged for long periods because of its nuclear-powered system.

MYSTIC

■ **Brilliant**
Mystic Seaport Museum
50 Germanville Avenue
1932

Built by Henry Nevins at City Island, New York, the *Brilliant*'s design was based on the great schooner-yachts of the 19th century. The two-masted schooner was used for racing and cruising except during World War II, when it served in the U.S. Coast Guard's picket patrol. The *Brilliant* was presented to Mystic Seaport in 1952 and currently serves as a training ship in its sail education program. NR. [Mystic Seaport Museum]

■ **Charles W. Morgan**
Mystic Seaport Museum
50 Germanville Avenue
1841

The last survivor of the 19th-century wood-hulled whaling vessels, the *Charles W. Morgan* was built for Charles Waln Morgan at the shipyard of Jethro and Zachariah Hillman in New Bedford, Massachusetts. The *Morgan* was launched

The last survivor of the 19th-century wood-hulled whaling vessels, the *Charles W. Morgan* sailed in pursuit of whales for almost 80 years.

during the peak years of the whaling industry. By the time it left on its second voyage, the whaling fleet numbered 678 ships and barks, 35 brigs, and 22 schooners, most from New Bedford and Nantucket. (Ships, barks, barkentines, brigs, and schooners were distinguished by the number of masts and arrangement of the sails.) Whale products were used for candles, whale oil lamps, cosmetics, buggy whips, canes, parasols, and corset stays. Later, whale oil also initially filled the need for a fine lubricant as the nation became industrialized. The *Morgan* was called a "lucky ship"—only once in its first 30 years of whaling did the gross value of its cargoes drop below $50,000.

On its maiden voyage the *Morgan* rounded Cape Horn and cruised the Pacific Ocean, returning to New Bedford three years and four months later with 2,400 barrels of oil and 10,000 pounds of whalebone. Thirty-seven voyages over an 80-year period yielded a total of 54,483 barrels of oil and 152,934 pounds of whalebone. The *Morgan* was home to more than 1,000 crew. Twenty-one masters commanded the vessel. Crews averaged 33 men per voyage, including officers, seamen, greenhands, and "idlers"—the cooper, carpenter, cook, steward, and ship's boy, who remained aboard to keep the ship headed toward the boats when the hunt for a whale was underway.

The *Morgan* was retired from whaling in 1921. After appearing in the motion pictures *Down to the Sea in Ships* and *Java Head*, it was laid up (that is, taken out of service) and forgotten until purchased by E. H. R. Green, the grandson of one of the *Morgan*'s former owners, who docked the vessel at his estate at South Dartmouth, Massachusetts. The *Morgan* became an exhibit open to those interested in whaling and maritime history until funds to maintain the vessel ran out upon Green's death in 1935. Brought to Mystic Seaport in 1941, the *Morgan* was studied, maintained, and completely restored. Relaunched in 1974, the vessel can now be toured as a floating exhibit. NR. NHL. [Mystic Seaport Museum]

Named after the young daughter of its captain, John Henry Berry, the *Emma C. Berry* was built in Noank, Connecticut, as a sloop-rigged "well smack" for the mackerel fisheries. The *Berry* fished the local waters between Montauk and Cape Cod for its first 30 years, was rerigged as a schooner in the 1880s, and was sold in 1894 to an owner in Maine, where the

■ **Emma C. Berry**
Mystic Seaport Museum
50 Germanville Avenue
1866

Presented to Mystic Seaport, the *Emma C. Berry* originally served the mackerel fisheries off New England.

vessel remained until it was "fished out" and abandoned in 1924. Rescued two years later, the vessel became a coaster, hauling coal, salt, and dried fish along the coast of Maine. Abandoned again in 1931, the *Berry* was purchased for use as a yacht and at times a freighter on the coast of New Jersey, in the Chesapeake, and as far south as the Carolinas. Presented to Mystic Seaport in 1969, the *Berry* has been restored to its original rig and condition. NR. [Mystic Seaport Museum]

■ **Florence**
Mystic Seaport Museum
50 Germanville Avenue
1926

An excellent example of the small motor fishing boats of the 1920s, the Florence was built by the Franklin G. Post and Son Shipyard in Mystic, Connecticut, for Morris Thompson of New London, Connecticut. These motorized craft gradually replaced the sailing schooners of the 19th and early 20th centuries. The Florence is a floating exhibit at Mystic Seaport. [Mystic Seaport Museum]

■ **Joseph Conrad**
Mystic Seaport Museum
50 Germanville Avenue
1882

Built as the *George Stage* by the firm of Burmeiser and Wain in Copenhagen, Denmark, this iron ship was used to train boys planning a career at sea. While cruising the Baltic and North seas, cadets learned navigation, ship handling, steam engine operation, rope work, and teamwork. After 52 years of training future Danish merchant officers, the *Stage* was purchased by the famous maritime historian and sailor Allen Villiers, who renamed the ship *Joseph Conrad*. Leaving England in 1934 with a crew of professional seamen, boys, and paying "cadets," the *Joseph Conrad* began a two-year journey to circumnavigate the globe, a voyage described by Villiers in *The Cruise of the Conrad*. Sold at the end of the voyage, the *Conrad* served briefly as a pleasure yacht harbored in Charleston, South Carolina. Turned over to the Federal Maritime Commission in 1939, the *Conrad* served as a merchant training ship out of St. Petersburg, Florida. Declared surplus in 1947, an act of Congress transferred its ownership to Mystic

Top: The *Florence*, an example
of a small early 20th-century
motor fishing boat. Left: The
Joseph Conrad has been providing sea training for young people
at Mystic Seaport since 1949.

Seaport Museum. After an extensive restoration, the *Conrad*
began its fourth training career in 1949. Young people aged
12 through 17 learn the basics of small boat sailing, navigation, seamanship, and maritime history through the *Conrad*
program. NR. [Mystic Seaport Museum]

Designed by Thomas F. McManus, one of the most important naval architects of the late 19th and early 20th centuries
and a significant figure in the design of the North Atlantic
fishing schooner, the *L. A. Dunton* was built at Essex, Massachusetts, by Arthur Story as a two-masted Grand Banks

■ **L. A. Dunton**
Mystic Seaport Museum
50 Germanville Avenue
1921

Exemplifying the New England fishing schooner, the *L. A. Dunton* was restored to its original rig and appearance as a Grand Banks fisherman in 1963.

fishing boat. Named for the Boothbay, Maine, sailmaker Louis A. Dunton, it sailed out of Gloucester as a dory fisherman until it was sold in 1935 to Canadian owners. The *Dunton*, whose home port is Grand Bank, Newfoundland, continued to fish, even making a voyage carting salt cod to Portugal, and ended its days under Canadian registry as a freighter, carrying general cargoes such as flour, feed, and coal. Rerigged as a ketch and powered by a 160-horsepower diesel engine, the *Dunton* changed considerably in a 40-year period. Purchased by the Marine Historic Association for Mystic Seaport in 1963, it returned to New England waters. Now restored to its original appearance as a dory trawler, the *Dunton* exemplifies the most common vessel and fishing method used on the Grand Banks during the heyday of the sailing fishing boats. The 124-foot-long wood schooner carries 14 dories nestled on its deck. NR. [Mystic Seaport Museum]

■ Sabino
Mystic Seaport Museum
50 Germanville Avenue
1908

The tiny, 57-foot-long *Sabino* is the last coal-fired, wood-hulled excursion steamer in the United States. Built as the *Tourist* in 1908 at East Boothbay, Maine, for the Damariscotta Steamboat Company, the *Sabino* ran on regular excursions on Maine's Damariscotta River and Linekin Bay. Sold in 1922 to the Popham Beach Steamboat Company, the steamer was renamed for a hill on its new route along Maine's Kennebec River. Sold again in 1927 for service on

The wood-hulled *Sabino*, a popular attraction at Mystic Seaport.

Casco Bay, it remained on the bay until 1960, when it was sold to new owners in Massachusetts. The *Sabino*, whose home port was Newburyport, was restored and operated on excursions along the Merrimack River, carrying as many as a hundred passengers on each trip. After sinking at its dock, the steamer was raised and restored by its owners and then in 1973 purchased by the Mystic Seaport Museum. Since then, the *Sabino* has operated on the Mystic River, making several short excursions each day. The tiny steamboat is tremendously popular; visitors watch the crew shovel coal into the boiler (each day the *Sabino* burns as much as a half ton of soft West Virginia coal) and observe the 75-horsepower compound steam engine as it turns the shaft leading to the single propeller. Although rebuilt several times by different owners, the *Sabino* remains an excellent example of the early 20th-century excursion steamers once common on the East Coast. The small steam system, unique in its continuing operation, offers visitors to Mystic Seaport a firsthand view of the earliest days of steamboating. NR. [Mystic Seaport Museum]

NEW LONDON

■ **Eagle**
U.S. Coast Guard Academy
Route 32
1936

Long after the navies of the world abandoned sail for steam, they deemed it important to continue training officer candidates before the mast. That tradition persists today, and several nations have square-rigged or fore-and-aft–rigged sail-training vessels. Many of these vessels are well known to American audiences because they have participated in the OpSails of 1976 and 1986 or have visited U.S. ports on official goodwill tours. Among the most famous is the United States' sail-training ship, the coast guard bark *Eagle*. The bark was designed and launched as a sail-training vessel for the Third Reich. Named the *Horst Wessel* in memory of the Nazi brownshirt martyr, the bark was constructed by Hamburg's

The *Eagle* was acquired by the U.S. Coast Guard at the end of World War II and has since served as a training ship for the Coast Guard Academy in New London, Connecticut.

Blom and Voss yard and launched on June 13, 1936. The *Wessel* survived the war and was acquired by the United States as a prize of war at the end of hostilities. Three other German sail-training ships, the same type of vessel as the *Wessel* but with some differences, were acquired by the victorious allies at the end of the war and continue to sail—Romania's *Mircea*, Portugal's *Sagres*, and the USSR's *Tovaritsch*. Taking the name of one of the coast guard's original 10 cutters, the *Eagle* is the seventh coast guard vessel to bear the name. The bark was originally awarded to the Soviet Union by drawing lots, but the U.S. representative quietly persuaded his Soviet counterpart to trade before the results were announced. The *Eagle* was sailed from Bremerhaven in 1946 to the United States, basically following Columbus's route. It took the place of the *Danmark*, which had served as the coast guard training ship through the war years. (Returned to a grateful Denmark at the end of the war, the *Danmark* had been visiting the United States at the outbreak of the war and had not been able to return to Europe.) Attached to the U.S. Coast Guard Academy at New London, Connecticut, the *Eagle* is a seagoing classroom for future coast guard officers. The bark accommodates up to 160 cadets, with a 50-member permanent crew and officer instructors. According to the coast guard, seamanship learned aboard the *Eagle* instills in the young men and women who come aboard more than just "their first taste of salt air and life at sea. The experience helps them develop skills of leadership and teamwork, as well as a healthy respect for the elements…. They are tested and challenged, often to the limits of their endurance; working aloft, they meet fear and learn to overcome it." The *Eagle*'s cadet cruises have taken the bark to ports throughout the United States and around the world; in 1990 it visited the Soviet Union. During the 1964, 1976, and 1986 OpSails the *Eagle* hosted the celebrations and led the seagoing parade. [U.S. Coast Guard]

SOUTH NORWALK

■ **Hope**
Maritime Center at Norwalk
10 North Water Street
1948

Built by Stanley G. Chard in Greenwich, Connecticut, the *Hope* is the last wood-hulled, sail-powered oyster sloop built on Long Island Sound. For most of its oyster dredging career, it was a familiar sight sailing into Norwalk's harbor, its decks piled high with cargo to be sold to one of the many oyster companies located on shore. Owned by an oyster company and moored at the Maritime Center at Norwalk, it is being restored by master shipwrights and volunteer apprentices as a floating exhibit with occasional operation for educational programs. [Tallmadge Brothers]

■ ■ ■ ■ ■ ■ **MAINE** ■ ■ ■ ■ ■ ■

BATH

■ **Sherman Zwicker**
Maine Maritime Museum
243 Washington Street
1941

Thousands of ships have worked the Grand Banks, sailing from New England and Canadian ports to work in the brutally harsh, cold, and often killing waters. In time the method of fishing the banks evolved into the deployment of flat-bottomed dories from larger schooners. Teams of fishermen on

A wood auxiliary fishing schooner constructed in 1941, the *Sherman Zwicker* was among the last of its type to be built.

dories cast out lines more than mile long and baited with hundreds of hooks. Hauling up fish until their gunwales lay low in the water, they then rowed back to pitch their catches on the schooner's deck. There the fish were split, gutted, and beheaded and then packed in salt in the hold. One of the premier Canadian fishing firms working the banks was Zwicker and Company. Two of the company's vessels survive as exhibits in the United States—the *E. F. Zwicker*, now the *American*, a restaurant in Cape May, New Jersey, and the beautifully maintained, unmodified *Sherman Zwicker*. Owned and operated by the Grand Banks Schooner Museum, *Sherman Zwicker* was built at the Smith and Rhuland yard in Lunenberg, Nova Scotia, in 1942. The 142-foot-long wood schooner worked until 1968, when it was presented to the museum. Beautifully restored and operational, the *Zwicker* regularly sails to Lunenberg and participated in the 1980 and 1986 OpSails. The schooner is occasionally berthed at the Maine Maritime Museum, where it is open to the public. [Grand Banks Schooner Museum of Boothbay Harbor, Maine]

CAMDEN

Originally built to carry lumber from southern ports to Long Island, New York, the two-masted schooner *Grace Bailey* is one of only three such historic ships in Maine. Built in Patchogue, Long Island, in 1882 by Oliver Perry Smith, the *Grace Bailey* was named for owner Edwin Bailey's daughter, born that year. In 1906 it was rebuilt and renamed for Bailey's granddaughter, Martha, nicknamed Mattie. From 1906 until 1990 the schooner sailed as the *Mattie*, but in the spring of 1990, after restoration, it assumed its original name.

■ **Grace Bailey**
Camden Harbor
1882

The *Grace Bailey*'s association with the Maine coast began in 1919, when Herbert L. Black of South Brooksville, Maine, purchased it. It was then sold to William F. Shepherd of Deer Isle, Maine, who continued to operate the schooner as a coaster until 1939, when it was chartered to Frank Swift of Camden for use as a passenger-carrying "windjammer." For all practical purposes the coasting schooner had ceased to be economically viable in the 1930s. No four-, five-, or six-masted schooner survives today except as a derelict hulk. On the Maine coast, however, the *Grace Bailey*, the *Mercantile*, and the *Stephen Taber* not only survive, but they turn a profit for their owners, because in 1936 Frank Swift conceived the idea of converting small two-masted cargo schooners into passenger vessels. Swift purchased the *Grace Bailey* in 1940 and the *Mercantile* in 1943. Today 15 windjammers operate out of midcoast Maine: 10 out of Rockland, 1 out of Rockport, and 4 out of Camden. Except for a brief interruption during the summer of 1942, when the vessel was chartered to the Maine Maritime Academy as its first training vessel, the *Grace Bailey* has been a part of the Camden fleet of cruise schooners since 1940.

Extensive renovation of the *Grace Bailey* began in the spring of 1989. The masts, deck, deckhouse, and ceiling were removed, and the deformation of its keel eliminated. It is not

Built as the *Grace Bailey* in 1882, the schooner sailed as the *Mattie* from 1906 until 1990, when its original name was restored.

known precisely what percentage of the *Bailey*'s 1882 fabric remains, nor is information available on how many rebuildings and refittings occurred between its documented 1906 rebuilding and the present set of repairs. However, the replacement of deteriorated elements of wood vessels is an ongoing process. No doubt this century-old wood schooner has been repaired on a number of occasions; this latest operation is one more in a continuing sequence. NR. [Ray Williamson]

■ **Mercantile**
Camden Harbor
1916

Originally built between 1913 and 1916 in Little Deer Isle, Maine, the two-masted schooner *Mercantile* is one of only three such historic ships in Maine. Designed for the "coasting" trade (that is, the transport of cargo from one Atlantic Coast port to another), the *Mercantile* carried lime kiln wood from the coastal islands to Rockland, Maine. Its later cargoes varied widely and included cordwood, lumber, coal, and boxwood. In 1943, when Ray Swift purchased the vessel to serve as a windjammer along Maine's midcoast, it was being used as a mackerel fishing boat in Warwick, Rhode Island.

Above: The *Mercantile* on one of its windjammer cruises Left: The bay coaster's anchor chain.

A week on a windjammer is more in the nature of a maritime experience than actual sail training. Passengers are encouraged but not required to lend a hand as needed. In addition to instilling a better understanding of America's maritime heritage, on a practical level the windjammers are an instrument for the preservation of schooner sail handling and maintenance and the shipwright's skills as well. In 1988–89 renovation of the *Mercantile* was carried out under the direction of Ray Williamson. NR. [Ray Williamson]

■ **Roseway**
Sharp's Wharf
1925

Built at the J. F. James Shipyard in Essex, Massachusetts, the principal community of New England fisheries shipbuilding, the *Roseway* was laid down and launched as a private swordfishing yacht for Harold Hathaway of Taunton. Hathaway, chief counsel for the Boston Elevated Railway, reportedly named his yacht for a female friend "who always got her way." In 1941 the Boston Pilots Association bought the 15-year-old schooner yacht and converted it to a pilot boat. For the next 32 years the *Roseway* was stationed off Boston Harbor, meeting inbound vessels and putting harbor pilots aboard to guide them through the channel. Working in tandem with the schooner *Pilot*, now a privately owned vessel in Gloucester, the *Roseway*, which has a large 2 emblazoned on the mainsail (the *Pilot* had *1*), stood off the Boston Harbor Lighthouse with a number of pilots and apprentices aboard. When hailed, the pilots were rowed to the incoming ship by yawl. The apprentices learned their trade, which included navigation, seamanship, pilotage regulations, and yawl handling, over a long period, some apprenticeships lasting as long as 10 years.

The *Roseway* had a long career that included rescues at sea and dismasting during a hurricane in 1970. The last pilot schooner active in the United States after 1970, the *Roseway* was retired in 1973 and replaced by a motor vessel. Bought on speculation for use as a windjammer, the *Roseway* passed to Jim Sharp of Camden, Maine, who owned the schooner *Adventure*. Sharp restored the *Roseway* and operated it as part of the Maine windjammer fleet of passenger schooners. Sold by Sharp in 1988, the *Roseway* continues to sail from Sharp's Wharf on passenger cruises that now range beyond the Maine coast to a winter season of Virgin Islands cruising. [Yankee Schooner Cruises]

■ **Surprise**
Public Landing
1918

Designed by the noted naval architect Thomas F. McManus, the *Surprise* is a scaled-down version of one of McManus's fishing schooners, as exemplified in the *L. A. Dunton*. Built by Waddell Brothers, of Rockport, Massachusetts, the 44-foot-long *Surprise* was commissioned by Martin S. Kattenhorn of New York, a Wall Street broker and founding member and later commodore of the Cruising Club of America. Rigged as a two-masted gaff schooner for fishing, the *Surprise* was sailed every season by Kattenhorn until 1959. Kattenhorn, writing McManus in 1925, praised the naval architect: "In *Surprise* you gave me a very clever boat and today outside of the latest Alden schooners, she is as fast or faster than most of the small cruising schooners." Now part of Maine's unique collection of windjammers, the *Surprise* sails three times a day during the summer on two- to three-hour cruises outside Camden Harbor. [Jack and Barbara Moore]

CASTINE

■ **Bowdoin**
Maine Maritime Academy Pier
Pleasant Street
1921

The 1921 auxiliary schooner *Bowdoin* was the brainchild of Adm. Donald Baxter MacMillan (1874–1970), an Arctic explorer, educator, aviator, author, anthropologist, and philanthropist who made 29 voyages to the Arctic between 1908 and 1954. Twenty-six of these voyages were made aboard the *Bowdoin*, the only American auxiliary schooner built specifi-

cally for Arctic exploration. In its career the *Bowdoin* logged more than 200,000 miles, while 300 crew members gathered information on Arctic ornithology, biology, anthropology, geology, meteorology, and oceanography, resulting in scores of scientific papers, articles, and books. Much of our current information about the Arctic, Labrador, and Greenland was gathered aboard the *Bowdoin*.

Built specifically for Arctic exploration, the schooner *Bowdoin* is one of a handful of historic Arctic vessels left in the world.

Small, sturdy, and built to MacMillan's specifications, this 88-foot-long schooner, named after his alma mater, was launched in 1921 and thereafter served as the base for MacMillan's explorations. The schooner's maiden voyage of 1921–22 was to the shores of Baffin Island, where it spent the winter iced-in and banked with snow while the crew conducted geomagnetic experiments for the Carnegie Institution. In 1923–24 the *Bowdoin*, under the sponsorship of the National Geographic Society, sailed for northern Greenland, where the vessel was frozen-in for a 330-day stay while the expedition gathered specimens, filmed wildlife, and gathered ethnographic information on Eskimos. The first short-wave transmissions from the Arctic were broadcast from the *Bowdoin* on this voyage.

Additional voyages north followed, and in 1925 MacMillan participated in another great feat in Arctic exploration. Under his command a joint National Geographic Society and U.S. Navy Expedition sailed north in two vessels, the *Bowdoin* and the *Peary*, to Etah, with a group of scientists while Loening amphibious airplanes under the command of Richard E. Byrd flew more than 6,000 miles over the Arctic, marking the beginning of polar aviation and garnering valuable experience for Byrd's future pioneer flights over both poles. The first natural color photographs of the Arctic were taken by National Geographic photographers on the expedition, which also broadcast daily reports by means of short-wave radio.

During World War II MacMillan and the *Bowdoin* were commissioned by the U.S. Navy to serve on the Greenland Patrol, assisting in the defense of Greenland and conducting a survey to establish air bases. Stricken from the U.S. Navy Register in May 1944, the schooner was sold in January 1945. Purchased by friends of MacMillan's, the battered schooner was refitted once again for Arctic exploration. MacMillan had established the MacMillan Moravian School at Nain in northern Labrador in 1927 to feed, clothe, and educate Eskimo children, and after the war he returned to his yearly supervisory and supply voyages. The Eskimos, who called him *Nagalek* ("leader"), came to admire MacMillan greatly. In 1929 the *Bowdoin* carried the lumber, desks, blackboards, books, radios, blankets, dishes, food, and sleeping bags to start the school. MacMillan provided an electric lighting system for the village and school, brought two organs (one for the school and the other for the village church), and once brought 20,000 false teeth and a dentist's chair.

The *Bowdoin* sailed north until 1954, when the 80-year-old MacMillan "retired." In 1959 Admiral MacMillan sailed the schooner to Mystic, Connecticut, where he turned it over to Mystic Seaport Museum for display. Unfortunately, the *Bowdoin* was not maintained, and it deteriorated. Taken off display, stripped of its gear, and its rig taken down, the laid-up schooner was covered with plastic. In 1967, at MacMillan's urging, the Schooner Bowdoin Association was formed by friends of the admiral's, including former crew members and others interested in saving the ship. Mystic Seaport relinquished the schooner to the association, which leased it to Jim Sharp of Camden, Maine. Sharp restored the schooner to operating condition and sailed it to Provincetown, Massachusetts, in 1969 on a sentimental journey to MacMillan's home, where the admiral, in his nineties, saw the *Bowdoin* sail again one last time. MacMillan died in 1970.

Sharp had restored what he could on the *Bowdoin* for $25,000, using it as a wharfside museum in Camden and sailing it on charters. In the mid-1970s, however, U.S. Coast Guard requirements for carrying passengers, which would have called for rebuilding the schooner and destroying its historic character, forced Sharp to return it to the Schooner Bowdoin Association. Used for sail training and leased by the association to various groups, the *Bowdoin* has persevered since then. A major restoration effort at the Maine Maritime Museum between 1980 and 1984 brought the schooner back to excellent condition. The restored schooner sailed in OpSail '86 in New York Harbor in the parade of ships that celebrated the Statue of Liberty's restoration. In 1987–88 the *Bowdoin* was leased to Outward Bound, an educational organization, and in 1989 was turned over to the Maine Maritime Academy in Castine. Used for sail training by the academy, the *Bowdoin*'s trips often include the waters that the vessel charted with Donald MacMillan at the helm more than 50 years ago. NR. NHL. [Maine Maritime Academy]

GREENVILLE

One of the few remaining lake boats once so common on Maine inland waters, the *Katahdin* was the last and biggest steam vessel operated on Moosehead Lake. As early as 1836 steamboats were introduced into this isolated region of central Maine, providing the only link between the northern and southern points of this 35-mile-long lake. The first steamer named *Katahdin* was built in 1896 following Moosehead Lake's rise in popularity as a summer resort and wilderness retreat. The second *Katahdin* was built by the Bath Iron Works to replace the earlier ship, which burned in 1912. The steel hull of the steamer was shipped in sections and assembled at the lake, where a wood superstructure was added. Launched in 1914 for the Coburn Steamboat Company, the *Katahdin* could carry up to 500 passengers to the hotels, villages, and hunting and fishing camps along the lake shore. The vessel also transported cargo and mail, as well as railroad cars on barges. When highway construction obviated the need for water transport, the *Katahdin* was retired from passenger service in 1938 and spent the next 38 years hauling logs for the paper industry, towing up to 6,000 cords of pulpwood in a single raft. Currently a working museum vessel, the *Katahdin* cruises daily on Moosehead Lake during the summer months. NR. [Moosehead Marine Museum]

■ **Katahdin**
Moosehead Marine Museum
Main Street
1914

Launched in 1914 for the Coburn Steamboat Company, the *Katahdin* carried passengers to the hotels, villages, and hunting and fishing camps along the shore of Moosehead Lake.

PORTLAND

■ **Lightship No. 112**
("Nantucket")
Maine Wharf on Commercial
Street near the Casco Bay
Ferry Terminal
1936

The nation's most significant lightship station for transatlantic voyages was Nantucket Shoals, established in 1854. Nearly 47 miles at sea, this remote station marks the limits of the dangerous Nantucket Shoals and the eastern end of the Ambrose shipping channel into New York Harbor. The Nantucket lightship was the last beacon seen by vessels when leaving the United States and the first when entering the country. Eleven lightships were assigned to Nantucket Shoals station during its history. It was the last U.S. lightship station in operation, having a lightship at anchor until 1983, eight years after most other lightships were retired. The *No. 112* is the oldest surviving lightship to have served on the Nantucket station, which it marked for 39 years.

Known by its former designation of "Nantucket," the *No. 112* was the largest lightship ever built.

The Nantucket Shoals station was the scene of the greatest lightship disaster in the history of the U.S. Lightship Service. In 1934 the RMS *Olympic*, sister ship of the *Titanic*, rammed and sank the *No. 117*, killing seven of the 11 crew members. The White Star Line paid $500,000 in compensation, of which $300,956 was expended to build the *No. 112* as an "indestructible" replacement for the lost *No. 117*. The *No. 112* was built with heavy reinforcement, a high degree of compartmentalization, a warning air whistle, and six exits to the upper deck, all safety features designed to avoid a repetition of the disaster.

Launched in 1936, the *No. 112* served the Nantucket station during the periods 1936–41, 1945–58, and 1960–75. During World War II the lightship was withdrawn from service and taken to Woods Hole, Massachusetts, where it was painted gray, armed with a 20-millimeter gun at the bow, and outfitted to examine incoming vessels at Portland, Maine. Withdrawn from service in 1975, the *No. 112* was replaced by the modern coast guard–built lightship *WLV-612*. Laid up at Chelsea, Massachusetts, the lightship later served as a floating museum operated by the Nantucket Historical Society until 1984, when it was leased to Nantucket Lightship, a nonprofit organization established to save the lightship from scrapping. Now fully restored, the *No. 112* is open to the public as an operational floating museum. NR. NHL. [Lightship Nantucket]

ROCKLAND

The auxiliary schooner *American Eagle*, built in 1930 as the *Andrew and Rosalie*, marked an important transition in the U.S. fishing industry, then and now centered primarily in Gloucester, Massachusetts, the port of the schooner's origin. A 300-year-old tradition of building sailing schooners at Gloucester and nearby ports was doomed by the rise of motor power. Beginning around 1900 the auxiliary schooner, a new type of vessel combining sails with motor power, was built. The auxiliary schooner was the forerunner of the modern trawler, introduced to the fishing industry in the 1930s and 1940s. The last auxiliary schooner built in Gloucester, the *Andrew and Rosalie*, now renamed the *American Eagle*, is the oldest known Gloucester combination power-and-sailing fishing boat left afloat and an excellent example of this transitional ship type.

The *Andrew and Rosalie* was built by the United Sail Loft Company in 1930 for Patrick Murphy, an 1880 immigrant to Gloucester and a well-known fishing schooner master. Named for his son and daughter, the new schooner was launched sideways from the company's wharf on June 2, 1930, as Rosalie Murphy christened it. The *Atlantic Fisherman*, covering the event, noted that the *Andrew and Rosalie* "will be used for swordfishing, netting and trawling." The occasion was a proud day for Gloucester—the schooner was the largest vessel built in the town in 20 years. The *Andrew and Rosalie* sailed on its maiden voyage June 24, "the craft going swordfishing."

Incomplete records of the schooner's fish landings at Boston from January 1934 until September 1952 show that the

■ **American Eagle**
North End Shipyard
Front Street
1930

After 55 years of service in the commercial fishing trade, including use as a motor-powered trawler, the *American Eagle* was restored to its auxiliary sailing rig and placed in service as a Maine windjammer.

Andrew and Rosalie landed 1,040,600 pounds of fish for the 16 months reported, a projected average of 780,450 pounds per year and a career total of 41,363,850 pounds of fish when the vessel was finally retired in 1983. Murphy died in 1938, and the schooner was worked by the family until 1941, when it was sold to the Empire Fish Company and renamed the *American Eagle*. The schooner fished as a trawler from 1942 until July 1983, the majority of that time under the ownership of John, Joe, and Gus Piscitello of Gloucester, who acquired the vessel in 1945.

In 1984 the *American Eagle* was purchased by John C. Foss of Rockland, Maine, then owner of the schooner *Lewis R. French*. After 55 years in service, including time as a motor-powered trawler, the *American Eagle* was restored to its auxiliary sailing rig and placed in service as a Maine windjammer. [John C. Foss]

■ **Isaac H. Evans**
North End Shipyard
Front Street
1886

The *Isaac H. Evans* is the oldest surviving oyster schooner in the United States and an outstanding representative of the early form of oyster schooner. It was built at Mauricetown, New Jersey, by J. W. Vannaman and Brother in 1886 as the *Boyd N. Sheppard* for use as an oyster freighter. Owned by Harrison Sheppard (the managing owner), Frank Sheppard, Moses Bateman, and Thomas A. Rogers, the schooner gradually passed to the two Sheppards and finally to Harrison Sheppard, who remained its managing owner and master until 1909. The *Sheppard* worked the oyster beds of Delaware Bay, carrying New Jersey oysters to market in New York throughout its career, although its home port was still Mauricetown.

After sale to Edgar, Norman, and Joshua Evans of Millville, New Jersey, early in 1909, the schooner continued oystering. The three Evanses, sons of the New Jersey oysterman Isaac H. Evans, renamed the schooner for their father in 1919. The schooner continued to work as a sailing ship until 1946, when a change in state law allowed oyster dredging under power. That year the *Evans*, like many other surviving oyster sloops and freighters, was converted to a motor vessel. The *Evans* continued to work through the decline of oystering, which was marked by the destruction of many of the fleet in the great hurricane of 1938 and World War II.

In 1971 the *Evans* was purchased by Doug and Linda Lee of Rockland, Maine, and restored to serve in the windjammer fleet. [Edward B. Glaser]

■ **J. & E. Riggin**
O'Hara's Wharf
End of Tillson Avenue
1927

The *J. & E. Riggin* is the youngest of the surviving oyster schooners in the United States and an outstanding representative of the oyster schooner's late and final form, representing the introduction of modern naval architectural theory and design. It was laid down and built at Dorchester, New Jersey, at Stowaman's Shipyard in 1927 for use as an oyster dredger and freighter. Owned by Charles Riggin, the schooner was named for Riggin's sons, Jacob and Edward. It worked the oyster beds of Delaware Bay under sail until 1946, when it was moored at Dorchester, New Jersey.

The *J. & E. Riggin* gained fame among oyster schooners in August 1929. During the only formal schooner race on the bay, the *Riggin*, with its owner and master Charles Riggin at the helm, won the event, covering 24 miles in four hours, 38 minutes, and 30 seconds. The Bridgeton, New Jersey, *Evening News* of August 24 noted that "this schooner of about 50 ton outstepped three larger boats of class A, which was open to craft of more than 95 feet long, and it did it in an emphatic manner, with its captain at the helm and a crew of twenty-five men."

The *Riggin* continued to work as a sailing ship until 1946, when a change in New Jersey laws allowed oyster dredging under power. That year, like many other surviving oyster sloops and freighters, it was converted to a motor vessel. The *Riggin* continued to work through the decline of oystering. After serving as a dragger out of Cape Cod, the *J. & E. Riggin* was purchased by David and Susan Allen of Rockland, Maine, in 1974, and restored to serve in the windjammer fleet. [David L. and Susan P. Allen]

The *Lewis R. French* is by a few months the oldest of the five surviving two-masted coasting schooners in the United States. The *French* and the *Governor Stone* are the only surviving examples of the fixed-keel, two-masted coasting schooner. The *French* is the oldest surviving sailing vessel built in Maine, the center for wood shipbuilding in the United States after the Civil War, and the only surviving schooner of the thousands constructed. Built and launched early in 1871 at Christmas Cove, South Bristol, Maine, by the French brothers, it was named for a part-owner, whose brother, Joseph W. French, commanded the new schooner. Registered at the port of Waldoboro on April 28, 1871, the *Lewis R. French* commenced a career in the coasting trade.

■ **Lewis R. French**
North End Shipyard
Front Street
1871

The *Lewis R. French* spent 50 years as a sailing freighter, was converted to a motorized freighter and used as such for another 50 years, and finally was rebuilt as a windjammer in 1973.

In 1877 the *French* entered the fishing trade, seining in the menhaden fishing grounds until 1888, when it resumed the general coasting trade. It remained in the general trade for the next four decades, carrying a variety of cargoes until 1928, when it was hauled, dismasted, and equipped with an engine and a pilothouse. Again entering the coasting trade, now as a motor vessel, the *French* remained in service until 1973, last working as a cannery tender, transporting fish from other large fishing vessels offshore to be processed in Eastport, Maine. It was sold to John Foss of Rockland, who intended to restore its schooner rig and enter it in the windjammer fleet of Maine. Restored between 1973 and 1976, the *French* was sold to Daniel Pease in 1986 when Foss bought and restored the *American Eagle.* [Daniel Pease]

■ **Stephen Taber**
Windjammer Wharf
Adjacent to Maine State
Ferry Terminal
1871

One of the oldest documented American merchant sailing vessels in continuous use under the U.S. flag, the *Stephen Taber* carried bricks and pulpwood in the northern Atlantic. It was built in 1871 by the Bedel Shipyard in Glenwood Landing, New York, on the north shore of Long Island, for the firm of Cox Brothers. In 1892 it was purchased by Bryan Hallock of East Setauket, New York. In 1900 and 1902, apparently when the coasting trade was slow, Hallock fitted out passenger accommodations below decks, with "ladies' accommodations" in the forward hold, and chartered the vessel to two wealthy families for the summer season.

From its launching until 1920 the *Taber* plied the waters of New York Harbor and its environs, carrying a variety of cargoes: coal, seed oysters, brick, and lumber. In 1920 Hallock sold the *Taber* to a Mr. Eaton of Deer Isle, Maine. It was subsequently sold to a Mr. Wood of Orland, Maine, and continued in the coasting trade until 1946, when it was purchased by Boyd Build of Castine, Maine, and converted to a passenger vessel. Subsequent owners in the passenger trade were Havilah Hawkins, Cy Cousins, Jim Sharp, Orville Young, Mike Anderson, and in 1979 Orville and Ellen Barnes.

At the close of the 1981 summer season, the Barneses hauled the *Taber* for a major refit. The vessel had been rebuilt in 1900 and in 1930. Using early photographs found on the *Taber* as a guide to its original sheer, the Barneses with David Johnson as foreman sought to do away with the "hog" in the keel that had developed over the years. Orville Barnes forged much of the necessary new ironwork for the project at his Camden, Maine, forge. In mid-April 1983 the refitted *Stephen Taber* was relaunched. NR. [Orville K. and Ellen S. Barnes]

■ **Victory Chimes**
O'Hara's Wharf
End of Tillson Avenue
1900

The last of the 30 Chesapeake Bay "ram schooners," the three-masted *Victory Chimes* was built as the *Edwin and Maud* at Bethel, Delaware, to carry cargo. Ram schooners were used from the end of the 19th century into the 1950s to haul cargo along the eastern seaboard and the Chesapeake Bay. These vessels were flat-bottomed to provide more cargo space and narrow-hulled to travel the Chesapeake and Delaware Canal. Use of a centerboard assisted them in sailing more efficiently on open waters, as well as enabling them to enter shallow-water ports.

After patrolling for enemy submarines operating in American coastal waters during World War II, the *Edwin and*

Maud was sold in the early 1950s for use as a passenger vessel. Sold again in 1954, it was renamed the *Victory Chimes*, and in 1959 it was purchased and modified to serve as a Maine windjammer for the next 26 years. Restored and renamed the *Domino Effect* in 1988, the vessel served briefly as a corporate yacht in Lake Huron for Domino's Pizza. Returned to Maine, sold, and renamed the *Victory Chimes* in 1990, the vessel once again operates on six-day cruises as a Maine windjammer. [Richard Files]

The *Victory Chimes*, built to haul cargo along the eastern seaboard and the Chesapeake Bay.

The newest arrival to the historic fleet of vessels sailing along the rocky Maine coast for charter, day, and overnight cruises is the schooner yacht *Wendameen*. Designed by noted naval architect John Alden for the Springfield, Massachusetts, socialite Chester Bliss, the 67-foot-long *Wendameen* cruised the New England coast, entertaining Bliss's guests and voyaging to Maine on hunting and fishing trips. Among the guests entertained aboard were the playwright Eugene O'Neill and the author Katherine Porter. Sold in 1916 to the Uihlein family of Milwaukee, the owners of Schlitz Breweries, the *Wendameen* sailed on Lake Michigan. When it was sold to Chicago attorney Paul L'Amoreaux during the 1920s, the yacht raced and sailed for the contentious attorney, noted for occasionally

■ **Wendameen**
O'Hara's Wharf
End of Tillson Avenue
1912

Rescued from a mud bank, the *Wendameen* has been restored for operation and offers cruises out of Rockport, Maine.

throwing a punch at his fellow barristers in an attempt "to settle out of court." Sold again in the 1930s and laid up on the East Coast, the *Wendameen* was acquired by the New York yacht broker G. W. Ford, who began to restore it. World War II intervened, and the *Wendameen* was left to slowly rot for the next 50 years. Rescued from a mud bank near New York by Neal Parker, its current owner, the *Wendameen* was brought to Rockland, Maine, where Parker carefully restored it. Launched once again in 1990, the *Wendameen* now sails on a regular schedule of one day–one night cruises from June through October. [Neal Parker]

ROCKPORT

■ **Timberwind**
Marine Park
Off Pascal Avenue
1931

Two of three remaining intact four-masted schooners in the United States, the *Hesper* and the *Luther Little*

Built by and for the Portland Pilots Association, the two-masted schooner *Timberwind* was originally named, appropriately enough, the *Portland Pilot*. The vessel spent its career guiding ships in and out of Maine's busiest port. It was retired in 1959, when the pilots switched to a modern motor vessel. Purchased that year by its current owner and renamed, the schooner has since worked as a Maine windjammer, carrying passengers for hire along the state's rockbound coast as a member of one of the nation's last two fleets of commercial sailing vessels. [Bill Alexander]

WISCASSET

■ **Hesper**
■ **Luther Little**
Along the waterfront between U.S. Highway 1 and Wiscasset Town Landing, off Water Street
1918 and 1917

Both hulks, the *Hesper* and the *Luther Little*, along with the *La Merced* in Anacortes, Washington, are the last remaining intact U.S. examples of a type of merchant vessel once common on both coasts and the Great Lakes. Between 1880 and the early 1920s, 400 four-masted schooners were built in the United States. Although designed for and operated in the coasting trade for the most part, four-masted schooners occasionally sailed to Europe and South America. The *Hesper* was built by the Crowninshield Ship Building Company at South Somerset, Massachusetts, to serve in the coastal coal and lumber trades. The *Luther Little* was built by the Read Brothers Company, also of Somerset. The careers of both ships were brief; the *Hesper* was laid up by 1928, the *Luther Little* in the mid-1920s. Later abandoned on the west bank of the Sheepscot River, both vessels can be seen from U.S. Highway 1 where it crosses the river. NR. [Town of Wiscasset]

■ ■ ■ ■ ■   **MASSACHUSETTS**   ■ ■ ■ ■ ■

BUZZARD'S BAY

Along the Cape Cod Canal at the Bourne Bridge approach next to Grandma's Restaurant rests the upper hull and pilothouse of the harbor tugboat *New York Central No. 16*. Built by the New Jersey Dock and Transportation Company at Elizabethport for the New York Central Railroad, the steel-hulled, 84-foot-long boat spent its entire working career in New York Harbor pushing railroad lighters, flat-bottomed vessels used to transport rail cars. It was retired in 1969, when the Pennsylvania Railroad merged with the New York Central. Purchased by the Witte Scrapyard, the tugboat sat idle and partially submerged in the mud at Witte's until Howard Shaw, the owner of Grandma's Restaurant, rescued the derelict hulk. Refloating the boat and taking it to East Boston, Shaw made the decision to cut the boat off at the waterline and lift the upper works on land for display at his restaurant as a monument to tugboats and their crews. In 1982 the hull, pilothouse, and stack, sandblasted and repainted, were placed ashore. Shaw, as reported in *Sea History* at the time, noted that "scholars may cringe at this type of restoration," but the magazine's editors lauded his saving a "very handsome bit of flotsam salvaged from New York Harbor's changing tides of history." [Grandma's Restaurant]

■ **New York Central No. 16**
Northbourne Rotary
1924

CHARLESTOWN

Representative of the *Fletcher*-class destroyers, the USS *Cassin Young* was built in 1943 by the Bethlehem Steel Corporation, San Pedro, California. One of the largest class of destroyers built during World War II, the vessel exemplifies the intense military-industrial effort geared to an Allied victory. The *Cassin Young* took part in most of the major naval battles in the Pacific in 1944 and 1945. It was the target of two kamikaze attacks, the second of which was the last of World War II.

■ **USS Cassin Young (DD-793)**
Boston National Historical Park
Charlestown Navy Yard
1943

Rehabilitated to its late 1950s appearance, the USS *Cassin Young* is berthed as a floating exhibit at the Charlestown Navy Yard.

Remaining in active service through the 1950s, the destroyer was decommissioned in 1960 and placed in the reserve fleet. In 1978 the destroyer was acquired by the National Park Service and rehabilitated to its late 1950s appearance. Berthed at the Charlestown Navy Yard Unit of Boston National Historical Park, the vessel is open to the public as a floating exhibit. The Charlestown Navy Yard specialized in building destroyers during World War II, and the *Cassin Young* visited this yard during the 1950s for maintenance and modernization. NR. NHL. [National Park Service]

One of six ships constructed to protect America's growing maritime interests in the 1790s, "Old Ironsides" is the oldest commissioned sailing ship and continues to be crewed by members of the U.S. Navy.

■ **USS Constitution**
Charlestown Navy Yard
1797

After independence the United States neglected, if not for all practical purposes abandoned, the idea of a navy. But the depredations of Barbary pirates against American merchant ships in the Mediterranean led Congress to pass its first act—to provide for a navy. Signed into law by President George Washington on March 27, 1794, the act authorized the construction of six frigates. One of those—"Old Ironsides"—is the oldest commissioned warship afloat. Building the *Constitution*, a 204-foot-long, 2,200-ton frigate, took three years; construction began on the *Constitution* in 1794 at Hartt's Shipyard in Boston after a design by Joshua Humphreys of Philadelphia, and the ship was launched on October 21, 1797.

Built of live oak, red cedar, white oak, pitch pine, and locust, the ship was fastened with brass and copper fittings manufactured in Boston by Paul Revere and could carry up to 500 crew members for a prolonged sea voyage of six months. The *Constitution* first cleared port on July 22, 1798, under the command of Capt. Samuel Nicholson, to engage French privateers in the Caribbean during the United States' undeclared war with France. The frigate's career was relatively undistinguished except for its service in the Mediterranean between 1803 and 1805, when it helped to break the power of the Barbary pirates. As a result, the *Constitution* earned widespread renown. However, the ship's greatest glory came during the War of 1812; it won its famous nickname after confronting the British man-of-war *Guerriere* on August 19, 1812. As the British ship's shot rained ineffectively against the *Constitution*'s stout oak hull, an American sailor reportedly yelled, "Huzza! Her sides are made of iron!" Throughout the war the *Constitution* survived the enemy's worst broadsides while battering British ships into surrender. The *Constitution*'s last great fights—its defeat of the British ship *Java* on December 29, 1812, and the subsequent capture of the frigate *Cyane* and the sloop *Levant* after the four-hour battle of Madeira on February 20, 1815—helped earn "Old Ironsides" an honored place in American naval history.

Put out of service after the war and sent to sea on two cruises, the *Constitution* was reported unseaworthy in 1830. The navy made plans to scrap the ship, but public sentiment was aroused to save it, thanks in large measure to a poem by Oliver Wendell Holmes (page 43). Rebuilt in 1833, the *Constitution* made several cruises, including a 52,279-mile, 495-day voyage around the world in 1844–45. Used as a training ship during the Civil War, it was rebuilt again in 1871. In 1878 the frigate made its last foreign cruise, to France, before returning home. Its seagoing career was concluded in 1881, and in 1883 the ship was a hulk being used as a receiving ship at Portsmouth, New Hampshire. Returned to Boston in 1897, the aged frigate was partially restored again in 1905 and then was rebuilt in 1927 with contributions from the nation's schoolchildren. After being towed coast to coast, the *Constitution* was moored at the Charlestown Navy Yard in 1932. The vessel was restored to its 1812 appearance in 1973 and a few years later led the parade of tall ships during OpSail '76 in New York Harbor. Annually on the Fourth of July, the *Constitution* is maneuvered in Boston Harbor for the Turnaround Cruise, while a 21-gun salute honors the nation's birthday. Manned by a U.S. Navy crew, the *Constitution* is open for public tours at the Charlestown Navy Yard. Although rebuilt several times, its basic lines have not been altered and its symbolic value has not been reduced. NR. NHL. [U.S. Navy; loaned to the USS Constitution Museum]

ESSEX

Essex was the heart of the North Shore's shipbuilding industry in the late 19th and early 20th centuries. More than 3,000 vessels, many of them two-masted fishing schooners, were launched into the Essex River to make their way to sea, working off the Grand Banks of Newfoundland or making

■ **Evelina M. Goulart**
Town Landing
Main Street
1927

coastal passages over three centuries. The Story family is prominent in the ranks of Essex shipbuilders, and in A. D. Story's yard the *Evelina M. Goulart*, one of the last of New England's commercial fishing schooners, was built in 1927. The schooner was launched without being christened by its namesake: 18-year-old Evelina, daughter of the ship's captain, Manuel Goulart, died shortly before the launch. The 83-foot-long, two-masted schooner, stoutly built of oak, had a 55-year career in which it fished the Atlantic from Nova Scotia to the Gulf Stream for swordfish. On one occasion it landed 64,348 pounds of fish, a record cargo worth $19,987 in August 1945, netting $1,262 per crew member for a 15-day voyage. Sold in 1946, the schooner passed through two owners' hands and was converted to a diesel-powered trawler before being laid up and abandoned in 1985 near the Acushnet Fish Plant in Fairhaven, Massachusetts. There it sank into the water and mud alongside a pier. Acquired and raised in 1989 by Bob Douglas, owner of the schooners *Alabama* and *Shenandoah*, the wreck was donated to the Essex Shipbuilding Museum. Hauled upriver to Essex, the *Evelina M. Goulart* was winched ashore to be stabilized. A canopy placed over it protects the timbers from further ravages, and the planks from half of the hull will be stripped so that the ship may remain in place as an exhibit demonstrating ship construction technique just 50 feet from where it was built and launched more than six decades ago. [Essex Historical Society and Essex Shipbuilding Museum)

FALL RIVER

The USS *Joseph P. Kennedy Jr.* is a World War II *Gearing*-class destroyer. Although none of the *Gearing* class was built in time to see much combat, these destroyers represented the ultimate stage in World War II destroyer design. Knowledge gained from the construction of the previous *Fletcher* and *Allen M. Sumner* classes was incorporated into the design of the *Gearing* destroyers, all of which remained in service after the war. All of the *Gearing* destroyers ultimately were subjected to fleet rehabilitation and modernization, and many were converted into specialized antisubmarine warfare ships.

Built by the Bethlehem Steel Company in Quincy, Massachusetts, the USS *Joseph P. Kennedy Jr.* was named for the eldest son of former Ambassador and Mrs. Joseph P. Kennedy. The younger Kennedy, a navy aviator, was killed off the coast of Normandy on a secret bombing mission in World War II. His brother Robert F. Kennedy served on the ship as a radarman, and President John F. Kennedy watched the America Cup races in 1962 from the second deck of the ship.

The USS *Joseph P. Kennedy Jr.* took part in the first United Nations counteroffensive of the Korean War. Later, the destroyer gained worldwide attention during the Cuban blockade when it intercepted a Soviet freighter. Stricken from the U.S. Navy Register in 1973, the *Kennedy* is now berthed at Battleship Cove with the battleship *Massachusetts*, *PT 617* and *PT 796*, and the submarine *Lionfish*. The *Kennedy* is a

■ **USS Joseph P. Kennedy Jr. (DD-850)**
Battleship Cove
Off Interstate 195, take exit 5
1945

The National Historic Landmark fleet at Battleship Cove in Fall River, Massachusetts, in 1990: from left to right, the USS *Joseph P. Kennedy Jr.*, the USS *Lionfish*, and the USS *Massachusetts*.

museum exhibit and also serves as the headquarters for Tin Can Sailors, the national organization of destroyer veterans of World War II. NR. NHL. [USS Massachusetts Memorial Committee]

■ **USS Lionfish (SS-298)**
Battleship Cove
Off Interstate 195, take exit 5
1944

The USS *Lionfish* is an intact example of the standard fleet boat of the *Balao*-class submarine, which played an important role in the war against Japan. Most other World War II submarines underwent complete exterior and interior alterations after the war as part of the Greater Underwater Propulsion Project (GUPPY) modifications. Commissioned in 1944, the *Lionfish* made two patrols in the Pacific during the war, receiving one battle star for its service. Late-war submarines were deployed off the coast of Japan as a cordon of "lifeguards" to rescue fliers who were shot down after bombing the Japanese home islands. In this capacity the *Lionfish* rescued the crew of a B-29. Ordered to inactive service in 1946, the submarine was recommissioned in 1951 as a training vessel with the Sonar School at Key West, Florida, and with the Atlantic Fleet out of Guantanamo Bay, Cuba. In 1952 it participated in NATO exercises in the Mediterranean. Inactive between 1953 and 1960, the submarine was placed in active reserve status to serve Naval Reserve Units out of Providence, Rhode Island. The *Lionfish* was declared obsolete in 1971 and in 1972 was donated to Battleship Cove. It is a floating exhibit moored between the *Joseph P. Kennedy Jr.* and the battleship *Massachusetts*. NR. NHL. [USS Massachusetts Memorial Committee]

■ **USS Massachusetts (BB-59)**
Battleship Cove
Off Interstate 195, take exit 5
1942

One of two surviving *South Dakota*–class battleships built by the United States in preparation for war (the other is the USS *Alabama*), the USS *Massachusetts* was built by the Fore River Shipyards of the Bethlehem Steel Company at Quincy, Massachusetts. Laid down on July 20, 1939, and launched on September 23, 1941, "Big Mamie" was commissioned on May 12, 1942, with Capt. Francis E. M. Whiting assuming command. After a shakedown cruise off the coast of Maine, the *Massachusetts* sailed to serve as the flagship of Operation Torch during the invasion of North Africa in World War II and as a unit of the Third Fleet in the Pacific. "Big Mamie" is credited with firing the first and last American 16-inch shells of World War II: the first fired in November 1942 during the invasion of North Africa, the last during the bombardment of Honshu in 1945. While cruising off Casablanca on November 8, 1942, the *Massachusetts* engaged the unfinished French battleship *Jean Bart*, then loyal to the Nazi-sympathizing Vichy government, silencing the French battleship's battery; the *Massachusetts* also sank two Vichy destroyers. After shelling coastal batteries and with a cease-fire arranged with the French on November 12, the *Massachusetts* returned to the United States. The gun duel with the *Jean Bart* was one of the few engagements between battleships during World War II.

Back home, the *Massachusetts* was prepared for duty in the Pacific. Arriving at Noumea, New Caledonia, on March 4, 1943, it operated for several months in the South Pacific, protecting convoys and supporting strikes against the Japanese at Tarawa and other islands in the Gilberts. As the U.S. Navy swept north across the Pacific, the *Massachusetts* joined

The USS *Massachusetts* awaits its launch at the Fore River Shipyards in 1941 (left) and on trials in Puget Sound in 1944.

other ships in bombarding the heavily defended Japanese base at Kwajalein before sortieing with the force that hit the naval stronghold at Truk. "Big Mamie" participated in the invasion of Hollandia before returning to the United States for an overhaul. Back in the Pacific in October 1944, the *Massachusetts* sailed to support the landings at Leyte, hitting Okinawa and Formosa and taking place in the decisive naval battle of Leyte Gulf. After operations in the Philippines and the South China Sea, the *Massachusetts* guarded U.S. carriers striking Japan. The battleship assisted in the Iwo Jima and Okinawa campaigns, "splashing" attacking kamikazes. In July 1945 the battleship sailed with the Third Fleet for what would be the fleet's last assault on the Japanese home islands. On this sortie the ship's 16-inch guns blasted an industrial complex at Kamaishi, Honshu, Japan's second-largest iron and steel center. After the Japanese surrender the *Massachusetts* sailed for Puget Sound.

During the war the battleship had steamed a quarter of a million miles, shot down 18 enemy aircraft, and sank five enemy ships, never losing a man in combat. It earned 11 battle stars for its combat service and participated in 35 engagements. After an overhaul at Bremerton it sailed in January 1946 for the East Coast, arriving at Hampton Roads in April. Decommissioned on March 27, 1947, the battleship was placed in reserve at Norfolk, where it remained until stricken from the U.S. Navy Register in 1962. Transferred to the Massachusetts Memorial Committee in 1965, "Big Mamie" was towed from Norfolk to Fall River and opened on August 14 of that year as the commonwealth's memorial to its citizens who gave their lives in World War II. The *Massachusetts* has been restored to its original World War II physical appearance. Its restored compartments, accessible to the public, include the berths for its 2,316 crew members and complete facilities for community life, including a 50-bed hospital, three dentist chairs, a large gallery, a shoe repair shop, a tailoring area, and a soda stand, as well as the various levels of one of the battleship's 16-inch gun turrets. NR. NHL. [USS Massachusetts Memorial Committee]

■ **Nobska**
Off Frontage Road past Fall River
Heritage State Park
1925

The *Nobska*, to be restored to
full operation.

The passenger ship *Nobska* was built by the Bath Iron Works for the New England Steamship Company. The last large coastal steamer of classic design operating in the eastern United States, it served the run between Woods Hole, Martha's Vineyard, and Nantucket, as the *Nobska* from 1925 to 1928 and as the *Nantucket II* from 1928 until retirement in 1973. Its steam engine still functional, the *Nobska* was returned to Massachusetts in 1988 after an unsuccessful restaurant venture in Baltimore. Moored not far from Battleship Cove on the Taunton River, Friends of the Nobska are restoring the vessel to full operation. NR. [Friends of the Nobska]

The motor torpedo boat *PT 617* is the sole surviving 80-foot-long type of PT boat built by the Electric Boat Company (Elco) Industries at Bayonne, New Jersey. Fully restored with its original wartime issue equipment and armament, the *PT 617* represents the nation's most heavily used, highly favored, and combat-tested PT boat of World War II. PT boats were highly effective craft built in large numbers to harass shore installations and landings on various islands and atolls of the South Pacific. During the war PT boats were involved in nearly every Pacific campaign, and their operations extended even into the Aleutians, the English Channel, and the Mediterranean. PT boats were vital partners in the United States' victory over Japan. They gained additional fame after the war

■ **PT 617**
Battleship Cove
Off Interstate 195, take exit 5
1945

The *PT 617*, an "Elco" type of PT boat on display.

following the successful political career of John F. Kennedy, skipper of the famous Elco-built *PT 109*.

Built in 1945, the *PT 617* was placed in service as part of Motor Torpedo Boat Squadron 42, the only squadron commissioned after the cessation of hostilities. The *PT 617* never reached the Pacific; instead, it and its crew were sent on a war bond drive by the navy, journeying as far as Florida before being decommissioned. Named "Dragon Lady" after Milton Caniff's sultry character of the comic strip "Terry and the Pirates," the boat remained in private hands for nearly four decades. The *PT 617* was found in Florida by PT Boats, Inc., where the boat was being used as a diving platform. After being carefully restored, the boat was placed on display at Battleship Cove. NR. NHL. [USS Massachusetts Memorial Committee]

The *PT 796* is the best preserved of three surviving Higgins-type PT boats. The vessel was built by the Higgins Company in New Orleans and was commissioned as a unit of PT Squadron 43 in July 1945. Delivered too late to see combat overseas, the *PT 796* remained in the United States during its years of active service (1945–70). The Higgins type, one of the two major types of PT boats used in combat during the war, showed a larger silhouette than the Elco type and differed in its deck arrangement and to a certain extent its hull.

■ **PT 796**
Battleship Cove
Off Interstate 195, take exit 5
1945

The *PT 796*, the best preserved of the three surviving "Higgins" type of PT boat.

The *PT 796*, painted over with the number *109*, was a prominent feature in the inaugural parade of President John F. Kennedy, who once served on a PT boat. The boat was acquired by PT Boats, Inc., restored with its original World War II equipment and armament, and placed on display at Battleship Cove. NR. NHL. [USS Massachusetts Memorial Committee]

GLOUCESTER

■ **Adventure**
Stae Fish Pier
Off Parker Street
1926

Along with the *Ernestina* in New Bedford, Massachusetts, and the *L. A. Dunton* in Mystic, Connecticut, the *Adventure* represents one of the last remaining examples of the Gloucester-type schooner. Designed by Thomas F. McManus, originator of the type and leading designer of fishing schooners from the 1890s through the 1920s, the *Adventure* was built at the John F. James and Son shipyard in Essex, Massachusetts, a town that supplied Atlantic fishing vessels for more than 300 years. The *Adventure*'s construction used traditional methods that had prevailed in Essex for generations. Leaving Gloucester on its maiden voyage on October 16, 1926, the schooner returned six days later with 70,000 pounds of haddock. It was the last schooner to use dory hand-trawling methods, carrying 14 two-man dories on its decks. The vessel fished out of Gloucester, America's oldest fishing port, from 1926 to 1934 and out of Boston from 1934 to 1953. In a 27-year fishing career, the *Adventure* stocked some $4 million worth of fish, believed to be an all-time high in the commercial fisheries up to that time. Having outlasted its aging crew, the *Adventure* began a second career as a Maine windjammer, carrying passengers out of Camden, Maine, on weekly cruises of 5½ days along the Maine coast from 1954 through 1987. In 1988 Jim Sharp, the vessel's owner and skipper for 24 years, donated the *Adventure* to the city of Gloucester under the proviso that it be cared for, promin-

The *Adventure* docked in Gloucester and the ship's steering gear

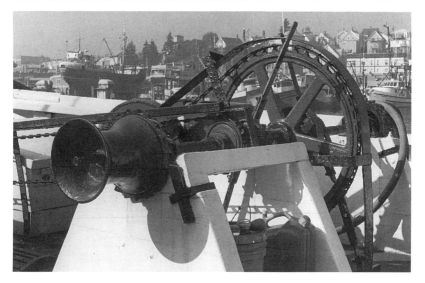

ently displayed as a monument to the history of Gloucester, and used for the education and pleasure of the public. Gloucester Adventure, a nonprofit group, is restoring the vessel and plans to operate it as a working museum and as a classroom offering a broad curriculum of sea- and environment-related issues. NR. [Gloucester Adventure]

The *Effie M. Morrissey*, now the *Ernestina*, sailing in the 19th century.

NEW BEDFORD

■ **Ernestina**
New Bedford State Pier
End of Union Street
1894

The schooner *Ernestina*, formerly the *Effie M. Morrissey*, is the oldest surviving Grand Banks fishing schooner and the only surviving 19th-century Gloucester-built fishing schooner. Moreover, it is one of two remaining examples of the *Fredonia*-style schooners, the most famous American fishing vessel type, and is the only offshore example of that type. It is also one of two sailing Arctic exploration vessels left afloat in the United States (the other is the schooner *Bowdoin*).

Laid down at the Essex yard of John F. James and Washington Tarr, who together built 139 vessels, the schooner was designed by George M. McClain after the *Fredonia* model. Commencing its career as a salt banker, the *Morrissey* fished for cod, at times bringing back from the Grand Banks as much as 320,000 pounds of fish packed in salt. Sold in 1905, it sailed out of Digby, Nova Scotia, with a Canadian crew to sell its catch in the United States. Frederick William Wallace described his experiences aboard the *Morrissey* in widely read accounts of his adventures among the schooners who fished the Grand Banks. "The Log of the Record Run," a ballad he wrote and published in the 1914 *Canadian Fisherman*, recounted a 225-mile, 18 1/2-hour passage that at times reached 16 knots in gale force winds that once knocked the schooner on its beam-ends, blew out sails, and snapped a spar, leaving only a headsail set for the last eight hours. Widely reproduced and sung up and down the banks, the ballad is now a firm part of Grand Banks folklore. In 1914 the *Morrissey* was converted to a cargo carrier, sailing between Newfoundland and Labrador with general cargo and coal, while occasionally making a sailing trip out to the banks.

After a long and distinguished fishing and cargo-carrying career, the *Morrissey* was purchased in 1926 by Robert A. Bartlett, a Canadian-born Arctic explorer and companion of Robert E. Peary. Bartlett navigated Peary and Matthew Henson to the North Pole in 1909 and was considered the greatest ice captain of the 20th century. Under Bartlett "the little Morrissey" made 20 regular voyages north, at one time reaching within 600 miles of the pole; during these voyages the crew documented the frozen north—its flora, fauna, and people—for patrons including the National Geographic Society, the

Smithsonian Institution, the Cleveland Museum of Natural History, the Museum of the American Indian, and others. Pathé newsreels and David Putnam's adventures for boys, *David Goes to Greenland* and *David Goes to Baffin Land*, spread the name and fame of the venerable master Robert Bartlett and his schooner.

After a long association with Bartlett that included World War II surveys of Greenland waters for the U.S. Navy and duty as a supply ship to U.S. airbases in the Arctic and to the Soviet port of Murmansk, the *Morrissey* entered a new career after Bartlett's death in 1946. As a Cape Verde packet, the schooner, renamed the *Ernestina* in 1948, regularly sailed between the Cape Verde Islands and the United States and was the last sailing ship in regular service to carry immigrants across the Atlantic to the United States. Donated as a gift to the United States by the newly independent West African Republic of Cape Verde in 1975, the *Ernestina* was restored and returned to the land of its construction in 1982, when it was presented to the Commonwealth of Massachusetts. After a four-year refit the *Ernestina* sailed in OpSail '86, held in honor of the restoration of the Statue of Liberty. Additional restoration in 1988 has retained the schooner's exceptional integrity. Now moored in New Bedford, Massachusetts, from which it sailed as a Cape Verde packet, the *Ernestina* regularly sails the New England coast, ranging as far north as Newfoundland. NR. NHL. [State of Massachusetts]

The last group of lightships built by the U.S. Lighthouse Service before it was made part of the reorganized U.S. Coast Guard was built between 1926 and 1938, embodying the changes wrought by direct diesel and diesel-electric technology. Five of these third-generation lightships survive, including the *No. 114*, now known as the "New Bedford." The *No.*

■ **Lightship No. 114**
(**"New Bedford"**)
State Pier
Off Herman Melville Boulevard
1930

The lightship *No. 114*, one of the last lightships built by the U.S. Lighthouse Service before the service was moved to the reorganized U.S. Coast Guard.

114 was built by the Albina Marine Works in Portland, Oregon, in 1930. It was the first lightship to complete a west-east passage via the Panama Canal. It served its first station, Fire Island, from 1930 to 1942, guiding mariners to New York Harbor. After serving as an examination ship at Bay Shore, New York, during World War II, it served the Diamond Shoal station, Cape Hatteras, from 1945 to 1947, replacing a lightship sunk by a German U-boat during the war. The *No. 114* returned to duty in the first district, serving as a relief ship until 1958. From 1958 to 1969 it was assigned to the Pollock Rip station off the eastern coast of Cape Cod and followed by the Portland station from 1969 until retirement in 1971.

When its title was transferred to the city of New Bedford in 1975, the *No. 114* became a part of the coast guard commemorative exhibit. Laid up on the New Bedford waterfront since 1985, plans call for restoring it as a floating exhibit. NR. [New Bedford Harbor Development Commission]

PLYMOUTH

■ **Sparrowhawk**
Pilgrim Hall Museum
75 Court Street (Route 3A) at
Memorial Drive
1626

The remains of the *Sparrowhawk*, the oldest identified vessel in the United States, are displayed indoors at the Pilgrim Hall Museum. Wrecked on the shores of Cape Cod near Orleans in the winter of 1626–27, the tiny colonial vessel was lost while en route to the Virginia colonies. Grounded outside Nauset Harbor, it became covered with sand. Winter storm erosion exposed its intact and well-preserved lower hull in May 1863. The timbers were excavated from marsh mud and sand and reassembled on the Boston Common. The "pilgrim ship" was identified as the *Sparrowhawk* by local residents on the basis of oral tradition passed from family to family since the 17th century. Whether or not it is the *Sparrowhawk*, the remains were positively identified as those of a 17th-century vessel. The reassembled ship was displayed in Boston and Providence and was taken on tour by P. T. Barnum. In 1889 the wreck was donated to the Pilgrim Society and placed in Pilgrim Hall. The display of the wreck was enhanced in a museum renovation in 1952; the *Sparrowhawk* now resides in a room devoted to 17th-century ships. [Pilgrim Society]

■ ■ ■ ■ ■ ■   **NEW HAMPSHIRE**   ■ ■ ■ ■ ■ ■

PORTSMOUTH

■ **USS Albacore (AGSS-569)**
Port of Portsmouth Maritime
Museum and Albacore Park
Market Street extension
1953

The experimental diesel-electric submarine *Albacore* represents a revolution in naval architecture. Designed to be a true submarine, in which surface characteristics were subordinated to underwater performance, it was much quieter, faster, and more maneuverable than any earlier submersible craft. Through a series of configurations the *Albacore* provided the model for all future U.S. Navy and most foreign nuclear submarines. Built at the Portsmouth Naval Shipyard, a yard located between Maine and New Hampshire in the Piscataqua River and specializing in submarine building and maintenance, the *Albacore* cost $20 million and took 33 months to build. The hull, constructed of a new alloy called low-carbon steel STS, allowed sustained underwater perfor-

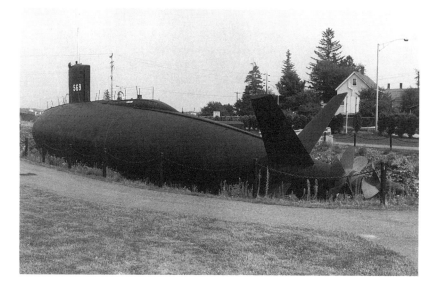

mance and was used in all subsequent submarines, including the USS *Nautilus*.

The *Albacore* possessed no weapon systems; its sole function was to conduct experiments. During its early trials it established a new underwater speed record with improved control. From 1955 to 1971 the submarine served in five distinct phases of experimentation, returning to Portsmouth between each phase for modifications and refitting. A 50-man crew carried out tests of speed, depth changes, and underwater maneuvering. U.S. Navy scientists used the *Albacore* as a floating laboratory to test sonar devices, hydrophones, diving brakes, emergency escape systems, and the first high-capacity silver zinc batteries for submarine propulsion. It also served as a high-speed, almost noiseless target for antisubmarine warfare. In 1966 the *Albacore* again set a new submerged speed record, thus earning a reputation as the world's fastest submarine. Having introduced new concepts in submarine design, the *Albacore* lived up to its motto, *praenuntius futuri* ("forerunner of the future"). Decommissioned in 1972, it was assigned to the inactive fleet for the next decade. When it was transferred to the Portsmouth Submarine Memorial Association in 1984, the submarine returned to its place of birth. After one year in the Portsmouth Naval Shipyard, the vessel was placed in a permanent dry-berth exhibit. NR. NHL. [Portsmouth Submarine Memorial Association]

The USS *Albacore*, whose components changed naval architecture.

■ ■ ■ ■ ■ ■   **VERMONT**   ■ ■ ■ ■ ■ ■

BASIN HARBOR

Operated on Lake Champlain by the U.S. Coast Guard to serve as an aids-to-navigation vessel between 1945 and 1980, the *CG 52302* worked as a buoy tender. Decommissioned in 1981, the 52-foot-long wood vessel was recently moved to Basin Harbor, where the Lake Champlain Maritime Museum will undertake a five-year restoration to use it as a floating classroom. [Lake Champlain Maritime Museum]

■ **CG 52302D**
Lake Champlain
Maritime Museum
The Basin Harbor Road
1944

BURLINGTON

■ **Adirondack**
King Street Dock
1913

The oldest operating American double-ended ferry, the *Adirondack* continues in service on Lake Champlain, where it has been located since 1954. Built at South Jacksonville, Florida, as the *South Jacksonville* and launched on January 15, 1913, the 130-foot-long, coal-fired ferry worked on the St. Johns River between Jacksonville and South Jacksonville. The Jacksonville Ferry and Land Company sold the vessel in 1921, when a bridge was built across the St. Johns. The Tacony-Palmyra Ferry Company of Philadelphia bought it and renamed it the *Mount Holly* for service on the Delaware River. Sold in 1927 to the 34th Street Vehicular Ferry Company of

The *Adirondack* has worked on waterways all along the Atlantic seaboard.

New York, the *Mount Holly* worked the busy East River ferry route between Manhattan and Long Island until the Great Depression intervened. The company declared bankruptcy in 1936, and in 1938 the *Mount Holly* was purchased by the Chesapeake Bay Ferry Company. The ferry's superstructure was rebuilt to carry automobiles more efficiently, and in 1945 the original steam engines and boilers were replaced with a pair of six-cylinder Atlas diesel engines. Rechristened the *Gov. Emerson C. Harrington II*, the ferry served the eastern Chesapeake Bay communities of Claiborne and Romancoke, first for the ferry company and then, after the early 1940s, for the state of Maryland. In 1952 the construction of yet another bridge intervened in the ferry's future. The completion of the Chesapeake Bay Bridge caused the *Gov. Harrington* to be put up for sale.

The boat's current owner, the Lake Champlain Transportation Company, bought the ferry in 1954. Renamed the *Adirondack*, it was partially dismantled to fit under the bridges of the Champlain Canal and was slowly brought to Lake Champlain. Restored to its 1938 configuration, the *Adirondack* now operates from Burlington to Port Kent, New York, the queen of a fleet of modern ferries that carry on a 200-year tradition of ferryboating on historic Lake Champlain. [Lake Champlain Transportation Company]

SHELBURNE

The only extant and basically unchanged side-paddle-wheel lakeboat in the United States, the *Ticonderoga* was the last coal-powered ship in service on Lake Champlain. Built by the Lake Champlain Transportation Company and launched in 1906, it was the 29th and last steamboat to be completed in the company's yards at Shelburne Harbor, Vermont. At full capacity the *Ticonderoga* carried 28 officers and crew and accommodated 1,200 passengers on its main, saloon or stateroom, and hurricane decks. It features a Morgan-type (feathering) paddle wheel, a "walking beam" steam engine, and elaborately designed passenger facilities. During its nearly half century of service it carried thousands of passengers, including residents and tourists, as a Lake Champlain excursion boat. When competition from both diesel-powered vessels and the automobile forced the Lake Champlain Transportation Company to close in 1948, it was the oldest operating steamboat company in the world.

The *Ticonderoga* was kept in service during 1949 and 1950 by private owners and concerned citizens, and in 1951 it was purchased by the Shelburne Museum. Founded by Electra Havemeyer Webb in 1947, the museum reflects her eclectic tastes, as seen in her "collection of collections" that she gathered to "show the craftsmanship and ingenuity of our forefathers." The museum, with its unique assortment of historic buildings and structures and early Americana, is now one of Vermont's most famous attractions. The Shelburne Steamboat Company, organized by the museum, was able to keep the boat in operation for another two seasons. The *Ticonderoga*, however, continued to run at a deficit, so Webb decided to put the boat on display. It was moved nearly two miles on a specially built steel cradle mounted on 16 freight car trucks (eight on each of two parallel tracks laid for the purpose). Moving the steamboat took 66 days and attracted national attention. Placed in a basin in the middle of the museum's grounds, the *Ticonderoga* is now a dry-berth exhibit. The steamer houses a collection of prints, paintings, and photographs illustrating the history of steamboating on Lake Champlain. NR. NHL. [Shelburne Museum]

■ **Ticonderoga**
Shelburne Museum
U.S. Route 7
1906

The side-wheel lakeboat *Ticonderoga* houses a collection of prints, paintings, and photographs illustrating the history of steamboating on Lake Champlain.

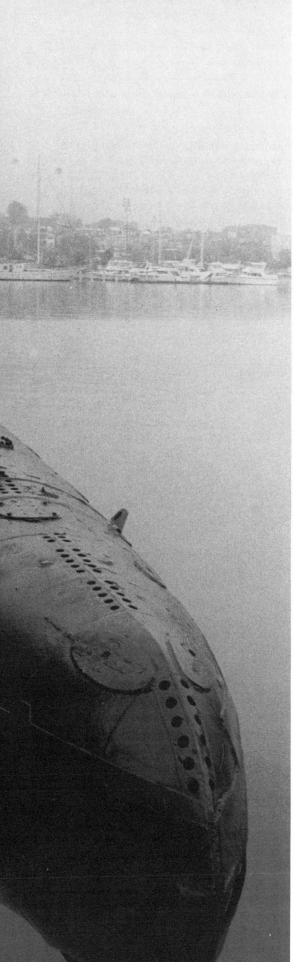

MID-ATLANTIC

The USS *Torsk*, one of two preserved examples of the *Tench*-class submarine, at Baltimore's Inner Harbor next to the aquarium.

■ ■ ■ ■ ■ ■   **DELAWARE**   ■ ■ ■ ■ ■ ■

LEWES

■ **Lightship No. 118**
("Overfalls")
Lewes-Rehoboth Canal
Between Shipcarpenter and
Mulberry Streets
1938

One of the last lightships ordered built by the U.S. Lighthouse
Service before it was merged with the U.S. Coast Guard in
1939, the *No.118* was constructed in 1938 at the Rice Brothers
Shipyard in East Boothbay, Maine. The lightship served first
and longest at the Boston Harbor station. The *No. 118* also
served at two stations near Long Island, New York-Pollock
Rip and Cornfield. Retired from active duty in 1973, the
lightship was given to the Lewes Historical Society for use as
a museum. Upon its arrival the vessel was named "Overfalls"
for a shoal located just outside Lewes Harbor and off Cape
Henolopen that had been marked by another lightship from
1892 until 1961. NR. [Lewes Historical Society]

The lightship *No. 118*, now
known as the "Overfalls,"
actually was never assigned to
that station in the Delaware Bay.

WILMINGTON

■ **USCGC Mohawk**
End of King Street
Opposite the Amtrak Station

The only member of the
Algonquin class of U.S. Coast
Guard cutters to be preserved,
the USCGC *Mohawk* now serves
as the Battle of the Atlantic
Memorial.

The U.S. Coast Guard cutter *Mohawk*, restored to its 1943
appearance, is a floating, operational memorial to the Battle
of the Atlantic. Beginning in 1940 Britain and its allies—
including, after 1941, the United States—were drawn into a
sea war against Hitler's submarine forces. With deadly effect
German U-boats struck convoys of ships ferrying fuel,
supplies, munitions, and troops to Europe. To counter this
onslaught the allies intensified their antisubmarine warfare
campaign, sending destroyers, destroyer escorts, corvettes,
and cutters into the Atlantic to seek out and destroy the
U-boats. The U.S. Coast Guard was an important participant
in the Battle of the Atlantic. The *Treasury*-class cutters *Ingham*
and *Taney*, now preserved at Mount Pleasant, South Carolina,
and Baltimore, are veterans of Atlantic service. The *Mohawk*
is the only restored example of an *Algonquin*, a 165-foot-long
class A cutter. Built in 1934 to break ice, the *Mohawk* was the
product of the noted shipyard of Pusey and Jones in
Wilmington and was launched on October 23. The cutter
was commissioned a few months later on January 19, 1935.
The *Mohawk* spent the next five years breaking ice, assisting

vessels in distress, and enforcing smuggling laws on the Hudson and the Chesapeake bays. As the clouds of war gathered, the *Mohawk* was temporarily transferred to the U.S. Navy on November 1, 1940, and assigned to the commander-in-chief of the Atlantic Fleet destroyers. Like the other cutters assigned to the navy for the coming conflict, the *Mohawk* retained its coast guard officers and crew. Assigned to the Greenland Patrol, it worked off the frozen northern coast, escorting vessels and on one occasion assisting torpedoed vessels and depth-charging German U-boats. The cutter also was used on weather patrol. Returning to the United States after the Japanese surrender, the *Mohawk* was returned to the coast guard in November 1945. The cutter was decommissioned in October 1947 and was bought by the Pilots Association of the Bay and River Delaware and renamed the *Philadelphia.* After a 24-year career as a pilot boat, the *Philadelphia* retired in 1981, and restoration of the cutter, once again renamed the *Mohawk,* began. Moored on the Christina River at Wilmington, the need for extensive repairs will place the *Mohawk* in dry-dock during the summer of 1991. Its future is uncertain, but plans call for moving the ship to Perth Amboy, New Jersey. [Air-Sea-Land, Inc.]

■ ■ ■ ■ ■   DISTRICT OF COLUMBIA   ■ ■ ■ ■ ■

The destroyer USS *Barry* is one of 18 *Forrest Sherman*–class destroyers built to be effective antisubmarine warfare platforms and fast-screening escort vessels for fast carrier forces. The third destroyer of this class, the USS *Barry* is one of only four remaining vessels of this class. These destroyers' design incorporated the combat lessons of World War II to create sleek, versatile craft that formed the backbone of U.S. destroyer forces in Korea and Vietnam. During its 26-year career, the *Barry* participated in numerous cruises and missions, including the U.S. blockade of Cuba during the Cuban missile crisis in October 1962 and the Vietnam War. Decommissioned in 1982, it was towed to the Washington Navy Yard in 1983 for public display next to the Navy Memorial Museum. [U.S. Navy]

■ **USS Barry (DD-933)**
Navy Memorial Museum
Washington Navy Yard
9th and M Streets, S.E.
1955

Decommissioned in 1982, the USS *Barry* was towed to the Washington Navy Yard in 1983 for public display next to the Navy Memorial Museum.

■ **Intelligent Whale**
Navy Memorial Museum
Washington Navy Yard
9th and M Streets, S.E.
1864

The U.S. government's first formal sponsorship of a submarine's construction came during the Civil War, when the exigencies of war provided the initiative for technological advances. A conflict that saw the development of undersea mines and ironclad warships, the Civil War also introduced the first submersible attack craft since Bushnell's Turtle of 1776 and 1812 and Robert Fulton's *Nautilus* of 1801. As the Confederacy worked to complete a submarine craft, beginning with the *Pioneer*, the Union navy authorized the construction of a small, iron-hulled vessel. Begun in 1864 and designed by a Mr. Halstead, the hand-cranked 30-foot-long craft was named the *Intelligent Whale*. Work on the small craft continued through 1872, when the designer died. Still uncompleted, the *Intelligent Whale* was abandoned that year as a failure, although $50,000 had been spent on its construction. Originally on display outside the Brooklyn Navy Yard, the *Intelligent Whale* was moved to the Washington Navy Yard in 1966. It is now displayed inside an annex to the Navy Memorial Museum.

The *Intelligent Whale* at the New York Navy Yard in 1915.

■ **Kaiten**
Navy Memorial Museum Annex
Washington Navy Yard
9th and M Streets, S.E.
1944–45

Japan's development of midget submarines culminated in the design and construction of manned torpedoes. Known as *kaiten* ("heaven shifters"), these craft were modified versions of Japan's oxygen-driven Type 93 torpedoes. A compartment amidships accommodated the pilot, helm, and a periscope. A lower hatch allowed the pilot to "lock in" from a mother submarine and launch submerged. There was also an upper hatch. Most of the kaiten was warhead; the smallest charges were 3,145 pounds of explosive, with the Type IV kaiten carrying nearly a two-ton charge. Plans for the kaiten were drafted in great secrecy in 1943, and as the tides of war turned against Japan in 1944, development of these weapons of desperation ensued. The 48-foot-long steel submarines had diameters of 3 feet, 3 inches and weighed 18.3 tons submerged. Nearly 400 kaiten were built, and several sorties with these weapons were made, damaging a handful of U.S. vessels but sinking only one, the fleet oiler *Mississenewa*, then at anchor at Ulithi in the Caroline Islands. When the war ended in August 1945, the Japanese had lost dozens of kaiten and 210 men, a huge failure when balanced against the U.S. losses of one ship and 50 men. Two kaiten are known to be displayed in the United States; others probably exist in museum collections. This kaiten is probably a Type I; the other, a Type IV, is displayed at Bowfin Park at Pearl Harbor. [U.S. Navy]

The *Philadelphia* is the only surviving gundelo, a small gunboat, built and manned by American forces during the Revolutionary War. Part of a hastily built fleet, it is one of 15 small craft with which Benedict Arnold fought 29 British vessels in the battle off Valcour Island, Lake Champlain, on October 11, 1776. The building of Arnold's fleet provided the colonists a year's grace period, and the Battle of Valcour Bay paved the way for the decisive American victory at Saratoga in the fall of 1777.

Sunk in Lake Champlain during the battle, the *Philadelphia* was remarkably well preserved by the cold water when it was identified and salvaged by Lorenzo Hagglund in 1934 and 1935. In addition to the guns and hull, hundreds of other relics were recovered from the vessel—shot, cooking utensils, tools, buttons, buckles, and human bones.

In the ensuing years the *Philadelphia* was exhibited at various points on Lake Champlain and the Hudson River before its installation as a permanent exhibit at Exeter, New York. Bequeathed to the Smithsonian Institution in 1961, the *Philadelphia* and its associated artifacts are part of the permanent collection of the National Museum of American History. NR. NHL. [Smithsonian Institution]

■ **Philadelphia**
National Museum of
American History
12th Street and
Constitution Avenue, N.W.
1776

■ ■ ■ ■ ■ ■   MARYLAND   ■ ■ ■ ■ ■ ■

ANNAPOLIS

Built by Otis Lloyd of Salisbury, Maryland, the *Stanley Norman* is one of a unique vessel type designed and adapted for use in the Chesapeake Bay during the 1890s. Known as skipjacks, these oyster dredge boats were popular during a period when boat-building costs were rising and the oyster catch was diminishing. The skipjacks were easier to construct than the earlier, traditionally framed bugeyes and other craft, and their shallow draft allowed them to navigate more easily the bay's coves and creeks. Local boatbuilders developed the skipjack by enlarging the hull of the traditional, unframed,

■ **Stanley Norman**
Annapolis Harbor
1902

square-sterned, and often flat-bottomed bay crabbing skiff and giving it a deadrise (or V) bottom, a deck, a cabin, and a single-masted sloop rig. Recently acquired by the Chesapeake Bay Foundation, the *Stanley Norman* hosts schoolchildren on educational cruises on the Chesapeake Bay. When not in operation, it is berthed in the Annapolis harbor. NR. [Chesapeake Bay Foundation]

Part of the Chesapeake Bay's famous fleet of skipjacks, the *Stanley Norman* has retired from oystering but continues to host schoolchildren on educational cruises on the Chesapeake Bay.

The *Baltimore*, the nation's oldest operating steam-powered tugboat.

BALTIMORE

■ **Baltimore**
Baltimore Museum of Industry
1415 Key Highway
1906

Built for the Port of Baltimore by the Skinner Shipbuilding and Drydock Company, a local yard, the iron-hulled, 81-ton steam tugboat *Baltimore* worked on the inner harbor for nearly six decades, breaking ice, pushing barges, moving pile-driving apparatus used to build the wharves that lined the waterfront, and carrying dignitaries on harbor tours for the municipal harbor board. Retired by the Maryland Port Authority in 1963, the tugboat was acquired for use as a private yacht. In 1979 ice damage to the hull's throughfittings caused it to sink. The owner donated the hulk, resting in 14 feet of water, to the Baltimore Museum of Industry. In 1981 the tugboat was raised by two 150-ton cranes and refloated. Since then it has been moored at the museum as one of its premier–but not stationary—artifacts. Restored to operational condition, the tugboat is a working example of 19th- and early 20th-century marine steam engineering. The 330-horsepower compound engine is powered by a Scotch boiler. Although it was converted to burn diesel fuel in 1957, toward the end of its working career, the *Baltimore* once again burns coal, one of a few steamers operated with this traditional fuel. [Baltimore Museum of Industry]

One of the first frigates of the fledgling U.S. Navy, the *Constellation* was built in Baltimore in 1797. Under the command of Thomas Truxton, the "Yankee Racehorse" quickly proved its capabilities in battle against the French in the Atlantic during an undeclared war with France from 1798 to 1800. Subsequent tours took the *Constellation* to the Mediterranean, the Pacific, and later to Africa to assist in the breaking up of the slave trade. During the Civil War the rebuilt ship blockaded southern ports. From 1894 to 1940 it was moored at the Naval War College in Newport, Rhode Island,

■ **USF Constellation**
Pier 1, Constellation Dock,
Inner Harbor
Off Pratt Street
1797

and used to train midshipmen. The *Constellation* was nearly forgotten until President Franklin D. Roosevelt recalled the vessel to duty as relief flagship of the Atlantic Fleet during World War II.

After the war the *Constellation* was dismasted and destined to be scrapped. Saved by concerned citizens and ultimately moved back to Baltimore, it is now moored in the city's Inner Harbor where it is being restored. The *Constellation* is one of the premier tourist attractions in Baltimore. NR. NHL. [U.S. Frigate Constellation]

Destined for scrapping, the USF *Constellation* was saved by concerned citizens. Moored in Baltimore's Inner Harbor, the vessel serves as a centerpiece for this waterfront development that has become one of the city's premier tourist attractions.

The *Norman T.*, a buyboat named for its first owner, was built in Perrin, Virginia, in 1928 and used for carrying freight, dredging crab, and fishing for flounder and conch on the Chesapeake Bay. Renamed the *Half Shell* in 1987, it operates educational cruises around the Chesapeake Bay, leaving from Baltimore during the summer months and from Salisbury, Maryland, during the fall months. Every spring the *Half Shell* joins the state of Maryland's oyster "spatting program,"

■ **Half Shell**
Harrison's Pier 5, Inner Harbor
711 Eastern Avenue
1928

dredging thumbnail-size baby oysters from natural seed beds and transporting them to harvest areas, where they can grow to maturity if water quality permits. [Ocean World Institute]

■ **John W. Brown**
Pier 1
Clinton Street
1942

One of two surviving Liberty ships preserved in the United States, the *John W. Brown* is the product of an emergency shipbuilding program of World War II that resulted in the construction of more than 2,700 Liberty ships. Designed as simple cargo steamers, the Liberty ships could be built quickly and inexpensively and formed the backbone of a massive sealift of troops, arms, material, and ordnance to every theater of the war. Built by the Bethlehem-Fairfield Shipyard of Baltimore for the Federal Maritime Commission, the *Brown* made wartime voyages to the Persian Gulf and the Mediterranean, including duty during the Anzio landings.

After the war the *Brown* carried government cargoes to help rebuild war-torn Europe. From 1946 to 1982 it served as a school ship. Acquired by Project Liberty Ship, the *Brown* arrived in Baltimore to serve as a museum ship and memorial in 1988. The only Liberty ship on the East Coast, the *John W. Brown* will be open to the public as a floating exhibit in Baltimore. NR. [Project Liberty Ship]

■ **Lightship No. 116**
("**Chesapeake**")
Pier 4, Inner Harbor
Off Pratt Street next to the
Baltimore Aquarium
1930

Owned by the National Park
Service but on a 25-year loan
to the city of Baltimore, the
lightship *No. 116* is now known
as "Chesapeake," its former
designation.

The years 1929 and 1930 saw the construction of several lightships powered by diesel-electric plants. This significant change in lightship power plants and propulsion marked the third generation of lightship design—the 133-foot-long lightship class—of which the *No. 116* is the best preserved example. The *No. 116* was built in Charleston, South Carolina, by the Charleston Drydock and Machine Company. Launched in 1929, it was sent to the Fenwick Island Shoal station off the Delaware coast. When that station was discontinued in 1933, the lightship was moved farther south to the Chesapeake station. The *No. 116* served here from 1933 to 1965, except for the period 1942–45, when war duty sent it north to Sandwich, Massachusetts, to serve as an examination vessel guarding the port of Boston. During this period the Chesapeake station was marked by a buoy.

From 1966 until 1970 the *No. 116* served at the mouth of Delaware Bay. Decommissioned in 1970, the lightship was transferred to the National Park Service in 1971. Refurbished at the Washington Navy Yard and displayed at Hains Point in East Potomac Park, Washington, D.C., it was used as a floating environmental living center until 1980. In 1981 the lightship was placed on a 25-year loan to the city of Baltimore and moored in the Inner Harbor as part of the Baltimore Maritime Museum. It is open to the public as a floating exhibit. NR. NHL. [Baltimore Maritime Museum]

The skipjack *Minnie V.*

One of the last operating skipjacks in the United States, the *Minnie V.* in the summer serves as an educational tour and charter vessel in Baltimore's Inner Harbor and in the winter dredges oysters out of Tilghman Island in the Chesapeake Bay. Originally built in Wewona, Maryland, where many active skipjacks continue to operate, the *Minnie V.* was rebuilt along its original lines in 1980 and 1981. On one- to two-hour tours the *Minnie V.* takes passengers on a seven-mile sail through the old port section of Baltimore, exploring the shoreline from the steamboat basin at the Inner Harbor to the original harbor entrance at Fort McHenry. NR. [Radcliffe Maritime Museum]

■ **Minnie V.**
Inner Harbor
Off Pratt Street
1906

■ USCGC Taney (WHEC-37)
Between Piers 4 and 5,
Inner Harbor
Off Pratt Street
1936

The USCGC *Taney* is the only surviving warship still afloat that witnessed the destruction at Pearl Harbor on December 7, 1941, when the Pacific Fleet was attacked. The *Taney* and the USCGC *Ingham* in Mount Pleasant, South Carolina, are the two remaining preserved 327-foot-long, *Secretary*-class, high-endurance cutters, a seven-ship class named for secretaries of the treasury. The *Secretary*, or *Treasury*, class was considered the most successful class of large U.S. Coast Guard–built cutters, making up the largest and most heavily armed coast guard warships until the delivery of their successors, the 378-foot-long *Hamilton* class in 1967. The *Secretary*-class ships were very large patrol gunboats designed to provide maritime law enforcement, search and rescue services, and communication and weather services on the high seas. These cutters also had a substantial wartime naval role, serving as convoy escorts, amphibious force flagships, shore bombardment vessels, and maritime patrol ships. Specialized law enforcement duties included fisheries patrol, interception of refugees, and interdiction of illegal drugs. Another specialized task was officer training. The *Taney* was an exemplary member of its class, serving in virtually all these roles during its half-century career.

Launched from the Philadelphia Naval Shipyard in 1936, the *Taney* was soon assigned to Honolulu, Hawaii. In 1938 it was chosen to establish fueling stations on Enderbury, Canton, Jarvis, and Baker islands for trans-Pacific seaplane service linking the United States with French New Caledonia and New Zealand. After the outbreak of World War II all cutters of the *Secretary* class except the *Taney* were transferred to the Atlantic to patrol the Grand Banks. The *Taney* remained in Honolulu to keep track of increasing Japanese fishing and intelligence gathering in the North Pacific. On December 7, 1941, it was moored next to the power plant when the Japanese began their attack. Within four minutes its guns were manned and firing at the attacking aircraft. After the attack the *Taney* was one of the few ships left to conduct antisubmarine patrols. Later the cutter was sent to the Atlantic as a convoy escort for the invasion of North Africa in 1944. Returning to the Pacific in 1945, the *Taney* participated in the Okinawa campaign, serving as the flag-ship for the commander of the naval forces.

At war's end the *Taney* was returned to the U.S. Coast Guard. Peacetime activities included serving as a weather ship and as a rescue and fisheries patrol and later providing narcotics interdiction. The *Taney* also served in the Korean conflict, providing communications and weather services to the U.S. forces in Korea. During the Vietnam War, the *Taney* underwent a brief deployment as part of a program to inter-dict the flow of enemy troops and material to South Vietnam from the communist-controlled north. After 50 years of active service the *Taney* was decommissioned in 1986. Acquired by the Baltimore Maritime Museum, it is open to the public as a floating exhibit. NR. NHL. [Baltimore Maritime Museum]

The USS *Torsk* is, along with the USS *Requin*, one of two preserved examples of the *Tench*-class submarines, a late war attempt by the U.S. Navy to improve the highly successful *Gato*- and *Balao*-class boats. The *Tench*-class ships were more strongly built and had a better internal layout, which increased their displacement by about 35 to 45 tons. Only 10 *Tench*-class boats were commissioned in time to fight in World War II. Completed at the Portsmouth Naval Shipyard in 1944, the *Torsk* embarked on its first war patrol in April 1945. On its second and final war patrol it fired the last two torpedoes of the war, sinking two Japanese coastal defense craft on August 14, 1945. The sinking of these last Japanese combatant ships of the war completed the navy's mission, begun on December 7, 1941, to sweep the seas of Japanese merchant vessels and warships.

After the war the *Torsk*'s operations as a training vessel at the submarine school in New London, Connecticut, helped it later establish a world record of 11,884 dives. Converted in 1951 to a GUPPY configuration (the navy's term for sub-marines modified as part of the Greater Underwater Pro-pulsion Program), the *Torsk* was equipped with a snorkel, which allowed the submarine to take in fresh air needed to operate the diesel engines underwater. Running on diesel engines allowed the submarine greater speed and range than was possible when running on battery power. All exterior guns were removed, and the original conning tower was enclosed by a new streamlined fiberglass sail casing designed to reduce underwater resistance. The *Torsk* was awarded the Presidential Unit Citation for operations during the 1960 Lebanon crisis and later took part in the Cuban blockade, which earned it the Navy Commendation Medal. In 1972 the *Torsk* was transferred to the state of Maryland. Manned and restored by Maryland sea cadets, it was established as a memorial in 1973. NR. NHL. [Baltimore Maritime Museum]

SOLOMONS

Used for fishing in the Chesapeake Bay, the 45-foot-long *Penguin* was built by Harvey Hurley in Wingate, Maryland. A wood workboat with a V-shaped bottom, locally known as a Hooper Island draketail, the *Penguin* is now displayed as a dry-berth exhibit along with the Calvert Marine Museum's small craft collection. [Calvert Marine Museum]

■ **USS Torsk (SS-423)**
Pier 4, Inner Harbor
Off Pratt Street next to the
Baltimore Aquarium
1944

The *Penguin*, a workboat referred to as a "Hooper Island draketail."

■ **Penguin**
Calvert Marine Museum
State Route 2
1935

Built as a bugeye in 1899, the *Wm. B. Tennison* was converted to a motor-powered buyboat between 1907 and 1911.

■ **Wm. B. Tennison**
Calvert Marine Museum
State Route 2
1899

A converted buyboat now afloat on the Chesapeake Bay, the *Wm. B. Tennison* was built by Frank Laird at Crab Island, Maryland, as a nine-log bugeye and converted to a motor-powered buyboat between 1907 and 1911. Its service has included oyster dredging, hauling produce, lumber, and live-stock in the off-seasons to Baltimore and Washington markets, and buying oysters from boats on the dredging grounds—a combination of uses typical of many Chesapeake Bay craft that have now disappeared. The *Wm. B. Tennison* is now operated by the Calvert Marine Museum as an educational and recreational passenger vehicle. NR. [Calvert Marine Museum]

ST. MICHAELS

■ **E. C. Collier**
Chesapeake Bay
Maritime Museum
Navy Point
1910

Now being restored to be a permanent dry-berth exhibit at the Chesapeake Bay Maritime Museum, the *E. C. Collier* is one of the oldest surviving skipjacks and, at 52 feet in length, one of the longest. Before its retirement the *Collier* spent 75 years dredging oysters on the Chesapeake Bay. Built for Eddie Collier by George Washington Horseman at Deal Island, Maryland, the *E. C. Collier* has been recorded by the National Park Service's Historic American Engineering Record through measured drawings, including an isometric drawing showing how dredging equipment is used. NR. [Chesapeake Bay Maritime Museum]

The skipjack *E. C. Collier*, awaiting restoration and as documented in one of the measured drawings from the National Park Service's Historic American Engineering Record.

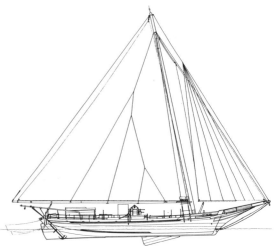

Built by John B. Harrison at Tilghman Island, Maryland, the *Edna E. Lockwood* is a nine-log sailing bugeye with partial frame sides, the oldest form of construction of these indigenous Chesapeake Bay workcraft. Bugeyes harvested oysters and were major participants in Maryland commerce, hauling freight before the development of improved highways. The evolution of the bugeye began with the widespread use of open sailing canoes on the Chesapeake Bay in the 18th century. Hewn out of one to three logs, these basic, inexpensively built workboats sold their harvest to larger, deep-keeled schooners, which in turn carried the product, chiefly oysters, to metropolitan markets. To increase profits, oyster boats were modified so that the oysters could be transported directly to market. A deck and forward cabin were added, providing increased storage capacity that enabled operators to deliver oysters in economical quantities. The bugeye that finally evolved had two raked masts, pronounced sheer (from the side, the longitudinal curve of the deck), a clipper bow with bowsprit, and a centerboard. The bugeye also featured low freeboard (from the side, the vertical distance between the top of the deck to the waterline) that allowed oyster dredges to be

■ **Edna E. Lockwood**
Chesapeake Bay
Maritime Museum
Navy Point
1889

Above: The *Edna E. Lockwood,* the only surviving example of an unaltered bugeye. Left: A hand winder used for oyster dredging aboard the *Edna E. Lockwood.*

hauled directly on deck. By 1893 the construction of bugeyes began to decline as smaller sloop-rigged skipjacks gained in popularity. By 1904 most bugeyes had been converted into motorized buyboats.

Moored at the Chesapeake Bay Maritime Museum, the *Lockwood* is the only unaltered example of an original bugeye, maintaining the integrity of its sailing rig and working appearance. Now a participant in many Chesapeake Bay festivities, the *Lockwood* visits ports all over the bay as part of a public awareness program. NR. [Chesapeake Bay Maritime Museum]

■ **Mustang**
Chesapeake Bay
Maritime Museum
Navy Point
1907

One of the last "brogan" oyster dredgers, the *Mustang* was built by the Moore brothers as the *Kate D.* in Saxis, Virginia. Predecessors of the bugeyes, brogans played an important role in the development of the Chesapeake Bay craft. Descended from Native American log canoes, they were larger and heavier to better pull an oyster dredge under sail. A brogan had two masts, a sharp stem and stern, a clipper bow, and bold sheer. Constructed of five loblolly pine logs pinned together with steel dowels, the *Kate D.* was one of largest of its type; its length is 45.9 feet (60 feet including the bowsprit and boomkins), and its beam is 10.8 feet. Used as a commercial vessel until the 1950s, it was sold and restored for educational and pleasure cruises out of Annapolis. Donated to the Chesapeake Bay Maritime Museum in 1989, it is to be restored as a dry-berth exhibit. NR. [Chesapeake Bay Maritime Museum]

■ **Old Point**
Chesapeake Bay
Maritime Museum
Navy Point
1909

The *Old Point*'s hull, a five-log construction, is an adaptive use of the round-stern bugeye construction. Built by and for J. G. Wornom in Poquoson, Maryland, the *Old Point* worked as a dredge for the Old Dominion Crab Company from 1910 until 1968, when it was sold to a private owner to carry light freight and passengers in the Turks and Caicos islands. The *Old Point* was restored as an operating exhibit and donated to the Chesapeake Bay Maritime Museum in 1984. [Chesapeake Bay Maritime Museum]

The *Old Point* worked as a dredge and a packet boat.

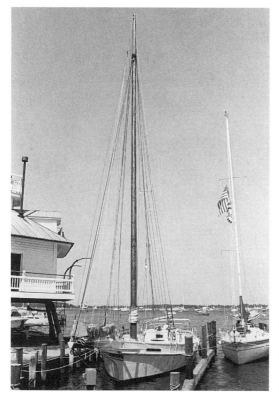

The skipjack *Rosie Parks*, a floating exhibit that is also operated occasionally at the Chesapeake Bay Maritime Museum.

Built by Bronza M. Parks for Captain Orville Parks in Wingate, Maryland, the *Rosie Parks* served as an oyster dredge. This skipjack is well known for having won nine out of 10 skipjack races between 1965 and 1975, when the captain retired. These races were revived during the 1960s as the centerpiece of the annual Chesapeake Bay Appreciation Days observance. The *Rosie Parks* is a floating exhibit at the Chesapeake Bay Maritime Museum. [Chesapeake Bay Maritime Museum]

■ **Rosie Parks**
Chesapeake Bay
Maritime Museum
Navy Point
1955

■ ■ ■ ■ ■ ■   NEW JERSEY   ■ ■ ■ ■ ■ ■

CAPE MAY

The Grand Banks of Newfoundland, a submerged plateau 35,000 square miles in area, has provided abundant pelagic harvests for centuries. Fishing vessels from Europe fished the banks, at times in sight of the New World, before Columbus's epic voyages, and in time the fisheries attracted French and British settlers to Newfoundland and Nova Scotia. Thousands of vessels have worked the banks, sailing from New England and Canadian ports to work in the brutally harsh, cold, and often killing waters. One of the premier Canadian fishing firms to work the banks was Zwicker and Company. Two of its vessels survive as exhibits in the United States—the *Sherman Zwicker* and the earlier *E. F. Zwicker*, now the schooner *American* of the Lobster House Restaurant in Cape May, New Jersey. Built in 1934 by Smith and Rhuland in Lunenberg, Nova Scotia, the heart of Canada's Grand Banks fishing industry, the two-masted auxiliary schooner

■ **American**
The Lobster House
Fisherman's Wharf
1934

Built in Nova Scotia as a Grand Banks fishing schooner, the *American* is currently a floating restaurant in Cape May's Inner Harbor.

worked until 1976, when it was sold to the Harry Lundeberg School, a maritime union training school in Maryland, which renamed it the *Captain James Cook* and used it for sail training. In 1988 the Lundeberg School sold it to the Lobster House Restaurant, which renovated it for use as a floating restaurant and renamed it the *American.* The schooner is now moored at Fisherman's Wharf on Cape May's Inner Harbor. [The Lobster House]

EDGEWATER

■ Binghamton
725 River Road
1905

Located on the Hudson River, overlooking the New York skyline and just three miles south of the George Washington Bridge, the 231-foot-long, double-ended ferry *Binghamton* retired from service on the Hoboken-to-Manhattan run on the Hudson in 1967 after a 62-year career, 125 million passengers, and 200,000 miles of operation. Renovated for use as a floating restaurant in 1975, the *Binghamton* has since served as a popular riverfront attraction and eatery. Designed by the New York naval architects Gardner and Cox and built by the noted Newport News Shipbuilding and Drydock Company in Virginia, the *Binghamton* was one of four sister ships constructed for the Hoboken Ferry Company as hulls 47, 48, 49, and 50 of the Virginia shipyard. The ferry's exterior is essentially unmodified, although the interior has been altered for restaurant use. The decks, which once carried 24 automobiles and 1,986 passengers when the *Binghamton* began service in March 1905, now accommodate dining rooms. Even the engine room, with its intact double-compound marine steam engines, is now open for dining. NR. [Hudson Landing]

HACKENSACK

The USS *Ling* is the last of the fleet boats that patrolled American shores during World War II in response to U-boat attacks off the eastern coast of the United States. A diesel-electric submarine of the *Balao* class, the *Ling* was built by the Cramp Shipbuilding Company of Philadelphia. Unlike many of its sisters, the *Ling* was built for Atlantic service and

■ **USS Ling (SS-297)**
New Jersey Naval Museum
Borg Park
Intersection of Court and
River Streets
1943

made one patrol before the war ended. Decommissioned in 1946, it became a part of the Atlantic Reserve Fleet until reactivation as a submarine training vessel in 1960. Redesignated as an AGSS (an auxiliary submarine assigned special duties), the *Ling* did not go out to sea but simulated all the aspects of submarine operations, including diving and surfacing.

The *Ling* was donated to the Submarine Memorial Association in 1971, arriving at its present home in New Jersey in January 1973. The boat is now displayed in the narrow headwaters of the Hackensack River and is the official state naval museum for New Jersey. It continues in service as a training aid for high school ROTC students. NR. [Submarine Memorial Association]

JERSEY CITY

Built for the Lehigh Valley Railroad Company, *Lehigh Valley Railroad Barge No. 79* is an excellent representative of a Hudson River railroad barge. Before railroad tunnels and bridges were built, a lighterage system was used on the Hudson River to transport goods to be consumed in New York City and cargo to be loaded on vessels for shipment overseas. Various railroad companies maintained large fleets of barges and tugboats, some numbering more than 500 vessels, to move these goods. With the demise of the lighterage system, wood barges were abandoned in the 1960s and 1970s. At one time the *No. 79* was acquired at a railroad auction and used for storage as a pile driver. Now on loan to the Hudson Waterfront Museum, it has been restored as a floating exhibit. Ports along the Hudson River include Piermont, New York, Hoboken, New Jersey, and Liberty State Park in Jersey City. NR. [David Sharps]

■ **Lehigh Valley Railroad Barge No. 79**
Liberty State Park
Exit 14B, off the
New Jersey Turnpike
1914

Top: The USS *Ling* patrolled American shores during World War II. Above: The *Lehigh Valley Railroad Barge No. 79*, a remnant of the Hudson River's lighterage traffic.

PATERSON

■ **Fenian Ram**
Paterson Museum
2 Market Street
1881

The U.S. Navy began a long and distinguished submarine tradition in 1898 when John P. Holland's 53-foot-long submersible, the *Holland*, was launched. When this tiny, 64-ton submarine was commissioned as SS-1 on April 11, 1900, it was the culmination of a decades-long ambition of the Irish-born educator and inventor from Paterson, New Jersey. Holland, who was born in 1841 and emigrated to the United States in 1873, was inspired by the exploits of Confederate-built semi-submersibles and dreamed of perfecting the submarine. In 1878 he tested a one-man, 14-foot-long prototype on the Passaic River. Three years later, financed by the Fenian Brotherhood, an Irish revolutionary movement in the United States that sought Ireland's independence from British rule, Holland built his second craft, a 19-ton, 31-foot-long riveted-iron submersible known as the *Fenian Ram*. The three-person ram, launched in 1881, made frequent dives in New York Harbor and led Holland to perfect four other experimental craft that resulted in his *Holland* submarine of 1898, which was adopted by the navy. Holland died in obscurity in 1914, but he had seen his dream of an effective submarine become a reality. The *Fenian Ram* was placed in Paterson's West Side Park in 1928 as a monument to the inventor, whose grave remained unmarked until 1976. In 1980 the rusting craft, covered with graffiti, was moved to the Paterson Museum, where it is now displayed indoors in the Rogers Locomotive Building as a reminder of the ingenuity of the "father of the modern submarine." [Paterson Museum]

■ ■ ■ ■ ■ ■ ■   NEW YORK   ■ ■ ■ ■ ■ ■ ■

HUNTINGTON

■ **Jean**
Huntington Harbor
1913

The *Jean* is an excellent example of an early 20th-century glass-cabin motor cruiser, a type developed and widely used to carry passengers as a yacht, ferry, or launch before the invention of the gasoline engine. Built at Red Bank, New Jersey, the *Jean* was constructed at the beginning of the motor boat era. The vessel was used as a family cruiser and small passenger vessel all of its active life. During the summer months the *Jean* assists in the educational programs offered by the Maritime Center on Long Island and is used for excursions by the general public. [Maritime Center on Long Island]

■ **Little Jennie**
Huntington Harbor
1884

Descended from the Native American dugout log canoe, the *Little Jennie* is a rare and largely intact example of a Chesapeake Bay bugeye, a sailing craft developed to meet the specialized needs and constraints of the Chesapeake Bay oyster industry during its heyday in the last quarter of the 19th century. The *Little Jennie* was built on Solomons Island, Maryland, by and for J. T. Marsh, a builder who specialized in the construction of bugeyes after launching the first regularly framed and planked bugeye with a distinctive duckbill stern in 1879. The *Little Jennie* was used continuously on the Chesapeake Bay from 1884 to 1930, first as an oyster boat and later as a sailing freighter hauling wheat and watermelons. It appears not to have been registered for 16 years, when it was rumored to be a rum runner, at least during the early 1930s. Conversion to a pleasure yacht after 1930 did not alter the vessel's distinctive bugeye lines and rig. Retired as a yacht in 1971, it was restored in the mid-1980s. Now an educational training vessel, the *Little Jennie* takes out fourth- and fifth-grade schoolchildren for courses in marine biology and ecology. NR. [Maritime Center on Long Island]

KINGSTON

Built as a Canadian steel steam tugboat, the *Mathilda* spent her entire career in or near Montreal Harbor. Vessels of this type once plied the Hudson River in large numbers, while none remains today. After being displayed for years at New York's South Street Seaport, the tugboat was donated to the city of Kingston, which has placed the *Mathilda* in a dry-berth exhibit as part of the restoration of its waterfront to early 20th-century conditions. NR. [Hudson River Maritime Center]

■ **Mathilda**
Hudson River Maritime Center
One Roundout Landing
1899

The *Mathilda*, a tugboat that once served Montreal Harbor.

NEW YORK CITY

The 1958 destroyer USS *Edson* (DD-946) is one of 18 *Forrest Sherman*–class destroyers. The destroyer is the oldest type of ship to have seen continuous service in the U.S. Navy. It was the focus of considerable design effort, planning, and construction from the mid-1880s through World War II, making it the most frequently built major surface warship in the history of the U.S. Navy. The final, ultimate class of destroyer, the *Sherman* class reflected combat lessons learned during World War II. These destroyers, many later modernized for more effective antisubmarine warfare (ASW) and antiaircraft warfare (AAW), served as the major all-gun, general-purpose destroyers during the Vietnam War and through the 1970s. They were in turn replaced by the frigates and cruisers of the modern nuclear navy.

Construction began in 1956 at the Bath Iron Works shipyard in Bath, Maine, and the ship was launched in 1958. The

■ **USS Edson** (DD-946)
Pier 86
Intrepid Sea-Air-Space Museum
West 46th Street
and 12th Avenue
1958

The USS *Edson* leaving Pearl Harbor before gunline duty in Vietnam.

USS *Edson* served with distinction from 1959 to 1989. Besides extensive Vietnam War gunline duty between 1964 and 1974, its service included training duty from 1977 until 1989, when it was retired and placed on display on the Hudson River. NR. NHL. [Intrepid Sea-Air-Space Museum]

■ **Fire Fighter**
Pier A
St. George Ferry Center
Staten Island
1938

One of 10 surviving fireboats in the United States 50 years of age or older, the *Fire Fighter* is the best-known fireboat associated with the port of New York, the most significant U.S. port since the 1820s and currently the primary port with respect to shipped and imported cargo. The *Fire Fighter* has never been modernized, making it the best example in the United States of a major port's large fireboat of the 1930s. The vessel represents the culmination of American fireboat design, as its long service without modification indicates.

New York became the first American port to use waterborne fire-fighting equipment in 1809, when its volunteer fire fighters placed a hand pump aboard a rowboat. In 1865 the city's Board of Metropolitan Fire Commissioners contracted for the services of a salvage tugboat as an "on-call" fireboat. In 1875 the city commissioned the building of its first fireboat and since then has assiduously followed modern developments in fireboat design and construction. In 1882 it ordered an iron-hulled fireboat, in 1898 a steel fireboat, in 1931 a gasoline-powered fireboat, and finally in 1938 the nation's most powerful diesel-electric fireboat, the *Fire Fighter*.

The *Fire Fighter* has responded to many fires and waterfront emergencies in its more than 50 years of service. Three of these fires—those on the SS *Normandie* in 1942 and the freighter *El Estero* in 1943, and the collision of the oil tanker *Esso Brussels* with the container ship *Sea Witch* in 1973— have brought considerable attention to the fireboat. For its critical role in fighting the fires and risking all to rescue the *Sea Witch*'s crew, the *Fire Fighter* and its crew were awarded the 1974 American Merchant Marine Seamanship Trophy. On May 22, 1975, the boat was presented with the Department of Commerce's Gallant Ship Award, the highest honor that can be accorded a merchant vessel, which cited the crew's extraordinary seamanship and heroism. The *Fire Fighter* is the only fireboat to win this award.

A popular exhibit at the 1939 World's Fair in New York, the *Fire Fighter* was also the subject of a popular and long-lived Revell plastic model, the only fireboat so honored. It has also been featured in children's books and leads parades welcoming arriving ships into New York Harbor. The fireboat participated in the tall ships celebrations—or OpSails—for the Bicentennial in 1976 and the rededication of the Statue of Liberty in 1986. NR. NHL. [Fire Department of New York, Marine Division]

Below: The *Fire Fighter*, a venerable tugboat that has never been modernized. Bottom: On February 10, 1942, the *Fire Fighter* worked to contain a fire aboard the capsized SS *Normandie*, successfully preventing the fire from spreading to the piers and along the waterfront.

■ **USS Growler (SSG-557)**
Pier 86
Intrepid Sea-Air-Space Museum
West 46th Street
and 12th Avenue
1954

An artifact of both the early Nuclear Age and the Cold War, the Grayback-Regulus II submarine *Growler* was laid down at the Portsmouth Naval Shipyard in 1954 to be a conventional attack submarine. In 1956, however, its construction was temporarily halted because of orders to convert it to a guided missile submarine to carry nuclear Regulus missiles, rail-launched missiles with an estimated 125-kiloton warhead deployed after a submarine had surfaced. Three other U.S. submarines also were modified to carry Regulus missiles in hangars. This program initiated a U.S. strategy of nuclear deterrent patrols in which large numbers of submarines, armed with nuclear missiles, patrolled the ocean from their constantly shifting, nearly undetectable positions. Launched on April 5, 1958, the 317-foot-long *Growler* was commissioned as SSG-577 on August 30 of the same year. Unlike the newly developed *Nautilus*, however, the *Growler* was not nuclear powered. Carrying either four of the Regulus I or two of the larger Regulus II missiles, it began deterrence patrols off China in March 1960 after test-firing exercises in the Caribbean in which the submarines surfaced, opened the hangars, and ran out the missiles on launching rails. The missiles unfolded their wings and were launched at targets with jet-assisted take off. After six patrols the submarine was retired, because both new missile and submarine propulsion technologies made it obsolete.

Decommissioned after four nuclear deterrence patrols and held in reserve after 1964, the USS *Growler* was placed on display at the Intrepid Air-Sea-Space Museum in 1989.

Decommissioned in May 1964, the *Growler* remained in reserve for 25 years. The navy turned the submarine over to the Intrepid Museum in 1988. The world's only guided-missile submarine open to the public, the *Growler* illustrates a concept that is still a cornerstone of America's strategic defense today. [Intrepid Sea-Air-Space Museum]

■ **USS Intrepid (CV-11)**
Pier 86
Intrepid Sea-Air-Space Museum
West 46th Street
and 12th Avenue
1943

The third *Essex*-class carrier built by the United States, the *Intrepid* is representative of the carriers that formed the core of the fast-carrier task forces of the Pacific theater of World War II. Early in the conflict, the *Essex*-class carriers were urgently needed to defend the vast areas of the Pacific quickly being conquered by the Japanese air and naval forces. The first group of operational *Essex*-class carriers arrived in Pearl Harbor in the later half of 1943. These six sister ships became the centerpieces of the newly formed fast-carrier task forces that would drive across the central Pacific. By the end of 1944 the 10 *Essex*-class carriers were the undisputed champions of the Pacific, as they and their air groups effectively destroyed the Imperial Japanese Navy. Operating in tandem, the *Essexes* joined the rest of the navy in sweeping the Pacific clear of the enemy.

Construction of the *Intrepid* began at the Newport News Shipbuilding and Drydock Company of Newport News, Virginia, just six days before the Japanese attack on Pearl Harbor. Named after a naval vessel lost during the Barbary Wars of 1803, the *Intrepid* won fame in the Pacific as the "Fighting I." It survived countless kamikaze hits and was said to have been hit more than any other ship during the war. The carrier played a significant role in the liberation of the Philippines, including the Battle of Leyte Gulf in 1944, the largest naval battle in history. It also played a significant role in the invasion of the Marshalls, Palau, and Okinawa and at the end of the war in the strikes against Japan's home islands. Early in the war its pilots flew in the devastating air raids against the naval stronghold at Truk. The carrier's combat record includes the sinking of two Japanese battleships and numerous other ships, as well as the destruction of more than 600 enemy aircraft.

The *Intrepid* has undergone several major rebuildings and overhauls for its various missions after World War II. It served during the Cuban missile crisis in 1962 and the Vietnam War from 1966 through 1968. Peacetime duties included numerous trips to the Mediterranean from 1954 through 1974 and service as a recovery ship for astronaut

Berthed in the Hudson River, the *Essex*-class aircraft carrier *Intrepid* houses exhibits for the Intrepid Sea-Air-Space Museum.

splashdowns in the Pacific in 1962 and 1965. Withdrawn from the active fleet in 1974, the *Intrepid* served as the official U.S. Navy and Marine Corps bicentennial exposition vessel at Philadelphia. Decommissioned in 1981, it was permanently loaned to the Intrepid Museum Foundation by the secretary of the navy. Now berthed in the Hudson River in Manhattan, the vessel houses a U.S. Navy Hall, Intrepid Hall, Pioneers Hall, Space Hall, numerous smaller galleries, and an assortment of aircraft, rockets, capsules, and other artifacts. NR. NHL. [Intrepid Sea-Air-Space Museum]

■ **Lettie G. Howard**
South Street Seaport Museum
207 Front Street
1893

Above: The *Lettie G. Howard*, being rebuilt as part of an extensive restoration by South Street Seaport Museum.

A wood fishing vessel, the *Lettie G. Howard* is one of two remaining examples of the *Fredonia*-model schooner, the ultimate clipper type named for the schooner *Fredonia*. Built in 1889, the *Fredonia* had a graceful, short clipper stem, a long bowsprit, a rockered keel, sharply rising floors, a gently rounded turn of bilge, and a long raked counter. Its smooth, graceful lines allowed great speed and maneuverability, and soon *Fredonia*-model schooners, designed with greater capacity, became the most common type in the New England and Gulf of Mexico fisheries. Although surpassed by later designs, the *Fredonia*-model endured as powered fishing boats replaced sailing boats in the 1920s.

The *Howard* was built in 1893 by Arthur D. Story, a famous New England shipbuilder in Essex, Massachusetts. It fished with dories on the Grand Banks until 1901, when it went aground on Brown's Island Shoal southwest of the U.S. Life-

Saving Service station at Gurnet, Massachusetts. Station workers carried its anchor out beyond the surf, and the vessel was refloated. The following year the *Howard* was sold south, like many other New England schooners. It was used in fishingfor red snapper on the Campeche Bank off Yucatan, Mexico, until too-frequent repairs made further service uneconomical, and it was put out of service until the Oscar Henderson Shipyard in Bayport, Florida, rebuilt it. The vessel was renamed the *Mystic C.* and rejoined its old fishing fleet in 1923. In 1924 it was given an engine and a new stern post and rudder to allow the schooner to compete against the power boats then entering the fisheries in great numbers.

The *Mystic C.* continued to work in the Gulf of Mexico fishery, downrigged and relying on its engine in later years. Many fishing schooners with sound hulls have been kept at work in this way. In 1966 it was sold to the Historic Ships Associates of Gloucester, Massachusetts, as a museum ship. Mistakenly identifying the vessel's former name, the Historic Ships Associates renamed it the *Caviare*, after a Gloucester schooner of that name built in 1891. The clipper bow, bowsprit, and main topmast were returned to the traditional *Fredonia* silhouette, and some interior restoration was done. The effort failed, however, and the schooner was sold to South Street Seaport Museum in 1968, which completed the restoration begun by Historic Ships Associates. After extensive research it identified the ship and renamed it *Lettie G. Howard* in 1972. NR. NHL. [South Street Seaport Museum]

Serving one of America's most important lightship stations, the *No. 87* had a profound impact on local, coastal, and international trade. It also was important in the history of radio, for it was the site of the first successful shipboard radio beacon used to guide ships for long distances in poor weather.

Built as part of a five-vessel contract by the New York Shipbuilding Company of Camden, New Jersey, the *No. 87* was built and launched in 1905. It served as the first lightship on the newly established station on the Ambrose Channel at the lower entrance to the lower bay of New York, the most important station in the country and thus was known as the "Ambrose." It guided mariners into this port until 1932, when it was replaced by a newer vessel. The *No. 87* became

■ Lightship No. 87 ("Ambrose")

South Street Seaport Museum
207 Front Street
1907

The lightship *No. 87* served the "Scotland" station near Sandy Hook, New Jersey, from 1936 to 1944 and from 1947 to 1964.

the "Relief" lightship for the third lighthouse district, working from St. George, Staten Island, for the next four years. In 1936 it was detailed to take over the Scotland station near Sandy Hook, New Jersey.

The *No. 87* was redesignated as LS 512 in 1939, when the U.S. Lighthouse Establishment was absorbed into the U.S. Coast Guard. Manned by coast guard crews, the lightship took on a more direct military role in 1942, when it served as an examination ship at Fort Hancock, New Jersey, following the U.S. entry into World War II. Returning to the Scotland station, the *No. 87* was replaced in 1964 by a new coast guard-built lightship. Renamed the *WAL 612*, the *No. 87*, was sent to the 1964 World's Fair, where it served as an exhibit for the coast guard. After the fair it was laid up in Curtis Bay, Maryland, until 1968, when it was given to the South Street Seaport Museum. Now interpreted as the "Ambrose," the lightship serves the port it guarded for 67 years. NR. NHL. [South Street Seaport Museum]

South Street Seaport Museum hopes to restore the *Maj. Gen. Wm. H. Hart* to its condition as an army vessel and use the interior for exhibits interpreting the history of ferries in New York Harbor.

■ **Maj. Gen. Wm. H. Hart**
South Street Seaport Museum
207 Front Street
1925

The city of New York was and is the largest user of ferries in the United States. At the beginning of this century more than 50 ferries moved people and vehicles across the harbor. The routes across the East River from Manhattan to Queens and Brooklyn linked major portions of America's greatest port, carrying people, automobiles, and commercial vehicles. The *Maj. Gen. Wm. H. Hart* was built as the *John A. Lynch*, a result of a contract between the City of New York Department of Plants and Structures and the Staten Island Shipbuilding Company to build five of the 16 identical double-ended steam ferries for services across the East River. The *Lynch* was used initially on the ferry crossing between College Point and Classon's Point, cutting the running time of its predecessor in half.

In 1932 all the city ferries named for living politicians were renamed for neighborhoods, and the *Lynch* became the *Harlem*. The routes of the 16 "151-foot tin-cans" were interchanged occasionally, and although the *Harlem* operated most often on the Astoria crossing, it was also used on the Rockaway, New York Bay, Hamilton Avenue, Classon's Point, Atlantic Avenue, and Broadway–Grand Street ferry crossings. In 1940 the *Harlem* was sold to the U.S. Quartermaster Corps for use on the ferry route to the base on Governor's Island. Renamed the *Maj. Gen. Wm. H. Hart*, the ferry served the army until Governor's Island was transferred to the U.S. Coast Guard in 1965. Laid up at Staten Island in 1968, it was given to the South Street Seaport Museum in 1970 for conversion into a school for maritime trades with machine shops in the teamways and classrooms in the lounges. The school was closed in 1979, but the machine shops are used for restoration support of the other vessels at South Street. The museum hopes to restore the *Hart* to its condition as an army vessel and use the interior for exhibits interpreting the history of ferries in New York Harbor. [South Street Seaport Museum]

One of the eight historic vessels whose home port is now New York's South Street Seaport on the Manhattan waterfront, the four-masted bark *Peking* dominates the scene with its lofty spars and yards towering above the freeway and the buildings that rise along the piers. Built for the noted German shipping firm of F. Laeisz Company of Hamburg, the *Peking* exemplifies the company's continuing commitment to the deep-sea sailing ship. Historian-seaman Alan Villiers once noted that Laeisz "showed that such vessels if properly conducted and well sailed, could still do their share of the world's work splendidly" in the age of steamships. Similar to the *Kurt*, now known as the *Moshulu*, the other German four-masted bark preserved in the United States, the *Peking* was constructed by Blohm and Voss of Hamburg and launched in 1911 for trade between Europe and South America, where general merchandise was exchanged for bulk cargoes of nitrate. The *Peking* continued in this trade until the outbreak of World War I. Laid up at Valparaiso, Chile, the bark was granted to Italy as a war reparation in 1921. After a single voyage under Italian control, the *Peking* was again laid up, this time at Antwerp, where F. Laiesz bought it back. Once again engaged in the nitrate trade, it gained fame when Irving

■ **Peking**
South Street Seaport Museum
207 Front Street
1911

One of the last surviving four-masted barks, the *Peking* was immortalized by Irving Johnson in his book *The Peking Battles Cape Horn.*

Johnson, a young American, shipped aboard for a voyage to Chile. His account, *The Peking Battles Cape Horn*, was published in 1932 by Milton Bradley and became a classic of sea literature.

Sold in 1932 to British Shaftesbury Homes and Arethusa Training Ship for use as a school ship, the bark was renamed the *Arethusa* in 1933 and served in this capacity, with a brief interruption during the war, until it was sold in 1974. Bought at auction in October 1974 by the J. Aron Charitable Foundation for South Street Seaport, the bark was towed across the Atlantic, arriving in New York on July 22, 1975. The *Peking* has been restored, and exhibits depicting its construction and history have been installed. [South Street Seaport Museum]

■ **Pioneer**
South Street Seaport Museum
End of South Street
1885

Of the eight historic vessels whose home port is now the South Street Seaport Museum, the two-masted schooner *Pioneer* is the only one to sail regularly the East River along the Manhattan waterfront as well as to various ports of call on the Delaware Bay. The only iron-and-steel-hulled 19th-century coastal schooner preserved in the United States, the *Pioneer* was built by the Pioneer Iron Company of Marcus Hook for the Chester Rolling Mills of Chester, Pennsylvania, in early 1885. Chester, center of the nation's building industry for iron ships, was the home of John Roach's Delaware River Iron Shipbuilding and Machine Works, the preeminent shipyard of the period. A 90-ton, 65-foot-long iron sloop, the *Pioneer* hauled sand for foundry and blast furnace work. A rarity in an age of wood schooners and sloops, it exemplified the new age of iron. George Matteson, *Pioneer* historian, stresses that at that "particular place there was a propensity toward elaboration and experiment, a fondness for the dark promises of iron. Great builders naturally gravitate toward symbols which bespeak permanence and ingenuity.... *Pioneer* may have been conceived as one more small challenge for iron."

The experiment of building a small coaster of iron was not repeated, however, and the *Pioneer* remained a rarity for its entire commercial career. Sold in 1895 to the Keystone Plaster Company of Chester, it continued to haul sand, this time for a different product. At this time, when it was 10 years old, the vessel was converted to a two-masted schooner. It was sold again in 1900, when it was used to haul stone, and again in 1903, when a gasoline engine was installed. By 1907 the former schooner, again under new owners, was now listed as a motor vessel carrying no sail; and as such worked in a variety of trades—for ship chandlers, an oil company, and a marine salvage firm. Purchased by Russell Grinnell, Jr., of Gloucester in 1966, the *Pioneer* was restored to a working two-masted schooner. The hull was replated in steel and a new engine was installed; at the same time two masts were installed so that the *Pioneer* could once again spread sail to the wind. When Grinnell was killed in an accident in 1970, his family offered the restored schooner to South Street Seaport, which raised the money to buy it. The vessel arrived at South Street in August 1970 and has since worked out of the seaport. First involved in a sail-training program that spurred the creation of the Pioneer Marine School at South Street, a program that trained hundreds in practical maritime trades such as engine repair, boat building, and welding, the *Pioneer* in

time began charter sailing. It now sails several times a day except in the winter, occasionally going back to its original sailing grounds on Delaware Bay and the Delaware River. [South Street Seaport Museum]

Also moored at South Street Seaport and visible from the pier is another historic vessel not open to the public. The small lighter *Vernie S.* has had a long and varied career. Built as the steam passenger launch *Four Sisters* at Glenwood, New York, in 1897, the tiny, 28-ton wood vessel was later converted to an oyster carrier. It was retired after being converted to a diesel-powered harbor lighter used by a ship chandlery to supply ships in the harbor. Now owned by the Wavertree Society, the *Vernie S.* makes occasional cruises of the harbor for the society's members. [The Wavertree Society]

The two-masted *Pioneer*, an iron-and-steel–hulled coastal schooner.

■ **Vernie S.**
South Street Seaport Museum
End of Fulton Street
1897

■ **W. O. Decker**
South Street Seaport Museum
207 Front Street
1930

The *W. O. Decker* began its career as a wood-hulled steam tugboat, the *Russell 1*, moving barges and scows in the industrial waterway that forms the boundary between Brooklyn and Queens. Since 1977 the diesel tugboat has been used for general towing work, shifting South Street Seaport Museum's larger vessels at the museum piers and moving smaller museum vessels to and from local shipyards for dry-docking. [South Street Seaport Museum]

■ **Wavertree**
South Street Seaport Museum
207 Front Street
1885

One of the last 19th-century square-rigged sailing merchant ships, the *Wavertree* was designed to carry low-priority, nonperishable bulk cargoes over long distances. Iron sailing cargo ships such as this, built to replace smaller, wood cargo-carrying ships, were larger, needed less maintenance, and lasted longer. During the period of their primary importance (1870–1920), they could be found in every major port in the world. The decline of the iron sailing ship was due primarily to its inability to compete with the steamship's larger cargo-carrying capacity, improved dependability, and greater efficiency.

Beginning its career as the *Southgate* in 1885, the vessel was built in Southampton, England, specifically for the jute trade between England and India. The jute market collapsed shortly after the ship was built, however, so it was sold and renamed the *Wavertree* in 1888. Carrying whatever cargoes were available to wherever the cargoes were needed, the *Wavertree* made 41 major ocean passages in its 25-year career, 16 of which were to or from American ports, including New York, San Francisco, several ports in Puget Sound, and Portland and Astoria, Oregon.

The *Wavertree* made its last voyage in 1910 and then was sold to a company in Punta Arenas, Chile. Towed to the Straits of Magellan, the vessel was used for storing coal and wool.

In 1948, after being sold for scrap iron, it was towed north to Buenos Aires, where its new owners converted the vessel into a sand barge and renamed it the *Don Ariano N.* The ship was rediscovered in 1966 and acquired by South Street Seaport Museum in 1968. The *Wavertree*'s restoration is a continuing process. The museum's goal is to rebuild the ship so that it will once again be capable of traveling under sail. NR. [South Street Seaport Museum]

Once square-rigged cargo ships such as the *Wavertree* were plentiful throughout the world.

WEST HAVERSTRAW

Similar to Mystic Seaport's steamer the *Sabino,* the motor vessel *Commander* was built in 1917 by the Beele Wallace Company of Morehead City, North Carolina, as a gasoline-powered excursion boat for service between Rockaway and Brooklyn, New York. A classic eastern small excursion boat, the 60-foot-long vessel provided an effective means of travel, as did many others, in the greater New York City and Hudson Valley areas. The *Commander* is a rare design link between the heavily built excursion steamers of the 19th and early 20th century and the more lightly built motor vessels of the early and later 20th centuries.

Arriving at New York City in November 1917, just before the United States' entry into World War I, the *Commander* had been leased by the U.S. Navy and assigned to the Brooklyn Navy Yard to outfit submarine chasers and tow barrage balloons from the Rockaway Air Station. Decommissioned on February 5, 1919, it was returned to its owners and began a six-decade career of excursion service between Rockaway and Brooklyn. That year the original engine was replaced with a Wolverine diesel engine. Apart from another engine replacement in or around 1957, the oak-framed, 70-ton vessel is largely unaltered. In 1981 the *Commander* was sold to its

■ **Commander**
Haverstraw Marina
Beach Road
1917

present owners after one of the longest uninterrupted careers in excursion service in the nation. Now operated on the Hudson River as a tour boat, the *Commander* offers a unique opportunity to explore the beauty of the Hudson River Valley by water. NR. [Hudson Highlands Cruise and Tours]

WEST SAYVILLE

■ **Modesty**
■ **Priscilla**
Suffolk Marine Museum
Suffolk County Park
Montauk Highway (27A)
1923 and 1888

Two of the last surviving vessels of the Long Island oyster trade, the sloop *Modesty* and the schooner *Priscilla* represent the important commercial oyster and scallop industry off Long Island that lasted from 1850 to the late 1920s. The *Modesty* was built by Wood and Chute at Greenport, New York, and the *Priscilla* was built by Elisha Saxon in Patchogue, New York.

Above: The *Commander*, a rare, intact example of the small wood passenger vessels that were common in the late 19th and early 20th centuries along the inland waterways of New York State. Right: The Long Island oyster sloop *Modesty* and the schooner *Priscilla* (opposite top) are still afloat and accessible to the public.

Moored next to a restored oyster house featuring equipment for harvesting shellfish, the vessels are floating exhibits that occasionally operate out of the Suffolk Marine Museum. [Suffolk Marine Museum]

■ ■ ■ ■ ■ ■   PENNSYLVANIA   ■ ■ ■ ■ ■ ■

ERIE

One of six warships built to regain control of the upper Great Lakes from the British during the War of 1812, the hastily built brig *Niagara* was Comdr. Oliver Hazard Perry's relief flagship during the bloody Battle of Lake Erie on September 10, 1813. Perry's forces destroyed two ships, two brigs, one schooner, and one sloop of the British fleet, thus eliminating the British threat to the Northwest Territory and opening supply lines to the beleaguered American military in Ohio. Perry sent his classic message of victory—"We have met the enemy and they are ours"—from the *Niagara*.

After a seven-year deployment as a station ship, the brig was stripped of its armament and laid up at Presque Isle Bay in Lake Erie, where it was allowed to decay and sink. To commemorate the battle's centennial the wreck was raised and rebuilt in 1913. The rebuilt ship gradually decayed and was moved ashore, where for many years it was on display. The brig was again completely rebuilt and relaunched in 1988 to commemorate the 175th anniversary of the battle. Sailing again, outfitted as when new, the *Niagara* serves as a reminder of one of the greatest U.S. naval victories of the 19th century

■ **USB Niagara**
164 East Front Street at end of Holland Street
1813

Completely rebuilt, the U.S. brig *Niagara* sailed once again on Lake Erie in 1990.

and of the nearly two centuries of peace between the United States and Canada that have followed. NR. [Pennsylvania Historical and Museum Commission]

PHILADELPHIA

■ **USS Becuna (SS-319)**
Penn's Landing
Delaware Avenue and
Spruce Street
1944

An example of the standard *Balao*-class submarines of World War II, the *Becuna* was constructed by the Electric Boat Company of Groton, Connecticut. The submarine was commissioned in 1944 and served as the flagship for the submarine forces in the Pacific under the command of Gen. Douglas MacArthur. The vessel's logo, a cigar-smoking fish clutching torpedoes, was designed by Walt Disney. The *Becuna* is credited with sinking the 1,945-ton Japanese tanker *Nichiyoku Maru* and received four battle stars for its World War II service.

Originally a presnorkel submarine operating underwater on batteries, the *Becuna* was converted from its basic fleet boat configuration to a streamlined underwater submarine known as a type 1A GUPPY (Greater Underwater Propulsion Project) in 1951. A new snorkel air system allowed it to operate its diesel engines underwater at a maximum speed of 20 miles per hour. The *Becuna* served during the Korean and

Berthed at Penn's Landing in Philadelphia, the submarine USS *Becuna* serves as an educational resource and tourist attraction with the cruiser USS *Olympia.*

Vietnam wars as well as in the Atlantic and Mediterranean. Struck from the navy list in 1973, it was acquired by the Cruiser Olympia Association in 1976. Now berthed at Penn's Landing in Philadelphia, the boat serves as an educational resource and tourist attraction along with the cruiser *Olympia.* NR. NHL. [Cruiser Olympia Association]

■ **Gazela Philadelphia**
Penn's Landing
End of Walnut Street
1883

Built as the barkentine *Gazela Primeiro* in Cachilhas, Portugal, the *Gazela Philadelphia* served first as a coastal trader in Europe and later as a Portuguese Grand Banks dory fishing boat. During its fishing career the vessel annually carried a complement of 40 crew members to the Grand Banks off Newfoundland, where they fished for cod from 35 one-man dories. Filling the ship's 350-ton capacity usually

Left: The *Gazela Philadephia*'s portside running light.
Above: In addition to serving as Philadelphia's maritime ambassador, the *Gazela Philadelphia* is used to preserve maritime skills through sail training and serves as a museum of sailing ship technology.

took from early spring until the beginning of fall. When the vessel was retired in 1969, a volunteer crew brought it to Philadelphia from Portugal. Supported and operated by volunteers, the *Gazela Philadelphia* serves as a living classroom in sail training, as Philadelphia's maritime ambassador, and as a museum of sailing ship technology. [Philadelphia Ship Preservation Guild]

The latest acquisition of the Philadelphia Ship Preservation Guild, which also owns the lightship *No. 79* and the fishing schooner *Gazela*, is the tugboat *Jupiter*. Built locally in 1902 by the firm of Neafie and Levy, the 91-foot-long steel tugboat was constructed for the Socony Oil Company, now Mobil Oil. Named and numbered *No. 14*, the tugboat worked

■ **Jupiter**
Penn's Landing
End of Walnut Street
1902

After a long career of pushing oil barges and tankers, the *Jupiter* was acquired by the Philadelphia Ship Preservation Guild as a working museum vessel.

in New York Harbor assisting oil tankers and barges until 1939, when it was sold to William Meyle for use on the Delaware River. Renamed the *Jupiter* as part of the Meyle tugboat fleet named for Roman gods, it worked for Meyle until 1981, when it was sold to a Boston towing company. In 1990 the *Jupiter*, its steam engine replaced by a diesel engine in 1949, was offered for sale and bought by the guild with the assistance of a state grant. It now serves as a working member of the guild's fleet, assisting the *Gazela* and taking members on harbor cruises when not docked at Penn's Landing. [Philadelphia Ship Preservation Guild]

A sister ship of the lightship *No. 83*, the lightship *No. 79* ("Barnegat") is one of the oldest surviving lightships in the United States. Built by the now defunct New York Shipbuilding Corporation of Camden, New Jersey, across the Delaware River from where it is now moored, the lightship was launched in 1904 with its four sisters, each of which cost the government $90,000. The new lightship was assigned to the Five Fathom Bank station off New Jersey, remaining there until 1924, whenit became a relief lightship serving all stations in the third lighthouse district for two years. The 129-foot-long, 668-ton vessel was modernized for the first time in 1921, when its lantern houses, formerly winched to the top of the masts to light the way for other ships, were replaced by acetylene lanterns permanently mounted to the mastheads. In 1928 these lights were electrified. In August 1927 the Barnegat lightship station was established eight miles east of the Barnegat Lighthouse, off the mouth of the Delaware River, and the *No. 79* remained on that station until it was retired in 1967. Its only prolonged interruption in service was from 1942 until 1945, when it was used as a harbor examination vessel during World War II. The original steam engine was replaced with a diesel engine in 1931, which helped keep the ship in service for an additional four decades.

Decommissioned in March 1967, "Old Barney" was displayed at St. Michael's, Maryland, until 1975, when it was

■ **Lightship No. 79**
("Barnegat")
Penn's Landing
End of Walnut Street
1904

The lightship *No. 79* ("Barnegat").

acquired by the Philadelphia Ship Guild. The lightship's bright red hull has been a Philadelphia riverfront attraction ever since. It has been recently restored and opened to the public. NR. [Philadelphia Ship Preservation Guild]

After a long period of neglect, the result of post–Civil War decrease in appropriations for the army and navy, Congress realized the need for a strong naval force and funded the development of a modern steel navy in the 1880s and 1890s. As a result of this program, a number of armored steel battleships and protected cruisers were built. In addition to

■ **USS Olympia (CA-15)**
Penn's Landing
Delaware Avenue and Spruce Street
1895

spurring the development of a U.S. steel ship industry, this program marked the emergence of the United States as a world power. Only one of these vessels survives today. The oldest steel-hulled American warship afloat, the cruiser *Olympia* was authorized in 1888 and was constructed at San Francisco's Union Iron Works in 1891. Launched in 1892, it continued to be fitted out for another three years and was not commissioned until February 5, 1895. The completed ship, built to an original American design that did not copy existing European cruisers, was a formidable 344-foot-long, 5,870-ton warship powered by two 9,000-horsepower triple-expansion marine steam engines and armed with a variety of medium-caliber, rapid-fire guns on two deck levels, most protected in armored casemates below the weather deck. In addition, the *Olympia* mounted four eight-inch, 35-caliber breech-loading rifles paired in turrets fore and aft. The cruiser also mounted above the waterline torpedo tubes, whose apertures, although closed, are still visible.

Built as the flagship of the navy's Asiatic Squadron, the *Olympia* served as Adm. George Dewey's flagship during the Battle of Manila Bay on May 1, 1898. In that engagement U.S. forces resoundingly defeated Spanish naval forces in the Philippines, securing the islands for the United States and launching the nation on an expanded role as a major force in not only Pacific but also world affairs. The *Olympia* is the sole surviving naval combatant of the Spanish-American War.

As the flagship of the U.S. Patrol Force, the *Olympia* served on escort and patrol duty during World War I. At the war's end it played a part in the little-publicized U.S. expeditionary force sent to aid anti-Bolshevik forces during the Russian Revolution when it joined Allied forces at Murmansk in 1918. After the war the cruiser carried home the casket holding the remains of the Unknown Soldier for burial at Arlington

The oldest steel-hulled American warship afloat, the *Olympia* served as Commodore George Dewey's flagship during the Battle of Manila Bay in 1898. It is shown here at Penn's Landing in 1989.

National Cemetery. The *Olympia*'s peacetime duties before retirement included serving as the flagship of the North Atlantic Squadron in 1907 and as a training ship at the U.S. Naval Academy. The ship was decommissioned for the last time in 1922 and was laid up at the Philadelphia Navy Yard. The rusting relic was saved from being scrapped during World War II when the decision was made to scrap the other surviving Spanish-American War vessel, the USS *Oregon*, but to preserve the *Olympia* in its place. Nonetheless, plans to save the cruiser languished until 1957, when it was acquired by the Cruiser Olympia Association and restored over the next few years. The ship is now displayed at Penn's Landing on the Philadelphia waterfront along with the World War II submarine *Becuna*. The *Olympia*'s triple-expansion marine steam engines are National Historic Engineering Landmarks. NR. NHL. ASME. [Cruiser Olympia Association]

PITTSBURGH

■ **USS Requin (SS-481)**
Buhl Science Center
Allegheny Square
1945

The *Requin* and the USS *Torsk* are the two surviving World War II *Tench*-class submarines, the largest of the fleet boats built during the war. Laid down in August 1944 at the Portsmouth Naval Shipyard, the *Requin* was launched on January 1, 1945, and was commissioned on April 28. Assigned to the Pacific Fleet, it arrived at Pearl Harbor at the end of July and was en route to Guam when the war ended in August. The submarine was then ordered back to the Atlantic without seeing combat. For the next two decades the *Requin* cruised the Gulf, Atlantic, and Mediterranean. Converted in 1946–47 into a radar picket submarine and modernized in 1959, it was decommissioned at Norfolk, Virginia, in 1968. The boat was sent to St. Petersburg, Florida, in February 1969 for use as a naval reserve training ship and served there until stricken from the navy list in December 1971. It was then transferred to the city of Tampa, Florida, for use as a naval memorial in 1973, later serving as the headquarters for local Sea Scouts. Construction on the waterfront closed the submarine to the public in 1983, and it did not reopen until late 1988. Transferred and towed up the Mississippi River en route to Pittsburgh, the *Requin* was again restored and opened to the public in October 1990 as a floating exhibit. [U.S. Navy; loaned to Buhl Science Center]

■ ■ ■ ■ ■   WEST VIRGINIA   ■ ■ ■ ■ ■

CHARLESTON

■ **P. A. Denny**
City Levee
Canal Boulevard
1930

Built in 1930 as the towboat *Scott* for the Louisville, Kentucky, district of the U.S. Army Corps of Engineers, the *P. A. Denny* has been greatly modified since its retirement from government service. The 109-foot-long, steel-hulled stern-wheeler was christened with its present name in 1975 and rebuilt in 1976. An additional deck has been added to the superstructure and the former towboat now resembles a riverboat. The *P. A. Denny* takes passengers on afternoon and evening river tours and brunch, lunch, and dinner cruises. [Charlestown Festival Commission]

SOUTH

The tugboat *John Taxis*, one of the oldest surviving tugboats in the United States and now on exhibit in Wilmington, North Carolina.

■ ■ ■ ■ ■ ■   GEORGIA   ■ ■ ■ ■ ■ ■

COLUMBUS

■ **CSS Chattahoochee**
Confederate Naval Museum
202 Fourth Street
1862

The gunboat *Chattahoochee*, one element in the Confederacy's river and coastal defense during the Civil War.

A 30-foot-long section of the stern and steam engines of the Confederate gunboat *Chattahoochee* was recovered in 1964 from its namesake river, where the vessel was scuttled by Confederate forces in 1865. A rare surviving example of Confederate shipbuilding, the *Chattahoochee* represents the Confederacy's innovative and resourceful improvisation as it built a fleet of river and coastal defense gunboats and ironclads during the Civil War. Its stern is displayed next to the hull of the armored ram *Jackson* at the Confederate Naval Museum. NR. [Confederate Naval Museum]

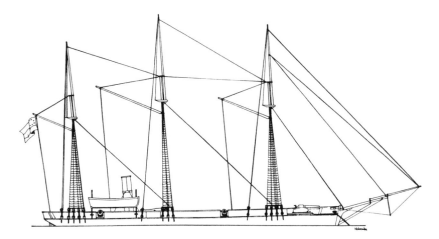

■ **CSS Jackson**
Confederate Naval Museum
202 Fourth Street
1864

A large portion of the hull of the ironclad ram *Jackson* is the prime exhibit of the Confederate Naval Museum. The design of the *Jackson*, an armored, steam-powered ram for river end coastal defense, was based on the successful model of the CSS *Virginia*, also known as the *Merrimac*. The *Jackson* exemplified the type of vessel used by the Confederacy in naval combat during the Civil War. The nearly completed hull sank in flames when set afire by Union raiders in April 1865. Rediscovered and raised in 1963, the *Jackson* is displayed along with the stern section of the gunboat *Chattahoochee*. NR. [Confederate Naval Museum]

■ ■ ■ ■ ■ ■   NORTH CAROLINA   ■ ■ ■ ■ ■ ■

KINSTON

■ **CSS Neuse**
Caswell-Neuse Memorial Park
On Highway 55/11
1863

Built by the Confederate government in 1862 to challenge Union control of North Carolina's coastal inlets and rivers, the ironclad gunboat *Neuse* was built as an armored floating battery at White Hall, North Carolina, on the Neuse River. Laid down in 1862, the incomplete hull was launched and taken down river in March 1863 to Kinston, where the engines, boilers, and cannon were installed and the first layer of iron armor was laid over the casemate. The unfinished *Neuse* never engaged the enemy. Lacking a second layer of armor, the gunboat was sent downriver toward the port of New Bern in April 1864. It ran aground on a sandbar just a half mile downriver, and not until May did the river rise enough to refloat the ironclad, which returned to Kinston. There the *Neuse* was finally completed, but it was too late. The river was too low, and Union forces were advancing. On March 12, 1865, Union troops were five miles from Kinston. The Confederate forces evacuated the town, leaving the *Neuse* to hold the line. The ironclad's guns opened up on the Union cavalry. Then, as the 18,000-troop Union line moved in, Capt. Joseph H. Price, surrounded and trapped on the narrow river with no hope of reinforcements, gave the order to abandon ship. The ironclad was set ablaze, and a powder charge was set in the bow. As smoke and flames poured from the casemate, an explosion tore open the hull, and the *Neuse* sank into the river. After the war the casemate, iron, engines and boiler, and guns were salvaged, but the hull remained at "Gunboat Bend" for nearly a century. In November 1961, at a period of low water, a local effort to recover the *Neuse* began and it was refloated, but the hulk sank again when the river rose. The wreck was not raised again until 1963, after portions of the hull had washed down the river. Cut into sections, the *Neuse* was transported to Caswell Memorial Park and placed on a cradle in May 1964. A piece of the casemate was recovered in 1966 and moved to the park. A large shelter covering the wreck was built in 1969, and a detailed program to conserve the hull was proposed. A small museum built on the site houses the artifacts recovered during the salvage as well as a model of the ill-fated gunboat. [State of North Carolina]

WILMINGTON

One of the oldest surviving tugboats in the United States, the *John Taxis* was built in 1869 at Chester, Pennsylvania, a leading center of shipbuilding in the United States after the Civil War. Constructed by Reaney, Son and Archbold, the tugboat was originally named the *William Stewart*. After a long and varied career it was retired and placed on display at Chandler's Wharf, a collection of restaurants and shops on the riverfront of Wilmington. The original steeple steam engine, previously removed, is on display at the Mariner's Museum in Newport News, Virginia. The wood-hulled tugboat itself, perched on a piling-supported cradle over the waters of the Cape Fear River, is an outdoor exhibit at Chandler's Wharf. [River Enterprises]

■ **John Taxis**
Chandler's Wharf
2 Ann Street
1869

The first of a modern class of American battleships built just before World War II, the USS *North Carolina* set a standard for new shipbuilding technology that combined high speed with powerful armament. Construction began on the *North Carolina*, the fourth warship to bear the name, at the Brooklyn Naval Yard in 1936. It was the first new battleship constructed since the Washington Naval Conference of 1922 limited the size and number of naval armaments among the five major naval powers. Commissioned in 1941, the *North Carolina*, also known as the "Show Boat," was considered "the most powerful warship afloat." It was more 728 feet long, it displaced 35,000 tons, and its maximum speed was approxi-

■ **USS North Carolina** (BB-55)
Three miles west of Wilmington, at the intersection of U.S. Highways 17, 74, 76, and 421
1940

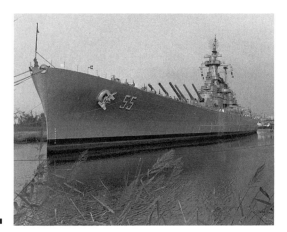

Combining high speeds with powerful armament, the USS *North Carolina* set a standard for new shipbuilding technology.

mately 27 knots. Its crew consisted of 108 officers and 1,772 enlisted personnel. The *North Carolina* entered Pearl Harbor in July 1942 to begin its 40-month participation in virtually all the major campaigns in the Pacific theater of World War II. During the Battle of the Eastern Solomons it was assigned to escort the carriers USS *Enterprise* and USS *Saratoga*. Its superior performance during this battle established the primary role of the fast battleship as a protector of aircraft carriers and led to the establishment of the fast-carrier task forces that struck Japanese forces with devastating results throughout the war. The battleship steamed 307,000 miles in the Pacific, stopping at 26 ports. The *North Carolina* has the best battle record of any surviving World War II battleship to serve in the Pacific, with 15 battle stars and credited kills of 24 aircraft, a merchantship, and the bombardment of nine Japanese strongholds.

During World War II air power and the newly developed aircraft carrier contributed to the obsolescence of battleships. In a sea battle airplanes launched from carriers could strike not only faster but also much farther than battleship guns. In 1947 the "Showboat" was decommissioned. In 1960 more than 700,000 North Carolinians contributed more than $325,000 to provide a permanent home for the ship. Now moored on the Cape Fear River off Wilmington, the battleship is a floating museum and memorial. NR. NHL. [USS North Carolina Battleship Commission]

■ ■ ■ ■ ■ ■   SOUTH CAROLINA   ■ ■ ■ ■ ■ ■

MOUNT PLEASANT

■ **USS Clamagore (SS-343)**
Patriots Point Naval and
Maritime Museum
40 Patriots Point Road,
off Highway 17
1945

The *Balao*-class submarine *Clamagore* is one of 132 fleet submarines built during World War II for the U.S. Navy. It was a typical fleet boat designed and constructed as part of a major program of submarine construction following the Japanese attack on Pearl Harbor. The submarine warfare pursued by the United States and supported by this construction program was instrumental in securing an American victory in the Pacific. After the war some of these submarines were modified to embody the lessons learned during the conflict. Arriving too late to serve in combat in World War II,

Above: Aerial view of the ships at Patriots Point . Left: The USS *Clamagore*, a typical World War II "fleet boat" built as part of the major submarine construction program following Pearl Harbor.

the *Clamagore* was modified in 1947 and again in 1962 into a FRAM II-GUPPY III submarine. One of only nine boats converted to a GUPPY III configuration and the sole survivor of these vessels, the *Clamagore* represents the navy's continued adaptation and use of war-built diesel submarines for the first two decades after the war. The GUPPY submarines comprised the bulk of the U.S. submarine force through the mid-1960s. Decommissioned in 1975, the *Clamagore* is open to the public as a floating exhibit. NR. NHL. [Patriots Point Development Authority]

The USCGC *Ingham* and the *Taney* are the two preserved *Secretary*-class cutters, probably the most successful large cutters built by the U.S. Coast Guard. Named after President Andrew Jackson's secretary of the treasury, the *Ingham* was launched from the Philadelphia Navy Yard. Based in Seattle and Port Angles, Washington, it patrolled the Bering Sea until it was reassigned to the East Coast in 1939 to help enforce neutrality laws. Patrolling the North Atlantic in the Grand Banks region of Newfoundland, the cutter gathered weather information for ships, planes, and stations. After the United States entered World War II the *Ingham* served on convoy

■ **USCGC Ingham (WPG-35)**
Patriots Point Naval and Maritime Museum
40 Patriots Point Road, off Highway 17
1936

duty, protecting ships ferrying vital supplies to Great Britain. It battled stormy weather and German U-boats and aircraft. The duty was hazardous; one of the cutter's sisters, the USCGC *Alexander Hamilton*, was sunk in 1942. That same year the *Ingham* sank the German submarine *U-626*. In November 1944 the *Ingham* was reassigned to the Pacific Ocean and served as the flagship for the Seventh Fleet amphibious operations. After the war the cutter returned to regular coast guard duties, primarily search-and-rescue operations, law enforcement, and ocean station patrols. Ocean station patrols consisted of weather forecasting, oceanographic research, mid-ocean communications, and search-and-rescue duty for transatlantic airline flights. In 1968 the *Ingham* operated off the coast of South Vietnam, conducting naval gunfire support missions and participating in Operation Market Time, a naval blockade of the South Vietnamese coast to prevent the smuggling of arms and supplies to the Viet Cong. Three years after becoming the oldest active commissioned naval vessel serving the United States, the *Ingham* was decommissioned in 1988.

The USCGC *Ingham* served with distinction during World War II on convoy duty, protecting ships carrying vital supplies to Great Britain.

Acquired by Patriots Point in 1989, the cutter joined the fleet of National Historic Landmark ships moored there and is open to the public. [Patriots Point Development Authority]

■ USS Laffey (DD-724)
Patriots Point Naval and
Maritime Museum
40 Patriots Point Road,
off Highway 17
1944

The *Laffey*, built by the Bath Iron Works of Bath, Maine, was laid down in June 1943, launched on November 21, and commissioned on February 8, 1944. The destroyer replaced an earlier ship named *Laffey*, lost in the night battle off Guadalcanal on November 13, 1942, after engaging a superior force of four Japanese warships, including the battleship *Hiei*, in what the U.S. Navy later termed a "no quarter duel at point blank range." The new *Laffey* was one of the first *Allen M. Sumner*–class destroyers, intended as an interim design between the *Fletcher* class and the more improved *Gearing* class. *Laffey* is the only remaining destroyer of the 58 vessels of the *Sumner* class.

The only surviving World War II destroyer to see action in the Atlantic, the *Laffey* served first as an escort for convoys to Great Britain. On D-Day the destroyer helped bombard Utah Beach at Normandy and Cherbourg in support of the Allied invasion. During the Cherbourg bombardment the destroyer was hit by a German shell that ricocheted off the water and penetrated its hull near the waterline but did not explode. Sent into the Pacific at the end of August 1944, the *Laffey* was involved in one of the most famous destroyer-kamikaze duels of the war. During the Battle of Okinawa, desperate Japanese pilots mauled U.S. destroyers off the island, inflicting heavy casualties of both ships and troops. On April 15, 1945, while screening the battleships of Task Force 54, the *Laffey* came under attack within 90 minutes from 22 Japanese kamikazes and bombers. Its gunner shot down nine attackers, but bullets from strafing runs and shrapnel from near misses riddled the superstructure, while five kamikazes and four bombs hit the ship. The first plane hit near the starboard 20-millimeter mounts amidships, splashing burning gasoline over the decks. The flames set off 40-millimeter shells, blasting holes in the decks. Burning gas flowed below decks. The second plane plowed into the fantail 20-millimeter mounts and rammed into the aft five-inch gun mount, tearing it open and splashing more burning gasoline on the decks. The third plane hit the same mount, destroying the side of the ship. Another plane then dove into the stern, tore apart the decks and jammed the rudder. The fifth plane, aflame, slammed into the after deckhouse. Racked by explosions and fires, the *Laffey* remained afloat only because of the valiant efforts of its crew. Thirty-two crew members died, and another 71 were wounded, but on that day the *Laffey* earned the sobriquet the "Ship That Would Not Die." Returning to the United States for repair, it did not return to action until after the war's end. The *Laffey* earned five battle stars and a Presidential Unit Citation for its World War II service.

The USS *Laffey*, the only surviving *Allen M. Sumner*–class destroyer that saw service in the Atlantic.

After participating in the Operation Crossroads atomic bomb tests at Bikini Atoll in 1946, the *Laffey* underwent radiological decontamination before being decommissioned and laid up in 1947. Recommissioned in 1951 for the Korean War, it bombarded the North Korean coast in 1952 and fought shore batteries at Wonsan. Deployed to the Mediterranean during the Suez crisis in November 1956, it operated in the Atlantic and Mediterranean on antisubmarine warfare deployments and NATO exercises until decommissioned in 1975. Stricken from the U.S. Navy Register in 1977, the *Laffey* was moved in 1981 to Patriots Point, where it is now displayed. NR. NHL. [Patriots Point Development Authority]

The NS *Savannah* and the USCGC *Ingham,* moored together at Patriots Point in 1990.

■ **NS Savannah**
Patriots Point Naval and Maritime Museum
40 Patriots Point Road, off Highway 17
1959

The combination passenger-cargo ship NS *Savannah*, the first nuclear-powered commercial ship, demonstrated to the world the safe and reliable operation of this new technology. Its success resulted in the establishment of a nuclear ship training program for civilian crew members and procedures for commercial nuclear ships to enter domestic and foreign ports. The *Savannah* also served a unique public relations role as a floating exhibit of the potential peaceful use of nuclear energy. In this context the vessel traveled more than 450,000 miles during its active career.

The development of this nuclear ship was authorized by Congress in July 1956 and administered jointly by the U.S. Maritime Administration and the Atomic Energy Commission. Launched in 1959, it was named after the SS *Savannah*, the first steamship to make a transatlantic voyage in 1819. From the outset the design for the ship's nuclear system placed safety and reliability above efficiency and economics. A primary goal was to design and operate a nuclear maritime vessel that was safe for crew, passengers, and the public. During its first five years of operation, the *Savannah* carried passengers and small amounts of commercial cargo. The ship made extended calls at 28 domestic and 18 foreign ports, hosting more than 1.4 million visitors.

In 1965 the *Savannah*'s passenger spaces were sealed and 1,800 tons of solid ballast were removed. First Atomic Ship Transport (FAST), a subsidiary of American Export-Isbrandtsen Lines, was licensed to operate the ship as a cargo vessel. To compensate for the expense of operating a demonstration vessel, FAST was given a one-dollar-per-year lease on the ship with no charge for the fuel.

In September 1965 the *Savannah* left New York for its first commercial voyage with a capacity load of 10,000 tons of general cargo. During 1967 its cargo activity generated $2.6 million in revenue. Nevertheless, while performing as a cargo vessel, it continued to fulfill its responsibilities as a goodwill ambassador, visiting ports in Europe, Africa, and the Far East. Then, just when the momentum for an enlarged U.S. nuclear merchant fleet should have been greatest, the single largest client for such a fleet—the U.S. government—decided to use traditionally powered vessels exclusively. The U.S. Department of Defense, a major customer of U.S. shipping, concluded that oil-fired freighters were more cost effective than nuclear ships.

By late 1970 the *Savannah* had consumed 163 pounds of uranium, estimated to have provided the equivalent power of nearly 29 million gallons of fuel oil. Among its accomplishments was the production of nearly $12 million in revenue during its first five years of cargo operation. The *Savannah* was deactivated in late 1971 and presented to Savannah, Georgia, in early 1972 as part of a proposed Eisenhower Peace Memorial, but adequate support for the peace memorial never materialized. Several years later Congress passed P.L. 96-331, which authorized the secretary of commerce to transfer the ship to the Patriots Point Naval and Maritime Museum in South Carolina. Since late 1981 the vessel has served as a floating exhibit in Charleston Harbor. In 1983 the *Savannah* was dedicated as an International Historic Mechanical Engineering Landmark by the American Society of Mechanical Engineers. NR. ASME. [Patriots Point Development Authority]

■ **USS Yorktown (CV-10)**
Patriots Point Naval and
Maritime Museum
40 Patriots Point Road,
off Highway 17
1943

The 10th aircraft carrier built and one of the U.S. Navy's best-known carriers, the *Yorktown* was constructed in 17 months at the Newport News Shipbuilding and Dry-Dock Company in Virginia. The second of the *Essex*-class carriers, the *Yorktown* replaced its namesake, which was lost at the Battle of Midway in June 1942. The *Essex*-class carriers formed the core of the fast-carrier task forces that struck Japanese forces in the Pacific with devastating results. The *Yorktown* was the first of the new post–Pearl Harbor aircraft carriers to enter the central Pacific counteroffensive, beginning with an assault on the Japanese airfield at Marcus Island in August 1943. It then joined a task force that hit Japanese-held Wake Island. The *Yorktown* sortied with Task Force 50 to the Gilbert Islands, and its aircraft supported the amphibious assaults on Tarawa, Abemama, and Makin before retiring to Pearl Harbor. In January 1944 the *Yorktown* returned to the Marshalls in support of Operation Flintlock. Now based in the Marshalls, the *Yorktown* raided Japanese bases and installations from the Marianas to New Guinea. In the Battle of the Philippine Sea the *Yorktown*'s pilots badly damaged the Japanese carrier *Zuikaku* but failed to sink it. After raids on Palau, Iwo Jima, Yap, and Ulithi, the *Yorktown* returned to the United States for an overhaul.

Returning to action in November 1944, the *Yorktown* sortied to support the invasion of the Philippines before entering the South China Sea to hunt for the Japanese and hit the empire's inner defenses. It then assisted in the assault on Iwo Jima before hammering Tokyo and airfields on Kyushu, Honshu, and Shikoku islands. Attacked by a kamikaze during these operations, the *Yorktown* was hit by a bomb on March 18, 1945, that tore two large holes in the carrier's side, killed five crew members, and wounded 26 others, but it remained operational and on station until it sailed to refuel on March 20. The *Yorktown*'s pilots then joined in the aerial pounding of Okinawa as U.S. forces took the island. The carrier's planes also participated in the destruction of the Japanese Navy's last sortie when the battleship *Yamato* and its screening ships were sunk in a devastating attack in which the *Yorktown*'s Air Group 9 placed several hits on the battleship and the cruiser *Yahagi*. The "Fighting Lady" ended the war by bombing Japan, hitting such targets as the Kure Navy Yard. After supporting the landing of occupation forces the *Yorktown* steamed into Tokyo Bay. As part of the

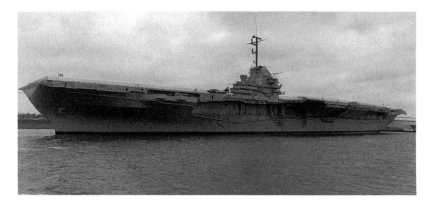

Active until 1970, the decommissioned aircraft carrier USS *Yorktown* forms the core of the National Historic Landmark fleet of ships at Patriots Point.

Magic Carpet demobilization program of 1945-46, the *Yorktown* ferried American troops home to the United States. It received 11 battle stars and the Presidential Unit Citation for its wartime service.

After the war the *Yorktown* and other *Essex* carriers formed the core of the U.S. postwar fleet. Placed in reserve in 1947, the carrier was reactivated in 1952 for duty during the Korean War but arrived after the armistice. Decommissioned in 1955, the *Yorktown* was modernized to support jet aircraft. Again modified in 1958 for antisubmarine warfare, it was then sent to demonstrate American strength when Communist Chinese forces shelled the Nationalist-held islands of Quemoy and Matsu at the end of 1959 and in early January 1959. The carrier spent much of its remaining active naval career off Vietnam, earning five battle stars. In 1967 the *Yorktown* joined other U.S. ships responding to the North Korean capture of the USS *Pueblo* (AGER-2). After its last Vietnam deployment on Yankee Station the *Yorktown* headed to sea in 1968 to recover crew members of Apollo 8, the first manned flight to orbit the moon, after their Pacific splashdown. After an Atlantic NATO cruise the *Yorktown* was decommissioned in 1970. Donated to Patriots Point in 1974, the carrier was towed from Bayonne, New Jersey, to Charleston in 1975 and was dedicated on October 13, 1975. The *Yorktown* forms the core of the National Historic Landmark fleet of ships at Patriots Point. Containing the carrier aviation hall of fame, it is itself a museum of carrier aviation, displaying vintage aircraft from all phases of its career and other planes that played a significant role in the war. The *Yorktown* has become an eagerly sought-after site for carrier crew and air group reunions. NR. NHL. [Patriots Point Development Authority]

■ ■ ■ ■ ■ ■ ■   VIRGINIA   ■ ■ ■ ■ ■ ■ ■

ALEXANDRIA

The colonial port of Alexandria on the Potomac River was at one time the third largest port in the United States. The advent of the railroad in large measure doomed Alexandria's maritime industry, although the port continued as an active center for local and regional maritime trade until early in the

■ **Alexandria**
End of Prince Street
1929

20th century. To celebrate and recall this now largely forgotten heritage the Alexandria Seaport Foundation was formed, and in 1983 it purchased the topsail schooner *Lindo* and renamed it the *Alexandria*. The 100-ton, 125-foot-long wood schooner was originally named the *Yngve* when launched from Albert Svennson's yard in Pukavik, Sweden, in 1929. A classic Scandinavian cargo schooner, it worked between various Baltic and Scandinavian ports and also fished for herring north of Iceland. Sold and renamed the *Lindo* in 1939, the schooner remained in the cargo trade until 1970, when it was bought for conversion into a passenger vessel. Taken out of service, it was converted in 1976 and entered the charter trade, also working in sail training and participating in OpSails of 1976 and 1986. Now a sailing ambassador for Alexandria and a sail-training vessel, the schooner is available for meetings, parties, and receptions. It is also open to the public when in port, docked at the foot of Prince Street on the city's restored riverfront. [Alexandria Seaport Foundation]

NEWPORT NEWS

■ **Dorothy**
4101 Washington Avenue
Newport News Shipbuilding
and Drydock Company
1890

Returned to the yard that
built it, the *Dorothy* stands as
a monument in front of the
Newport News Shipbuilding
and Drydock Company's
office headquarters.

The *Dorothy* was the first vessel built by the Newport News Shipbuilding and Drydock Company, noted particularly for the large number of warships it built for the U.S. Navy and now the largest private shipbuilding concern in the United States. When launched in 1891, the *Dorothy* was a tugboat typical of the period. Its iron hull was strongly built and well powered for the time. Horace See, its designer, was well known for his seaworthy vessel designs and modern engine plans. See designed the first quadruple-expansion steam engine compact enough to be fitted into a tugboat.

The *Dorothy* began its career as a railroad tugboat, towing car floats around New York Harbor. After many owners and renamings it was laid up after colliding with a cargo ship in 1964. In 1974 Newport News Shipbuilding was persuaded to buy, raise, and restore the tugboat. Work was finished in time for the vessel to be unveiled on its 85th birthday, April 30, 1975. The *Dorothy*, Hull Number 1, stands on a concrete-and-steel pad on the lawn between the present ship-

yard office headquarters, built in 1974, and the original shipyard offices built in 1891. [Newport News Shipbuilding and Drydock Company]

PORTSMOUTH

The lightship *No. 101* was built in 1916 by Pusey and Jones of Wilmington, Delaware, along with its sister lightship the *No. 102*. This new class of lightships was not immediately successful, and both sisters required a number of trips to the yard before they were finally seaworthy. The *No. 101*, for example, required a complete rebuilding. All its defects

■ **Lightship No. 101**
(**"Portsmouth"**)
London Slip
Portsmouth Lightship Museum
End of London Boulevard
1915

eliminated, *No. 101* served off Cape Charles, Virginia, at Smith Island Shoal to mark the entrance to the Chesapeake Bay from 1916 to 1925.

In 1925 the *No. 101* was transferred to the less exposed station at Overfalls that marked the end of the Delaware Bay breakwater. The *No. 101* was unusual in that it served at its station in its peacetime colors all during World War II and until 1951, actually staying on station for a number of years without relief and accumulating a phenomenal amount of marine growth on its bottom. In 1951 it became the "Relief" vessel for the Nantucket station, but its short hull proved unsuitable to this open ocean station, and in 1952 it was reassigned to the Stonehouse station, in a more protected area of Nantucket Bay. The *No. 101* served on Stonehouse station until 1953, when it served briefly on the Crossrip station until its machinery broke down at sea the next year. It was retired on July 18, 1960.

Used briefly by the U.S. Coast Guard as a museum in Portsmouth, the ship was renamed "Portsmouth" for its new location, although a station by that name never existed. Ownership was transferred to the city of Portsmouth, and the lightship is now open to the public as a dry-berth exhibit next to the Elizabeth River. NR. NHL. [Portsmouth Lightship Museum]

After being transferred by the U.S. Coast Guard to Portsmouth, the lightship *No. 101* ("Portsmouth") was named after the city, rather than an actual station.

GULF OF MEXICO

The battleship USS *Alabama* and the submarine USS *Drum*, moored off the Mobile Ship Channel at the Battleship Memorial Park.

■ ■ ■ ■ ■ ■ ■   ALABAMA   ■ ■ ■ ■ ■ ■

ALICEVILLE

■ **Montgomery**
Tom Bevill Visitor Center
Tennessee-Tombigbee Waterway
Off Route 14, south of
Pickensville
1926

The steam-propelled, stern-wheel snagboat *Montgomery* is one of a handful of steam-powered stern-wheelers in the country and one of only two surviving U.S. Army Corps of Engineers snagboats (the other is the *W. T. Preston* in Anacortes, Washington). Snagboats cleared the western rivers of countless obstructions, including submerged logs, and allowed the spread of navigation to regions previously inaccessible.

The *Montgomery* was built in 1926 for the Corps of Engineers' Montgomery district by the Charleston Drydock and Machine Company of Charleston, South Carolina. The vessel worked mainly on the Alabama and Coosa river systems clearing channels of snags, dredging, and repairing river locks. The Montgomery district was absorbed into the Mobile district in 1933, but the *Montgomery* continued to work the same rivers, as well as the Black Warrior and Tombigbee rivers. Its home port was shifted from Montgomery to Tuscaloosa at that time. In 1959, when the *Montgomery* was transferred to the Panama City area office, its home port was shifted to Florida. From Panama City the vessel worked to keep the Apalachicola, Chattahoochee, and Flint rivers clear of obstructions. During the 1970s the *Montgomery* played a major part in the creation of the Alabama-Tombigbee-Tennessee river project, an alternative river system to the Mississippi. Completed in 1984, the entire waterway is 234 miles long and to some ports is 400 to 800 miles shorter than the Mississippi route. In 1979 the *Montgomery* shifted home ports again to White City, Florida, where it continued to work on the same waterways until its retirement in 1982.

The U.S. Army Corps of
Engineers' snagboat
Montgomery, at work in
Pickensville, Alabama, c. 1980.

The *Montgomery* is the prize exhibit at the Tom Bevill Visitor Center, where it helps interpret the role of the U.S. Army Corps of Engineers in the development of America's waterways. NR. NHL. [U.S. Army Corps of Engineers]

MOBILE

Commissioned in August 1942, the *Alabama* is one of only two surviving *South Dakota*-class battleships built as part of America's preparations for the possibility of war (the other is the USS *Massachusetts*). The fourth naval vessel to carry the name *Alabama*, BB-60 was laid down at the Norfolk Navy Yard on February 1, 1940, and was launched two years later on February 16, 1942. The *Alabama* was commissioned at Portsmouth, Virginia, on August 16, 1942, with Capt. George B. Wilson assuming command. The *Alabama* served with the Atlantic Fleet and with the British Home Fleet in the North Atlantic until mid-1943, protecting lend-lease convoys to Britain and the Soviet Union. After a brief overhaul at Norfolk it departed for the Pacific and crossed the Panama Canal in August 1943, bound for Pearl Harbor. As part of the Third Fleet, it then joined forces bombarding the islands of Roi, Nauru, Kwajalein, and Majuro in early 1944. In February 1944 the *Alabama* supported the task force hitting the Japanese naval stronghold at Truk before heading to the Northern Marianas. Bombardment and invasion-support missions followed, including the invasion and reconquest of Guam in August 1944. The *Alabama* also supported the invasion of the Philippines, sailing with carrier forces that wreaked havoc on Japanese installations in the Philippines and the South China Sea. It later participated in the battle off Cape Engano on October 25, 1944, part of the larger Battle of the Philippine Sea, in which a Japanese naval force sent to threaten the U.S. invasion of the Philippines was beaten back.

After two years in the combat zone, the *Alabama* underwent a lengthy overhaul at Bremerton, Washington, before returning to the Pacific in May 1945 in time to support the Okinawa Gunto operations. The battleship ended its wartime service bombarding Japan. On June 17, 1945, its 16-inch guns hurled 1,500 tons of shells into enemy mills and factories on Honshu. At the end of the war the *Alabama* steamed into Tokyo Bay and helped occupy the Japanese capital before returning veterans home as part of Operation Magic Carpet. The *Alabama* spent 40 months in active service in the Pacific, participating in 26 engagements, and earned nine battle stars. Despite 37 months of active duty, the battleship, known by its crew as "Lucky A," was never damaged by enemy fire.

Decommissioned after the war in January 1947, the *Alabama* spent 17 years in the reserve fleet at Bremerton, Washington. In 1964 the it was presented to the state of Alabama as a memorial to World War II and Korean War veterans from that state. The vessel was towed 5,600 miles from Bremerton to Mobile and moored at its present site off the Mobile ship channel. NR. NHL. [U.S.S. Alabama Battleship Commission]

Named for a large sea bass found off the North Atlantic coast, the submarine *Drum* was launched from the Portsmouth Naval Shipyard in 1941. A *Gato*-class, fleet-type, presnorkel submarine, the vessel was built to maintain speeds averaging 17 knots. It was operated underwater on batteries and powered on the surface by a diesel-electric system. The *Gato*-class submarines proved to be fast, strong, well armed, and suited to the long-range patrols necessary for warfare in the Pacific.

■ **USS Alabama (BB-60)**
Battleship Memorial Park
Battleship Parkway (U.S. 90),
off Interstate 10
1942

■ **USS Drum (SS-228)**
Battleship Memorial Park
Battleship Parkway (U.S. 90),
off Interstate 10
1942

The vessel had a long and illustrious war career. In the spring of 1942 the *Drum* patrolled the Bungo Straits with deadly efficiency, attacking and sinking four enemy ships. In later actions it operated with wolf packs in the "Convoy College," scoring additional hits and sinkings. The submarine made 13 patrols, nine of which were designated "successful," and is credited with sinking 15 enemy ships weighing a total of 80,580 tons, making it one of the top 25 high-scoring U.S. submarines of World War II: ranked 20th with respect to the number of ships sunk and eighth with respect to the tonnage sunk.

Decommissioned in 1946, the *Drum* began service in 1947 to members of the naval reserve in the Potomac River Naval Command in Washington, D.C. Stricken from the U.S. Navy Register in 1967, the vessel was donated to the USS Alabama Battleship Commission in 1969. Moored beside the battleship *Alabama*, the *Drum* is open to the public at the Battleship Alabama Memorial Park. NR. NHL. [USS Alabama Battleship Commission]

The USS *Drum*, a fleet boat submarine with a long and illustrious war career that began soon after Pearl Harbor.

■ ■ ■ ■ ■ ■ ■   FLORIDA   ■ ■ ■ ■ ■ ■ ■

APALACHICOLA

■ **Governor Stone**
Battery Park Boat Basin
Bay Avenue
1877

Of the five surviving two-masted coasting schooners in the United States, the *Governor Stone* is the only surviving Gulf of Mexico–built schooner of thousands constructed and used in the busy and nationally important gulf fishing and general freight trades. It is the sole known survivor of the indigenous sailing schooners of the American South still afloat.

The schooner was built at Pascagoula, Mississippi, for the merchant Charles Anthorn Greiner and was named for John Marshall Stone, the first post-Reconstruction governor of Mississippi and Greiner's close friend. It was built to haul materials from Greiner's ship chandlery and sawmill in Pascagoula out to deep-water sailing ships anchored off the mouth of the shallow Singing River. Until harbor improvements and dredging projects in the late 19th century improved conditions, shallow-draft schooners such as the *Governor Stone* formed an important part of the maritime commerce of the South and the Gulf Coast, particularly the upper Gulf Coast, where shallows and sandbars made the use of shoal centerboard schooners essential for the transfer of freight and goods to and from large, ocean-going sailing vessels that could not come into port. After the harbors were improved the upper gulf coasting schooners were adapted to fishing and oystering, and their form and lines inspired the next generation of fishing schooners, many of which were built in Biloxi and thus are known as "Biloxi schooners."

Sold in 1880, the *Governor Stone* carried freight and as a buyboat purchased oysters from tongers off Alabama. Sold several times after 1882, it continued to work as an oyster buyboat until 1939, when it sank at Bay St. Louis, Mississippi. Later that year the schooner was raised and repaired at De Lisle, Mississippi. Renamed the *Queen of the Fleet* in 1940, it was used for the next two years as a day sailer for guests at Inn by the Sea, a summer resort near Pass Christian, Mississippi. In 1942 it was based in Biloxi and leased to the War Shipping Board for use as a Merchant Marine Academy sail-training vessel and based in Biloxi. The vessel's former

Schooners such as the *Governor Stone* formed an important part of maritime commerce along the southern and Gulf coasts.

owner reclaimed the vessel in 1947, and his estate sold it in 1953. The schooner then passed through five owners, each of whom changed its name to, respectively, *The Pirate Queen*, *Sea Bob*, *C'est la Vie*, and *Sovereign*. The last owner, John Curry, conducted research that identified the vessel as the *Governor Stone* and began a program of restoration that lasted through the 1970s and 1980s.

An effort to complete the vessel's restoration and display it at Pascagoula, where it was built, failed, and after two years the schooner was deeded to the current owner, the Apalachicola Maritime Institute. The schooner was restored between September 1989 and June 1990 and brought to Apalachicola, once a thriving port and center of southern shipbuilding, to serve as a sail-training vessel and sailing goodwill ambassador along the Gulf Coast. [Apalachicola Maritime Institute]

TARPON SPRINGS

■ **St. Nicholas III**
Old Sponge Docks
Dodecanese Boulevard
1939

One of only five remaining sponge diving boats of the many constructed in Tarpon Springs between 1907 and 1940, the *St. Nicholas III* was built in 1939. Its unusual and functional design resulted from modifying a traditional Mediterranean prototype to combine the benefits of a highly maneuverable sailing craft with the efficiency of motorized power.

When the *St. Nicholas III* was constructed in the shipyards along the Anclote River in 1939, nearly 100 sponge diving boats operated out of Tarpon Springs, most of them similar in design. The fall in the demand for sponges after 1946 and the microbiotic diseases that devastated the Tarpon Springs sponging grounds a short time later caused a severe decline in the sponge industry. After 1947 the *St. Nicholas III* was fitted with a canopy and benches to work as a tour boat. The *St. Nicholas III* continues to work as a sponger and an excursion vessel demonstrating traditional sponging techniques to tourists. NR. [Ted Billiris]

The *St. Nicholas III* works as a sponger and an excursion vessel demonstrating traditional sponging techniques to tourists.

■ ■ ■ ■ ■ ■ ■   LOUISIANA   ■ ■ ■ ■ ■ ■ ■

BATON ROUGE

■ **USS Kidd (DD-661)**
Louisiana Naval War Memorial
and Nautical Center
305 South River Road
1943

Representative of the *Fletcher*-class destroyers that formed the backbone of U.S. destroyer forces in World War II, the USS *Kidd* is named for Rear Adm. Isaac C. Kidd, Jr., who was killed aboard his flagship, the USS *Arizona*, when the Japanese struck Pearl Harbor on December 7, 1941. The two major classes of destroyers used by the U.S. Navy during the war were the *Allen M. Sumner* class, of which 70 were built, and the *Fletcher* class, of which 175 were built. (Most of the 105 *Gearing*-class destroyers were built too late to see action.) Other surviving *Fletcher*-class destroyers include the USS *Cassin Young* and the USS *The Sullivans*. The *Fletcher*-class destroyers made up the largest number of ships to be built to a single design by the U.S. Navy during World War II. Developed to protect larger ships against surface, submarine, and air attack, they also proved effective in an offensive role. During the war they were used mainly for screening task forces, bombarding shore targets, serving on radar picket duty, and battling enemy airplanes. This class formed the backbone of destroyer forces throughout the war. The *Fletcher*-class destroyers were larger than any previous class of destroyers and when fully loaded carried sufficient fuel, ammunition, and stores needed for extensive sea duty in the Pacific. No aircraft carrier or battleship would proceed into hostile waters without an escort of destroyers; the destroyer was an all-purpose ship, ready to fight off attacks from the air, on the surface, or underwater. It also could give fire support to troops, deliver mail, transport personnel to other ships, rescue pilots downed at sea, and dispense early warnings to the rest of the fleet in enemy waters.

The *Kidd* saw heavy action in World War II, participating in nearly every important naval campaign in the Pacific. The

The USS *Kidd* retains its World War II appearance.

ship and its crew gallantly fought during the invasion of the Gilbert and Marshall islands, the Philippines, at Leyte Gulf, and off Okinawa, where the destroyer screened the badly damaged carrier *Franklin* after a devastating kamikaze attack. On April 11, 1945, while on radar picket duty, a Japanese plane rammed the *Kidd* amidships, killing 38 crew members and wounding 55. The crippled destroyer managed to stay afloat and rejoined the task force to continue the fight. Decommissioned in December 1946, the *Kidd* earned four battle stars for its World War II service.

In 1951 the destroyer was recommissioned and deployed to Korean waters, where it won four more battle stars for service that included shore bombardment. From 1953 to

1959 the battleship served in the Pacific Fleet. In 1961 it served with fleet operation forces during the Berlin crisis and patrolled off the Dominican Republic. Decommissioned in 1964, it entered the Atlantic Reserve Fleet and was berthed at Philadelphia until 1982, when its ownership was transferred to the Louisiana Naval War Memorial Commission. The destroyer was not extensively modernized, and now, after careful and meticulous restoration, it is the only destroyer to retain its World War II appearance. The *Kidd* is now on public view as a combination floating and dry-dock exhibit. A shoreside museum interprets the story of the *Kidd* and other warships, as well as the story of Louisiana's contributions to the nation's defense. NR. NHL. [Louisiana Naval War Memorial Commission]

NEW ORLEANS

■ **USS Cabot (CVL-28)**
End of Jackson Avenue
1943

The sole survivor of the nine *Independence*-class light aircraft carriers of World War II, the *Cabot* was built on the converted hull of the incomplete cruiser *Wilmington* at the Camden, New Jersey, yard of the New York Shipbuilding Corporation. Commissioned in 1943, "The Iron Lady" participated in some of the fiercest sea battles in the Pacific— Leyte Gulf, Okinawa, and off Iwo Jima, where it survived kamikaze hits. The war correspondent Ernie Pyle brought the carrier war to millions through dispatches from the *Cabot*'s decks. The *Cabot* served with distinction from 1943 to 1947, earning nine battle stars and the prestigious Presidential Unit Citation for its wartime service.

A World War II light aircraft carrier, the USS *Cabot* participated in some of the fiercest sea battles in the Pacific.

The *Cabot* was reactivated in 1948 and commissioned as a naval air reserve carrier until 1955, serving in the Gulf of Mexico, the Caribbean, the Mediterranean, and the North

Atlantic. Decommissioned for the last time by the U.S. Navy in 1967 and turned over to Spain, it served as the SNS *Dedalo*, the flagship for that nation's navy until 1989, when the Spanish government returned the carrier to the United States as a gift. The ship, whose home port is now New Orleans, is undergoing restoration and refitting as a naval memorial on the Mississippi River. Despite long service in two navies, the *Cabot* is essentially unmodified. It is a working museum of World War II naval technology, whose operating equipment includes elevators, navigational instruments, electrical systems, and armament still electrically linked and capable of tracking by means of the Mark 51 and Mark 7 gun directors on the gallery decks. NR. NHL. [USS Cabot–SNS Dedalo Museum Foundation]

Following the boom created by the gold rush, the California Transportation Company built up a successful fleet of steamers. In the 1920s the company made plans for a pair of steamboats to serve on the Sacramento and San Joaquin rivers as luxury overnight transportation between San Fran-

■ **Delta Queen**
No. 30 Robin Street Wharf
1926

cisco and Sacramento, California. Built at Glasgow, Scotland, and shipped unassembled to the United States, the steamboats were reassembled and launched in 1927 from the C. N. & L. shipyard in Stockton, California. The stern-wheel river steamboats *Delta Queen* and *Delta King* began service between San Francisco and Sacramento on a schedule in which one left San Francisco for Sacramento and passed the other along the way. Each boat left at 6 p.m. and arrived at 6 a.m., returning the next day. The *Delta Queen* could accommodate 234 passengers, 40 automobiles on the main deck, 15 on the outside decks, and 350 to 400 tons of cargo. The passengers were accommodated in 117 staterooms for two persons and a large men's dormitory area forward. In 1940 the *Delta Queen* was chartered for use as a mine-sweeping training ship in San Francisco Bay. Requisitioned for use by the U.S. Navy in 1941, both the *Delta Queen* and the *Delta King* were used to carry large groups of troops around the San Francisco Bay area. They were also used as gigantic lighters to carry 3,000 troops at a time out to liners anchored in the bay.

The *Delta Queen* was retired from naval service on August 21, 1945, declared surplus on August 28, 1946, and sold to the Greene Line, of Cincinnati. Modified for service on the western rivers, the Greene Line sent the *Delta Queen* on passenger cruises west to Omaha, Nebraska, south to New Orleans, north to Stillwater, Minnesota, and Joliet, Illinois, and west to

The *Delta Queen* is one of only two stern-wheel river passenger boats operating under steam and is the sole remaining example of a western rivers overnight passenger boat in operation.

Charleston, West Virginia, and Knoxville, Tennessee. The Greene Line underwent management changes and sold most of its other steamboats but continued to operate the *Delta Queen* until finally it sold the steamboat to Edward J. Quinby and Richard S. Simonton on February 22, 1958. The steamboat, however, continued to operate on the same sort of strenuous tramping passenger excursion trips. Some minor improvements to make the boat more attractive and comfortable to passengers were made.

The Safety at Sea Law of 1966 threatened the *Delta Queen*'s continued operation because one clause forbade operations of vessels with wood superstructures in overnight passenger service. Legal maneuvering fueled by a tremendous public outcry resulted in a special congressional exemption for the *Delta Queen* in 1970. Several subsequent extensions of this exemption have focused tremendous national attention on this problem. Many modifications for safety have been made to the boat, although all are short of the complete rebuilding sought by the U.S. Coast Guard.

Every year since 1962 the *Delta Queen* has raced the only other surviving stern-wheel passenger steamboat, the *Belle of Louisville*, as part of the Kentucky Derby celebrations. The *Delta Queen* has attracted many distinguished passengers. In 1979 President Jimmy Carter and his family took a highly publicized cruise on the upper Mississippi from St. Paul, Minnesota, to St. Louis, Missouri, as the president worked on his energy policy and prepared for the upcoming election. Princess Margaret of Great Britain and a royal party made a similar cruise in 1986. Today the *Delta Queen*, the sole remaining western rivers overnight passenger boat, is an important reminder of the region's cultural and historical heritage. NR. NHL. [Delta Queen Steamboat Company]

■ **Deluge**
Port of New Orleans
Opposite the French Quarter
1923

The fire-fighting tugboat *Deluge* is the oldest surviving fireboat associated with the port of New Orleans, the most significant Gulf Coast port in the United States since the 1840s and currently the second-ranked U.S. port "in value of total foreign and domestic waterborne tonnage." Launched in 1923, the *Deluge* was authorized during a period of unprecedented growth of harbor activity. The previous fireboat—the 1881 iron-hulled fire tugboat *Samson*, a 108-foot-long, 22-foot beam, 560-horsepower vessel mounting a single monitor—was not capable of meeting the needs of a harbor whose load had tripled in tonnage in a 10-year period. The *Deluge*, a large, powerful modern fireboat, was designed by the New Orleans naval architect H. E. Cornell and built by the Johnson Iron Works, Drydock, and Shipbuilding Company of New Orleans.

In addition to responding to fires along the waterfront and aboard vessels docked in the harbor, the *Deluge* also was authorized at the captain's discretion to respond to emergencies "requiring assistance in saving human life or property" and to serve as a tugboat "for moving floating equipment owned by this Board…and for other miscellaneous services, such as the washing of the river banks by propeller or hose lines." Other duties have included inspection and goodwill tours after the sale in 1966 of the *Good Neighbor*, an inspection vessel of the Port of New Orleans Dock Board.

The fire-fighting tugboat *Deluge* with crew in 1928 and heading into harbor today.

The *Deluge* has worked hard in its role as a fireboat; as recorded in 1958, it fought an average of 40 fires a year. These included fighting a two-day fire in March 1930, when the freighter *Scantic* burned, killing 10 of the freighter's crew; pumping a quarter of a million gallons of water from the river to help fire companies ashore extinguish a school fire in Algiers in March 1958; and extinguishing a fire on a water-side dock when a man making carburetor repairs set his engine on fire in February 1957. Typical of the *Deluge*'s hazardous duty was Christmas Eve, 1950. A crude oil-laden barge being towed upriver had broken loose and smashed into the Standard Oil tanker *Baltimore* steaming downriver, also carrying oil. Arriving at the scene at 9:40 p.m., the *Deluge* opened up with all monitors. Hailing a nearby tugboat to tow the charred barge to shore, the *Deluge* then quickly ran downriver to the burning *Baltimore*, still spewing burning oil from a gaping hole in the bow. Maneuvering alongside the burning tanker, the *Deluge* began to pour water onto and into the *Baltimore*. For more than four hours the battle raged; the danger of an explosion seemed imminent, but the *Deluge* clung firmly to the *Baltimore*'s side until the fire was extinguished at 2:25 a.m. Christmas Day. Other notable fires combatted by the *Deluge* were the *African Star* and *Union Faith* fires in 1968 and 1969.

The *Deluge*'s logbook for the period between October 1, 1954, and September 30, 1955, reveals a typical year's operation: 310 towing jobs, 33 jobs "washing out silt" from beneath docks, four jobs "digging with wheel" (that is, a propeller), and 44 emergency responses, including drifting barges, escorting a leaking oil barge, extinguishing burning objects in the river, revetment and levee fires, and five vessel fires, including burning oil barges, a yacht, a dredge, and two tugboats.

Its propulsion systems modernized in 1962, the *Deluge* has, with the exception of minor repairs and maintenance, remained in active service. Its crew, some long-time veterans of service, keep their historic fireboat operating in the best traditions of the maritime fire service. NR. NHL. [Port of New Orleans Dock Board]

■ **Pioneer**
French Quarter
1862

Displayed outdoors in the French Quarter next to the Cabildo is the Confederacy's first submersible craft, the appropriately named *Pioneer*. Following the tradition of undersea attack craft first developed by David Bushnell and Robert Fulton, Horace L. Hunley of Mobile, Alabama, financed the construction of the *Pioneer* in 1862. The 30-foot-long, three-person craft was propelled by hand cranking. Built to counter Union moves toward New Orleans's Lake Ponchartrain, the tiny craft, made from quarter-inch plates cut from old boilers and riveted together, made several successful practice attacks. Before the *Pioneer* could be deployed, however, New Orleans was captured, and the craft was scuttled. Hunley went on to build another submersible, often called the *Pioneer II*, which was lost near Fort Morgan at the entrance to Mobile Bay while en route to attack Union blockaders. Hunley's third submersible, named for him, was a 40-foot-long, hand-cranked vessel mounting a spar torpedo at the bow. Moved to Charleston, it accidently sank three times during testing, twice drowning the crews. On the third occasion Hunley himself was lost. Raised a fourth time, the ship avenged its inventor's death on February 17, 1864. Casting off at nightfall, the tiny craft approached the corvette *Housatonic*. At 8:45 p.m. the *Hunley* ran for the warship as alert Union sailors peppered it with rifle fire. The spar torpedo, pressed up against the hull, was detonated in a blinding flash that sent a cascade of water up into the sky and sank both vessels. The *Hunley* thus became the first submarine craft to successfully sink an enemy vessel in combat. A modern replica of the ill-fated craft is displayed outside the Charleston Museum in South Carolina. However, the craft that began Hunley's quest, the *Pioneer*, was raised after the Civil War and placed on display at its present location. [Louisiana State Museum]

■ ■ ■ ■ ■ ■ ■   **MISSISSIPPI**   ■ ■ ■ ■ ■ ■ ■

VICKSBURG

■ **USS Cairo**
Vicksburg National Military Park
Adjacent to the Vicksburg
National Cemetery
1861

An important contribution to the Union's victory in the Civil War was the seizure and control of New Orleans and the lower Mississippi River and its tributaries. Adopting a proposal by James Eads of St. Louis to build armored gunboats to steam up the river and capture Confederate ports, the U.S. government contracted with Eads for seven of his "city class" vessels. Powered by steam and surmounted by an oak casemate covered with railroad iron, the USS *Cairo*, built at Mound City, Illinois, after a design by the naval architect Samuel M. Pook, was one of these seven bulky, 512-ton, 175-foot-long warships that, like their more famous iron-hulled coastal cousins, the monitors, inaugurated the naval age of iron in the United States. The vessel was named for the nearby city of Cairo, Illinois. The concept of armored, casemated vessels dated to the War of 1812, but it was not until the Civil War that such vessels were built in the country. Another feature of the gunboat was its recessed wheel, housed inside a protected raceway that kept it safe from cannon fire.

The *Cairo*'s career was short-lived. Launched in December 1861 and commissioned January 15, 1862, the gunboat was sent to help the naval and land campaign to take the important river port of Vicksburg, Mississippi. Heading up the Yazoo River on a reconnaissance trip, the *Cairo* was lost to a Confederate innovation of the war, the "torpedo." These electrically detonated mines, made from five-gallon glass demijohns filled with black powder with primers in their necks and linked to shore by waterproof copper wire,

Raised from the mud of the Yazoo River in 1964, the wreck of the USS *Cairo* was rebuilt as an outdoor display for Vicksburg National Military Park.

were moored along the river and suspended from the bottom. The *Cairo* moved ahead, despite warnings of the presence of the Confederate "infernal machines," where the ironclad's commander, Thomas O. Selfridge, in the words of a fellow officer, "found two torpedoes and removed them by placing his vessel over them" at 11:55 a.m. on December 12, 1862. Thus the *Cairo* became the first warship sunk by a mine. The gunboat went down in 12 minutes as the 175-person crew hastily abandoned everything in their rush to leave the sinking vessel. Settling into the mud, the *Cairo* was abandoned and passed into obscurity.

The intact wreck was rediscovered in November 1956 by Edwin C. Bearss, historian of the Vicksburg National Military Park, and two colleagues, Warren Grabau and M. D. Jacks. Their discovery inaugurated a four-year project, begun in 1960, to survey and raise the *Cairo*. The iron pilothouse was raised from the river in October 1960, and by December 1963, after the hulk had been freed by dredging, the first attempt to raise the gunboat was made. A second attempt in July and August 1964 broke the *Cairo*'s hull, which was raised, shattered, and placed on a barge. The wreckage was sorted and placed in storage in Pascagoula. In 1973 the National Park Service received the wreck and its artifacts, which were moved to Vicksburg in 1977. When funding became available the Park Service began the process of reassembling the iron-clad in a covered outdoor display and built a nearby museum to house the artifact collection. The museum opened in1980, when rebuilding the *Cairo* commenced. Missing members were replaced with an open skeleton of laminated beams to which the original timbers, armor, engines, boilers, paddlewheel, and cannon were mounted. Work was completed by 1986, and the "hardluck ironclad" is now a prominent feature of the national park. [National Park Service]

■ ■ ■ ■ ■ ■ ■ ■   TEXAS   ■ ■ ■ ■ ■ ■ ■ ■

FORT WORTH

■ MSB-5
Pate Museum of Transportation
On U.S. Highway 377, off U.S. Highway 17 between Fort Worth and Cresson
1952

A minesweeper from the Korean and Vietnam wars, the *MSB-5* is now on exhibit.

The introduction during the Civil War of submarine "torpedoes," now better known as mines, and their subsequent adoption by the world's navies led to the need for craft that would "sweep" the seas and harbors to remove these moored or drifting menaces. The U.S. Navy first formally assigned and designated vessels as "minecraft" in 1911. World War I introduced the need for a large fleet, and between 1917 and 1919 dozens of mine planters and layers were commissioned, while more than a hundred minesweepers were built or converted from other craft. None of the early minesweepers survives as a preserved historic vessel in the United States, although two World War II minesweepers, the *Hazard* and the *Inaugural*, are preserved and displayed at Omaha, Nebraska, and St. Louis, Missouri, respectively. The

only other of these specialized vessels preserved and on display is the *MSB-5*, built as part of a Korean War buildup of mine craft. Launched in 1952 by the yard of John Trumpy and Sons of Annapolis, Maryland, better known for its yacht designs, the *MSB-5* saw service during the Vietnam War. Laid up in the navy's reserve fleet at Orange, Texas, the *MSB-5* was acquired by the Pate Museum of Transportation in 1973. Moved ashore, the minesweeper is displayed at the museum, along with aircraft, automobiles, and railroad cars. [Pate Museum of Transportation]

The *HA-19*, a captured Japanese midget submarine aground at Bellows Beach on the northern, or windward, side of Oahu, December 19, 1941.

FREDERICKSBURG

The display of captured prizes of war has been a common feature of most societies; among the more notable prizes are enemy warships. A participant in the Japanese attack on Pearl Harbor on December 7, 1941, the *HA-19* was the only Japanese vessel captured intact during the battle. Yielding significant intelligence information as well as the United States' first prisoner of war, Ens. Kazuo Sakamaki, the pilot and commanding officer, *HA-19*'s story is a significant part of the "day of infamy" at Pearl Harbor and its immediate aftermath.

Built as part of Japan's expansion of its armed forces in the 1930s, the Type A midget submarine *HA-19* was an important component of the Imperial Japanese Navy in the 1930s. Following Adm. Isoruko Yamamoto's determination to attack the U.S. Pacific Fleet at Pearl Harbor as the opening blow of a war with the United States, military and naval planners began assembling the plan for the attack, designating it Operation Hawaii. Initially conceived as solely an air strike, the plan was modified to combat test the hitherto untested Type A midget submarines.

Five I-class fleet submarines of the First Submarine Squadron, Sixth Submarine Fleet, each carrying a Type A midget—*I-16*, *I-18*, *I-20*, *I-22*, and *I-24*—were designated the Special Attack Force. The midget submarines' mission was to slip

■ **HA-19**
Admiral Nimitz Museum of the Pacific War
340 Main Street
1938

From 1942 to 1945 the *HA-19* toured the United States to promote the sale of war bonds.

covertly into Pearl Harbor, wait until the attack, and then each launch their two torpedoes. They would then navigate submerged counterclockwise around Ford Island, escape, and meet up with their mother submarines some seven miles west of Lanai Island. The last midget submarine launched was the *HA-19*, commanded and piloted by Sakamaki and crewed by CWO Inagaki. While still aboard the *I-22*, Sakamaki and Inagaki had learned that the *HA-19*'s gyrocompass, a critical navigational aid, was out of order. Running at periscope depth, Sakamaki managed to navigate the entrance without being spotted by patrol craft but could not reach Pearl Harbor before the air attack commenced. Striking submerged coral reefs at the entrance three times, Sakamaki surfaced just after 8 a.m. There, the *HA-19*, aground and with propellers spinning in reverse, was spotted by the USS *Helm*, which blasted the midget off the reef, disabled one of the torpedo firing mechanisms, and knocked Sakamaki unconscious.

The submarine, again aground on the reef, was unsuccessfully bombed by army planes, but once again U.S. forces succeeded in freeing the vessel. Drifting ashore, the *HA-19* was captured by a salvage party from the submarine base at Pearl Harbor. Naval investigators recovered several documents from the submarine's interior, including a navigational chart of Pearl Harbor. Sakamaki, imprisoned at Fort Shafter, was interrogated by naval intelligence staff. While "his revelations were less than earthshaking," the captured submarine provided Allied intelligence with its first view of Japan's secret submersible weapon. The initial report on the captured midget submarine was produced on December 26, less than three weeks after the attack.

Very soon after the midget submarine's capture and studies to assess its capabilities, the *HA-19* was pressed into another duty. Shipped to the mainland in January 1942, mounted on a trailer and modified for public display, the midget submarine toured the United States for three years as a promotion for war bond sales, an integral part of the nation's effort to win the conflict. Admission to the "Japanese suicide" submarine was secured by the purchase of war bonds and war stamps. More important, however, the captured midget was a potent symbol. The *HA-19* helped create an image of a clever, perfidious enemy and ensure that the nation remembered Pearl Harbor.

The *HA-19* ended the war in Chicago, lying at the navy pier until transferred at the request of the commanding officer to the submarine base at Key West, Florida. Arriving at Key West on January 20, 1947, five years after its arrival on the mainland, the submarine served as a stationary outdoor exhibit at the base until 1964, when it was loaned to the Key West Art and Historical Association, at its request. On December 2, 1964, the submarine was placed on indefinite loan to the association and put on outdoor display at the Key West Lighthouse Museum on Whitehead Street. Moved when the lighthouse was restored, the *HA-19* was transferred from the U.S. Navy to the National Park Service. Now on temporary loan to the Nimitz Museum, the submarine will be moved again to Honolulu for display at Pearl Harbor in 1993. [National Park Service; leased to the Admiral Nimitz Foundation]

GALVESTON

Galveston's Seawolf Park, located on Pelican Island opposite the city's historic Strand, is the home port for two historic World War II vessels, the *Cavalla* and the *Stewart*. Launched from the Groton, Connecticut, yard of the Electric Boat Company, the *Balao*-class submarine *Cavalla* (SS-244) was commissioned on February 29, 1944. Sailing from New London on April 11, it arrived at Pearl Harbor nearly a month later and on May 31 began a war patrol that would win its crew a Presidential Unit Citation. On June 17 it made contact with a large Japanese task force en route to the Philippines. Tracking the enemy fleet, the *Cavalla* relayed its position to a waiting American task force that met and stopped the Japanese during the Battle of the Philippine Sea, also known as the "Marianas Turkey Shoot," which ended in victory for U.S. forces. Pursuing the Japanese fleet, the *Cavalla* caught the carrier *Shokaku*, the sole survivor of the six Japanese carriers that struck Pearl Harbor, and sank it with three torpedoes. The *Cavalla* made six war patrols, sinking a total of 34,180 tons of enemy shipping, including the destroyer *Shimotsuki*, which was destroyed in a daring surface attack on November 25, 1944.

■ **USS Cavalla (AGSS-244)**
Seawolf Park
Pelican Island
1942

The *Cavalla*, which sank the last of the Japanese carriers to attack Pearl Harbor.

Stationed off the coast of Japan when the war ended on August 15, 1945, the *Cavalla* was present for the Japanese surrender in Tokyo Bay on September 2. Decommissioned and placed in reserve in March 1946, the submarine was recommissioned during the Korean War. Converted to an SSK (hunter-killer) submarine between late 1952 and early 1953, the *Cavalla* was again recommissioned in July 1953. The submarine remained in the Atlantic on active duty until 1963, when it was decommissioned and its ownership transferred to the U.S. Submarine Veterans of World War II. Moved to Seawolf Park and placed ashore, the submarine was opened to the public in April 1971. [U.S. Submarine Veterans of WWII]

■ **Elissa**
Pier 21
The Strand
1877

The bark *Elissa* was built in Aberdeen, Scotland, as a "tramp" sailer to carry available cargoes, such as coal, lumber, sugar, rice, cotton, and miscellaneous merchandise, usually handling goods not yet carried by the steamships that were beginning to dominate the seas. During that career it sailed to U.S. and Canadian eastern seaboard ports, as well as to South America and the Caribbean and later Indian, Burmese, Australian, and even Chilean ports.

The second oldest operational sailing vessel in the world and one of the three oldest merchant vessels still afloat, the square-rigged bark *Elissa* regularly sails from Galveston, Texas.

The *Elissa* brought cargoes to and from Boston, New York, Savannah, Georgia, Pensacola, Florida, and Galveston, Texas. It remained under British sail until 1897, when, after being damaged in a storm, it was sold to a Norwegian firm. Renamed the *Fjeld*, the vessel operated as a sailing bark until 1911, when it was sold to a Swedish owner, who renamed it the *Gustaf*, cut down the rig to a barkentine, and in 1918 installed an engine. In 1930 it was sold to its first Finnish owner, who cut its rig down to a schooner. Sold to Greek owners in 1959, the former bark was renamed the *Christopherous* and then the *Achaios* in 1967. It was then sold to smugglers who briefly changed its name to *Pioneer* in 1969. Laid up at Pireaus, Greece, in 1970, the vessel was slated for scrapping when it was discovered and rescued by the maritime historian and archeologist Peter Throckmorton in Athens, Greece, in 1961. The ship was purchased in 1975 by the Galveston Historical Foundation, which had been seeking a square-rigged vessel to complement the restoration of the Strand, the city's 19th-century historic district, and honor the city's maritime past. Restoration work began in Greece in 1977. The *Elissa* was towed to Gilbraltar in December 1978 and to Galveston in June 1979. There it was slowly restored to operating condition. On July 4, 1982, the *Elissa* opened to the public as a floating museum.

The *Elissa* is the second oldest operational sailing vessel in the world and one of the three oldest merchant vessels still afloat, surpassed only by Britain's *Cutty Sark* (1869), now in a dry berth, and the *Star of India* (1863). Of the nine historic square-rigged vessels preserved in the United States, only the *Elissa* and the U.S. Coast Guard training ship *Eagle* regularly sail. The *Elissa* alone is regularly open and accessible to the

Square-rigger technology, maritime lore, and the language of the sea are kept alive in a working context aboard the *Elissa*. Visitors assist crew members in hauling on a line during a 1989 cruise.

public; people not only are able to watch the ship but also are allowed to participate as working crew members, thus gaining a compelling and unusual perspective on square-riggers, maritime culture, seafaring, and maritime preservation. NR. NHL. [Galveston Historical Foundation]

The last destroyer escort in the United States, the USS *Stewart* is a representative of this austerely designed, hard-working type of vessel. Built for antisubmarine warfare, the destroyer escorts were considered by the U.S. Navy's general board at the beginning of World War II, largely because of the success of Britain's *Hunt*-class destroyer escorts. A British request for U.S.-produced destroyer escorts led to the construction of the first in 1942, and in time more than 500 ships were built. Divided into six nominal classes, the destroyer escorts were in fact variants of a basic type. Fast and lacking the single or paired five-inch guns the destroyers carried, escorts nonetheless bristled with three-inch, 40-millimeter and 20-millimeter antiaircraft guns and depth charge projectors, the so-called Y-guns, and a hedgehog, which fired depth charge projectiles ahead of the ship. The only antiship weap-

■ **USS Stewart (DE-238)**
Seawolf Park
Pelican Island
1942

ons they carried were three 21-inch above-deck torpedo tube launchers. The destroyer escorts were used in both the Atlantic and Pacific theaters but came too late to influence substantially the Allies' ultimate victory against German U-boats in the Battle of the Atlantic. Nonetheless, the ships and their crews performed heroic service, and a dozen destroyer escorts were lost during the war. After the war they remained an important part of the fleet, although they were gradually retired, sent to other nations, or broken up.

The *Stewart* was built at Houston, Texas, by the Brown Shipbuilding Company in 1942. After a lengthy training period on the Gulf and Atlantic coasts, the *Stewart* alternated convoy escort duty to Europe with training exercises throughout the war. Sent to the Pacific after Germany's surrender, the escort was in training at war's end. Sent back to the East Coast, the *Stewart* was decommissioned in 1947 at Philadelphia and laid up in Florida. Shifted to Norfolk, Virginia, in 1958, Charleston, South Carolina, in 1959, and Orange, Texas, in 1969, the aging ship was found to be in poor condition and was stricken from the navy list in 1972. Donated to the state of Texas in 1974, it was placed in a dry berth, surrounded by landfill, on Pelican Island as part of Galveston's Seawolf Park for display with the *Cavalla*. The long-term survival of the ship, now stripped and in poor condition, is questionable. [State of Texas]

The USS *Stewart* served in the North Atlantic as a convoy escort during World War II.

LAPORTE

■ **USS Texas (BB-35)**
San Jacinto Battleground
State Historical Park
3527 Battleground Road
1914

Built as one of six ships similar to the *New York* class, the *Texas* is the sole survivor of the American dreadnoughts. The battleship was one of the last two American warships built with reciprocating steam engines; the other was its sister ship, the USS *New York*, sunk during a training exercise in 1948. According to the American Society of Mechanical Engineers, these engines were the last and most sophisticated reciprocating steam engines to be installed in an American warship. Britain completed the first turbine-powered battleship, the HMS *Dreadnought* in 1906, and the U.S. Navy followed suit with five turbine-powered dreadnoughts that preceded the *Texas*. The *Texas* was built during a period of a dramatic upsurge in global military escalation. The dreadnoughts set the stage for a naval arms race that measured battleship strength by gun size. Within 10 years

An American dreadnought, the USS *Texas*, completed in time to participate in the American landings at Veracruz, served in both world wars. It is shown here as a newly restored floating exhibit in 1991.

of its launching the *Texas* was superceded by much larger, better-armed warships.

The *Texas* was completed by the Newport News Shipbuilding and Drydock Company in Virginia in time to participate in the American landings at Veracruz and served during World War I as a member of the Atlantic Fleet, hunting down German warships. Between wars it was the first battleship to launch an aircraft from its decks, accomplishing this feat at Guantanamo Bay, Cuba, on March 9, 1919. Later that year the *Texas* escorted the navy's seaplane NC-4 on its first trans-Atlantic flight. In 1925 the vessel's coal-burning engine was converted to an oil-burning one, and its original 14 boilers were replaced by six more efficient oil-fired ones. In 1927 the *Texas* was named the flagship of the American fleet. When the United States entered World War II, it became the flagship of the Atlantic Training Squadron. During the war it served on Atlantic convoy duty and bombarded shore positions during the invasions of North Africa, Normandy, and southern France. In late 1944 the vessel proceeded to the Pacific, where it participated in the bombardment of Iwo Jima and Okinawa, fighting off kamikazes at Okinawa and firing four shiploads of ammunition in a six-week deployment.

Returning to the United States at the close of the war, the battleship brought home 4,267 troops and then was laid up at the Norfolk Navy Yard. Decommissioned and stricken from the U.S. Navy Register in 1948, it was presented to the state of Texas as the flagship of the "Texas Navy." The first battleship to be made into a state shrine, the *Texas* is moored at San Jacinto Battleground State Historical Park. Recently restored as a floating exhibit at Todd Shipyard in Galveston, the battleship is open to the public. The "Mighty T" has been restored to its appearance during the Pacific Theater of World War II, and more than two-thirds of its living and working spaces are interpreted. Its reciprocating marine steam engines are National Historic Engineering Landmarks. NR. NHL. ASME. [State of Texas Parks and Wildlife Department]

MIDWEST

A dry-berth exhibit on the Omaha waterfront, the minesweeper USS *Hazard* retains all of its original equipment with the exception of the minesweeping cable.

■ ■ ■ ■ ■ ■ ■ ■ IOWA ■ ■ ■ ■ ■ ■ ■ ■

CLINTON

■ **City of Clinton**
Riverview Park
1401 11th Avenue, North
1936

A sister of the towboat *John W. Hubbard* (now the Mike Fink Restaurant in Covington, Kentucky), the *City of Clinton* was built by the Dravo Corporation of Pittsburgh. Launched sideways into the river in 1936 as the towboat *Omar*, the steel-hulled, 173-foot-long stern-wheeler pushed barges laden with coal upriver from West Virginia to Cincinnati for the Ohio River Company. After a quarter century of service the towboat was presented to the state of West Virginia as a centennial exhibit. The state converted the *Omar* into a showboat, raising the pilothouse to build a third deck that housed the theater and renaming it the *Rhododendron* after the West Virginia state flower. In 1966 West Virginia sold the show-boat to the city of Clinton. Towed 1,600 miles down the Monongahela River to Pittsburgh, up the Ohio River to Cairo, Illinois, and then up the Mississippi River to Clinton, the former towboat was moored at the city's Riverview Park, where it offered summertime plays. Moved from the riverfront in 1980 during a five-year U.S. Army Corps of Engineers project, the vessel was renamed the *City of Clinton* on its return in 1985. Set atop the riverfront dike built by the corps, the showboat rests on dry land; it is open for tours and continues to serve as a theater. [City of Clinton Department of Parks and Recreation]

DAVENPORT

■ **President**
End of Brady Street
1924

The steamboat *President* is the only remaining large western rivers side-wheel excursion boat. Such boats served as packets, carrying passengers on day outings while providing entertainment and pleasant diversion. The Louisville and Cincinnati Packet Company, the oldest steamboat company on the western rivers, ordered two steam-propelled side-wheel packet boats, the *Cincinnati* and the *Island Queen*, to be completed in 1924. The most expensive and luxurious packets constructed until then, the vessels were designed by the marine architect Tom Dunbar and built by Midland Barge Company of Midland, Kentucky. The *Cincinnati*, the surviving vessel, began its career with a grand excursion to New Orleans for Mardi Gras. Following this annual trip it provided packet service between Louisville and Cincinnati and occasionally excursion charters in the summer.

Deluxe packet boats were expensive to run, and the *Cincinnati* was the last large packet to operate on the western rivers. Sold in 1932 to Streckfus Steamers of St. Louis, Missouri, it was rebuilt as an excursion boat. Tougher safety requirements encouraged Streckfus to rebuild the entire superstructure of steel, and Art Moderne ornamentation and styling replaced the Victorian Gothic. Renamed the *President*, the boat was advertised as "The Wonder Ship of the Mississippi–where life is gay, vivacious–alive with exciting thrills–with dancing and romancing...the ultimate in excursion pleasure." Famous jazz bands played aboard, providing entertainment in the open-air grand salon. A popular way to beat the summer heat, river cruises were enjoyed by city dwellers before the advent of air conditioning. The

President went tramping during the majority of the year and traveled to New Orleans for the winter months, when low water and cold weather made northern operation difficult.

During World War II the boat discontinued tramping and made day and night cruises near New Orleans. When the war ended, it remained in New Orleans as a popular night spot. In 1978 the side wheels were removed and replaced with 1,000-horsepower diesel engines. In 1985 the *President* returned to St. Louis, its new home port. The vessel served as a popular attraction on the St. Louis waterfront, carrying excursion charters, educational tours, and promotional tour groups on day and night trips down the Mississippi River until 1990. Converted from an excursion boat to a cruising casino, the President Riverboat Casino began operation out of Davenport in April 1991. NR. NHL. [Gateway Riverboat Cruises]

Before being converted to a gambling casino operating out of Davenport, the side-wheel river excursion steamboat *President* was a popular attraction on the St. Louis waterfront.

DUBUQUE

The steam-propelled, stern-wheel dustpan dredge *William M. Black* is one of a handful of steam-powered side-wheelers in the United States and one of only four surviving unmodified historic U.S. Army Corps of Engineers river dredges. Dredges deepened and redirected the western rivers, fought levee failures to prevent floods, and allowed the spread of navigation to regions previously inaccessible. The *Black* was built by the Marietta Manufacturing Company of Point Pleasant, West Virginia, for the Corps of Engineers following unsuccessful attempts to use the inland waters for shipping wartime supplies during World War I. It was one of a pair of 34-inch pipeline dredges built at the same time for service on the Missouri River (the other was the *William S. Mitchell*) and one of four boats used to complete the navigable channel on the Missouri River.

Dredges, designed to improve navigation, consist of a hull supporting some sort of excavating equipment. Many are self-propelled for easier movement. The most common type today is the suction dredge, which moves large amounts of sediment using streams of water and an enormous suction pump. The sediment is removed to deepen rivers, remove shoals, or cut new channels. Dredges can also be used to

■ **William M. Black**
Port of Dubuque River Museums
2nd Street at Ice Harbor
1934

improve levees or close dangerous breaches in them. The *Black* is commonly referred to as a dustpan dredge, because the shape of the suction head is similar to a common dustpan. The Army Corps of Engineers developed this design and adapted it to the dredging conditions of inland rivers.

Decommissioned in 1973, after 37 years of service on the Missouri River, the *Black*, almost unchanged from its original appearance and condition, is now a floating exhibit at the Port of Dubuque River Museum. The museum and dredge interpret the history and development of the western rivers and the role of the Corps of Engineers. NR. [Dubuque County Historical Society]

The dustpan dredge *William M. Black*, built to improve inland waterways for shipping wartime supplies during World War I.

KEOKUK

■ **Geo. M. Verity**
Keokuk River Museum
Victory Park
1927

Used to move barges on all the navigable waters of the western rivers, towboats have been an important component of the American transportation system since the 1850s. Few examples of paddle wheel-propelled vessels remain in the United States, and the *Geo. M. Verity* is one of only three steam-powered towboats extant in the country.

River transportation declined after the Civil War and nearly disappeared during World War I. Built as the SS *Thorpe* by the Dubuque Boat and Boiler Works of Dubuque, Iowa, the *Verity* and its three sisters, using modern equipment and management methods, reopened barge freight service on the upper Mississippi. The *Thorpe* helped expand service capabilities by pushing larger tows than had been previously possible. In 1929 the vessel was the first to push upriver eight barges loaded with the equivalent of 200 railroad boxcars of freight. The *Thorpe* at first operated between Dubuque and Minneapolis, later traveling to St. Louis and even to New Orleans. The service was so successful that private investors copied its methods and equipment, thus building a huge new industry.

By the late 1930s changes in technology made the *Thorpe* relatively expensive to run. The vessel began a second career in 1940, when the American Rolling Mill Company (ARMCO) bought it and renamed it for George M. Verity, the company's founder and first president. ARMCO was able to operate the boat cheaply because coal, which it burned, was to be its chief cargo. The *Verity* towed barges loaded with coal and scrap iron on the Ohio and Mississippi rivers and several tributaries. The transportation of raw materials and finished products was a vital function to the American steel industry and, because of the importance of steel to American industrial expansion, to the growth and well-being of the entire economy. In 1960 ARMCO discontinued river operations in favor of railroads and sold the *Verity* to the city of Keokuk for one dollar. The boat was placed in a dry-berth exhibit on the Upper Mississippi riverfront in 1961. NR. NHL. [Keokuk River Museum]

Placed in a dry-berth exhibit in 1961, the *Geo. M. Verity* is a steam-powered towboat.

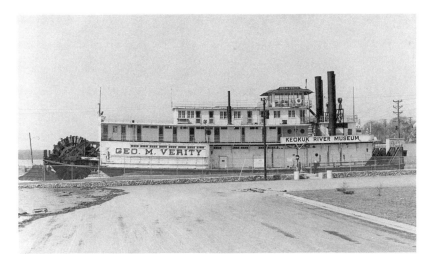

LE CLAIRE

In 1868 Sam Mitchell of Lyons, Iowa, built a small stern-wheel packet designed to provide the versatility needed in the postwar business slump. He called the boat the *Lone Star* and ran it as a short-trade packet between Davenport and Buffalo, Iowa. After its second season on the river the *Lone Star* was taken out of the packet business and was used for towing log rafts along with general river passenger and towing duties for six years. Mitchell sold the boat in 1876 to Goss and Company of Davenport, which converted it into a regular towboat for dredging sand from the river bottom. The *Lone Star* towed a digger and a sand barge between sand deposits and the company yard at Davenport.

In 1890 Goss and Company had the boat enlarged and rebuilt at Rock Island, Illinois, to better serve the company's purposes. The sand pump required more space in the engine

■ **Lone Star**
Buffalo Bill Museum
201 River Drive North
1868

The *Lone Star* is the sole remaining example of a wood-hulled steam towboat, a vessel type that played an important part in the westward expansion of the United States.

room and additional length for it to be mounted. This type of rebuilding provides owners with the chance to have a vessel redocumented and allows less expensive insurance rates as well as longer periods between time-consuming safety in spections. Goss and Company took advantage of the rebuilding to obtain a new enrollment.

The *Lone Star* was the first boat through the Illinois and Mississippi Canal, which joined the Mississippi River at Rock Island with the Illinois River at Hennepin. Goss and Company became Builder's Sand and Gravel about 1900 and continued to operate the *Lone Star* in the sand business. When the boat hull wore out and required rebuilding, the company once more took advantage of the chance to enlarge the boat. The owners again reenrolled the *Lone Star*, received a new official number, and changed its home port to Chicago. The rebuilding allowed the *Lone Star* to operate until 1956 without much repair work. That year the hull was replanked and the boat was reconditioned for continued work. In 1968, when the steamboat failed a U.S. Coast Guard safety inspection, the head of Builder's Sand and Gravel sought a home that would preserve and display it. The LeClaire Businessmen's Association, of LeClaire, Iowa, bought the *Lone Star*, moved it to its new home under its own power, and placed it in a dry berth on the LeClaire waterfront.

The *Lone Star* is the sole remaining example of a wood-hulled steam towboat, a vessel type that played an important part in the westward expansion of the United States and was used on all the western rivers. Although enlarged, the *Lone Star* retains much of its original fabric; its appearance depicts the vessel's appearance after its last major rebuilding in 1922. The *Lone Star* is the oldest of three remaining western rivers steam towboats. NR. NHL. [Buffalo Bill Museum of Le Claire]

SIOUX CITY

■ **Sergeant Floyd**
Chris Larsen Park
Adjacent to the Missouri River
Off Hamilton Boulevard, exit
from Interstate 29
1932

The *Sergeant Floyd* is one of only a handful of surviving U.S. Army Corps of Engineers vessels dating from the 1920s and built to control the nation's inland waterways. One of only two remaining army inspection boats and the only one originally built specifically for that purpose, although later used as a towboat, the *Floyd* is one of the best preserved examples of a nearly vanished form of American transportation that aided the development of the entire Midwest.

The passage of the Flood Control Act of 1928 was part of a comprehensive plan by the federal government to control flooding and improve navigation on the Mississippi and Missouri rivers. Following authorization for work on the Mississippi River's upper tributaries, the U.S. Army Corps of Engineers expanded its fleet of dredges and other vessels. Among the new boats was the *Sergeant Floyd*, which was built at a cost of $131,970 by Howard Shipyards, in Jeffersonville, Indiana. Launched on May 31, 1932, the boat was named for Sgt. Charles Floyd, the only member of the Lewis and Clark expedition to die during the expedition.

In August 1932 the *Sergeant Floyd* was delivered to the Corps of Engineers' Kansas City district, which operated it on the Missouri and occasionally on the Mississippi River. The *Sergeant Floyd* was used as a workhorse of the district, moving men, equipment, and supplies up and down the river, marking navigable channels, assisting in dredging and flood control work, doing some towing, and making inspection voyages. The *Floyd* continued work in the Kansas City district until 1975, when, on the verge of being retired, Congress authorized it to be remodeled as a portable Army Corps of Engineers museum for the U.S. bicentennial. Following a $300,000 conversion the *Floyd* traveled the Mississippi and Missouri rivers with exhibits depicting the wide range of Corps of Engineers activities in the United States and at the Panama Canal. During this tour the boat was visited by more than 550,000 people in 250 communities along more than 20,000 miles of America's inland waterways.

After its tour ended in December 1976 the *Sergeant Floyd* was berthed along the levee on the waterfront of St. Louis, Missouri, where it continued to operate as a corps museum. In 1982 its title was transferred to the city of Sioux City, Missouri. The *Floyd* was brought ashore in November 1983, and its restoration as a dry-berth exhibit was completed in 1989. NR. NHL. [City of Sioux City]

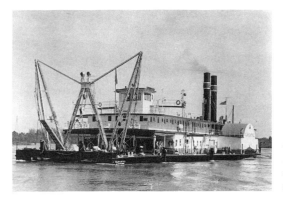

A sister ship to the *William M. Black*, the *William S. Mitchell* is also a dustpan dredge.

■ ■ ■ ■ ■ ■ ■   KANSAS   ■ ■ ■ ■ ■ ■ ■

KANSAS CITY

Built along with its sister ship, the *William M. Black*, at the Marietta Manufacturing Company in Mount Pleasant, West Virginia, the *William S. Mitchell* is a dustpan suction dredge designed specifically to create and maintain the widths and depths of the Missouri River, providing the desired navigation channel dimensions and facilitating the passage of commercial barges. The *Mitchell*'s superstructure is wood with a steel framework, and the hull is steel. Its large side wheels were propelled by high-pressure, in-line compound, reciprocating steam engines. An inverted, direct-acting, triple-expansion reciprocating steam engine powered the main dredge pump. In its time the *Mitchell* could move 80,000 cubic feet in 24 hours.

The need for dredging decreased in the mid-1960s, and by 1973 the *Mitchell* alone maintained the Missouri River. In 1979 the boat was retired to the U.S. Army Corps of Engineers' harbor in Gasconade, Missouri, where infrequent dredging took place until 1981. Still undergoing stabilization, the *Mitchell* is moored 100 yards from the confluence

■ **William S. Mitchell**
River City USA
One River City Drive
1934

of the Kansas and Missouri rivers, where it serves as a floating exhibit interpreting the history of the Missouri River and the role of the Corps of Engineers in its development. In 1990 it hosted 4,000 schoolchildren as part of its education program. NR. [Kaw Point Historical Association]

■ ■ ■ ■ ■ ■ ■ KENTUCKY ■ ■ ■ ■ ■ ■ ■

COVINGTON

■ **Mike Fink**
End of Greenup Street
1936

Brightly lighted at night and easily seen by day because of its bright red superstructure, the stern-wheel towboat *John W. Hubbard* is now the *Mike Fink*, a restaurant ship permanently moored on the Covington riverfront. It offers a stunning view of the Cincinnati skyline on the opposite bank of the Ohio River. Built in 1936 by the Dravo Corporation of Pittsburgh, the *Hubbard* was built for the Campbell Transportation Company (later the Mississippi Valley Barge Line) to push barges full of coal upriver from Huntington, West Virginia, to Cincinnati. Sold in 1947 to the Ohio River Company, the towboat was renamed the *Charles Dorrance* but continued in the same trade. Sold in 1957 to the Point Towing Company of Point Pleasant, West Virginia, the towboat was stripped of its machinery and boilers and used as a harbor boat. In 1959 the boat was acquired by John L. Beatty, who converted the superstructure into a restaurant that he named after the legendary riverman, Mike Fink. Since then the restaurant, which lies close to the National Historic Landmark Covington-Cincinnati Suspension Bridge, has been part of Covington's historic riverside district. NR. [Mike Fink, Inc.]

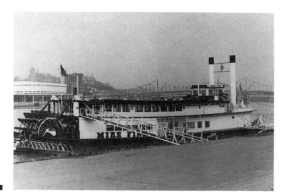

A typical example of a 20th-century stern-wheel river towboat, the *Mike Fink*, the former *John W. Hubbard*, was remodeled in 1960 to become a restaurant.

LOUISVILLE

■ **Belle of Louisville**
Fourth Street and River Road
1914

The *Belle of Louisville*, which operates on the Ohio River, is one of only two stern-wheel river passenger steamboats and is the sole remaining western rivers day packet boat. Such boats performed a variety of tasks to earn a livelihood. When built in 1914 as the *Idlewild*, it served primarily as a ferry between Memphis, Tennessee, and Hopefield Point, Arkansas. The ferry business at Memphis ended when a bridge joined the shores the *Idlewild* served. Sold to the Tri-State Ferry Company of Cairo, Illinois, the boat was again used chiefly for ferry service and some excursion business. Sold

again, it ran mainly on the Ohio, carrying excursion parties and occasional produce and, when not employed in excursion work, towing barges. The vessel's versatility helped it survive the hard times of the 1930s. World War II brought more towing jobs providing badly needed oil in barges to various points on the Ohio and Mississippi rivers.

Sold in 1947 and renamed the *Avalon,* the vessel sought excursion business on the western rivers system. Improvements and modifications to make the vessel more attractive to passengers allowed it to operate into the late 1950s. Sold at auction in 1962, the *Avalon* was reconditioned and rechristened the *Belle of Louisville* before a crowd of 3,000. Today the *Belle of Louisville* works as a goodwill ambassador for the city of Louisville, carrying excursion charters and educational and promotional tour groups on the Ohio River. Annually the *Belle* races the steamboat *Delta Queen* during the celebrations surrounding the Kentucky Derby. NR. NHL. [Belle of Louisville Operating Board]

The *Belle of Louisville* works as a goodwill ambassador for the city of Louisville, carrying excursion charters and educational and promotional tour groups on the Ohio River.

The U.S. Life-Saving Service was established in 1848 to rescue and provide aid to shipwrecked mariners by constructing lifesaving stations near dangerous waters. The first such station on the western rivers was established at Louisville, Kentucky, in 1881, to guard the treacherous falls of the Ohio River. Frequent fluctuations in the level of the river made it advisable to use a floating struction for the station. The U.S. Coast Guard Lifesaving Station *No. 10* was the third vessel to serve at this location. Built at Dubuque, Iowa, in 1928, it served the Louisville station from 1929 until 1972 when the station was closed. The floating station was equipped with two lifesaving skiffs, a six-oar surf boat, and a motorized utility boat. The skiffs were used on protected waters for missions requiring only a few crew members, while the two powered boats were used to assist the larger vessels. The Louisville station also assisted in enforcing prohibition by transporting prohibition agents to remote islands in the Ohio River to search and destroy illicit alcohol distilleries.

From 1881 to 1936 the station was located at the end of Second Street but construction of the George Rogers Clarke

■ **Mayor Andrew Broaddus**
41 River Street
End of Fourth Street
1929

Memorial Bridge made the station's relocation necessary, and in 1936 the moorings were moved downriver to the end of Fourth Street. During the 1960s and 1970s the requirements for coast guard assistance in search-and-rescue activities diminished yearly. Because of severe cuts in operating budgets, the Louisville station was put on a reduced personnel and boat allowance in 1971 and closed in 1972. Once

Decorated for Christmas, the lifesaving station *No. 10*, now the *Mayor Andrew Broaddus*, serves as the backdrop for a crew inspection in 1941.

inactive, the station was transferred to the city of Louisville, renamed the *Mayor Andrew Broaddus*, and converted to serve as the offices and wharfboat for *Belle of Louisville*. The only floating lifesaving station extant and one of the few remaining floating lifesaving stations of any kind left in the United States, the *Broaddus* remains at its historical moorings on the Ohio River. NR. NHL. [Belle of Louisville Operating Board]

■ ■ ■ ■ ■ ■ ■ ■   MISSOURI   ■ ■ ■ ■ ■ ■ ■ ■

ST. CHARLES

■ **Goldenrod**
Intersection of Boonslick and
Riverside Drives
1910

Showboating was a means of bringing dramatic musical entertainment to frontier families who lived along the rivers of the Midwest. Showboats flourished during two distinct eras: the first began in the 1830s and ended with the outbreak of the Civil War; the second era began in the 1870s and continued into the 1920s. The *Goldenrod* and the *Majestic* are the two remaining examples of showboats of the latter. The *Goldenrod*, the largest and most elaborately decorated of the two, was built by the Pope Dock Company in Parkesburg, Pennsylvania, for W. R. Markle, the era's most success-

Moored on the St. Charles River, the *Goldenrod* continues in its role as a showboat.

ful showboat owner. The exterior was plain by contemporary standards, but its interior was lavishly decorated; 5,000 lights illuminated the theater, and full-length mirrors exaggerated the room's size. Gilding, friezes, red velour, draperies, and bright carpets also contributed to the illusion of opulence. The showboat, which originally seated 1,400, provided entertainment in the form of minstrel shows, vaudeville, and serious drama to hundreds of thousands of people in 15 states.

Motion pictures, increased mobility, and the Depression contributed to the decline of showboating. In 1937 the *Goldenrod* was permanently moored on the St. Louis riverfront but continued its traditional role. Sold to the city of St. Charles in 1990, it has been renovated to offer off-Broadway productions and serve as a restaurant and lounge at its mooring on the Missouri River. NR. NHL. [City of St. Charles]

The U.S. Army Corps of Engineers played a vital role in the development of the nation's inland waters as highways for maritime trade and commerce. Steam-powered dredges cut navigable channels through mud-clogged rivers and straightened their courses to enable barges to pass through what previously had been dangerous if not unnavigable waters. Most of the dredges built to work the rivers were suction dredges that vacuumed up mud loosened by jets of water. Other dredges with greater cutting power, called cutterhead dredges, were also built. Cutterhead dredges had a central "ladder" and a semispherical cutterhead with detachable blades mounted on the end. This cast-steel head, six feet four inches in diameter, rotated and cut through sediment with such force that even hardened clay and sand were loosened and sucked up the suction head. A long pipeline towed behind the dredge deposited the spoil wherever the operator desired. A typical cutterhead could cut a 250-foot-wide swath 35 feet deep, moving up to 1,200 cubic yards of spoil an hour. The *Ste. Genevieve* is the last Corps of Engineers cutterhead dredge in the United States. Constructed in 1932 by the Dravo Corporation of Pittsburgh, long a supplier of inland rivers craft and dredges, it was built for the corps's St. Louis district and worked primarily on the Mississippi for its entire 52-year career.

Retired in 1984, the "Genny" was transferred to the city of Davenport, Iowa, as a museum display vessel, arriving there in 1985. Recently transferred to St. Charles, the dredge continues to interpret the story of the Corps of Engineers' century of work taming the rivers and its now obsolete but nonetheless impressive technology. [Marine Learning Institute]

■ **Ste. Genevieve**
End of Boonslick Road near Frontier Park
1932

ST. LOUIS

During the streamlined decade, the 1930s and early 1940s, buildings, automobiles, appliances, and ships were designed with sleek, flowing lines that gave the style its name. After beginning life as the railroad transfer ferry *Albatross*, the *Admiral* was remodeled between 1937 and 1940 in the streamlined Moderne style by its new owners, Streckfus Steamers. What was then the largest excursion boat in the world, the sturdy side-wheeler accommodated 4,400 passengers. When

■ **Admiral**
North Leonore K. Sullivan Boulevard
End of Washington Avenue
1907

When rebuilt in 1940, the *Admiral* was the epitome of streamlined modernity and claimed to be the largest excursion boat ever built.

relaunched in 1940, the *Admiral* was described as a "superlatively modern" vessel "as new as tomorrow." Its rounded, smooth superstructure is aluminum-painted steel sheathing, and it was the first river steamer equipped with air conditioning. Other modern features included a 1,200-square-foot dance floor with a ceiling covered with star-shaped lights and the signs of the zodiac; bulkheads covered with laminated artificial leather, then a new product; chrome-plated railings; satinized metal; and neon lights. The *Admiral*'s day and evening excursions on the Mississippi for 40 years made it a St. Louis legend and an important part of the city's quest for a modern image that culminated in Eero Saarinen's stainless steel Gateway Arch. Laid up in 1979, the *Admiral* was converted into a permanently moored floating entertainment center near the Gateway Arch. The riverboat's gleaming aluminum-colored hull and massive bulk dominate the St. Louis riverfront. [Gateway Riverboat Cruises]

■ **USS Inaugural (AM-242)**
400 North Leonore K. Sullivan Boulevard
1944

The USS *Inaugural* is one of two surviving vessels of this type of American minesweeper.

One of two surviving *Admirable*-class minesweepers, the largest and most successful class of American minesweepers, the *Inaugural* was fitted for both wire and acoustic sweeping and could double as an antisubmarine warfare platform. Minesweepers, the first ships to arrive in enemy waters, swept the area free of mines and then remained to continue sweeping after the fleet arrived. The *Admirable*-class minesweepers were also used as patrol and escort vessels. Launched from the Winslow Marine Railway and Shipbuilding Company in Winslow, Washington, the "Augie" first distinguished itself at the bloody Battle of Okinawa, where it sank or badly damaged a Japanese submarine. During its patrols off Okinawa the *Inaugural* often fired at enemy planes that were attempting to halt American ground forces by destroying their sea support. After riding out the great typhoon of December 1944, which struck the U.S. Third Fleet with devastating results, the *Inaugural* remained in the dangerous waters off Okinawa until the war's end. It then swept the seas off Japan and Korea, clearing mines for the occupation forces. By the time it returned to the United States the vessel had cleared a total of 82 mines. Decommissioned in Galveston, Texas, in September 1946, the *Inaugural*

entered the Atlantic Reserve Fleet as MSF-242. Stricken from the U.S. Navy Register in 1961, it is now displayed on the Mississippi River near the north leg of the famous St. Louis Gateway Arch as an educational museum open to the public. NR. NHL. [St. Louis Concessions]

■ ■ ■ ■ ■ ■ ■ NEBRASKA ■ ■ ■ ■ ■ ■ ■

BROWNVILLE

One of only a handful of surviving U.S. Army Corps of Engineers vessels built to control the nation's inland waters, the *Captain Meriwether Lewis* is one of the best preserved examples of an inland waters dredge and the best preserved pipe-line suction cutterhead dredge in the United States. Its unique structure was significant to river development in the 20th century. The *Lewis* did dredging and flood control work on the river to provide better navigation and flood control for the Missouri River basin. Assigned to the Kansas City district, the *Lewis* worked without interruption from 1932 to 1965. The typical work schedule for the dredge was

■ Captain Meriwether Lewis
Brownville State Recreation Area
Five miles west of Interstate 29
on Highway 136
1932

The *Captain Meriwether Lewis* worked to improve navigation along the Missouri River.

24 hours a day from April to November, five to seven days a week. Three crews totaling 50 to 65 persons were required to maintain the work schedule. Retired after 1965, the *Lewis* was laid up until 1976, when it was declared surplus and sold for one dollar to the Nebraska State Historical Society. Shifted onto its dry-berth cradle in 1979, the *Lewis* has been the home of the Museum of Missouri River History since 1981. The vessel is open to the public during the spring, summer, and fall. NR. NHL. [Meriwether Lewis Foundation]

OMAHA

The United States built 106 *Admirable*-class minesweepers, of which only the USS *Hazard* and the USS *Inaugural* survive. Built by the Winslow Marine Railway Company in Winslow, Washington, the *Hazard* was equipped to perform a full range of patrol, radar-picket, convoy escort, and antisubmarine duties in addition to clearing mines. The *Hazard* began its World War II service escorting a convoy from San Francisco to Pearl Harbor and then running with convoys to Eniwetok and Ulithi. In March 1945 the minesweeper was sent to Okinawa, where it performed antisubmarine patrol duties before sweeping the area off Kerama Retto in keeping with its slogan, "No sweep, no invasion."

■ USS Hazard (AM-240)
2497 Freedom Park
1600 Abbott Drive
1944

At the war's end the ship cleared the seas off Korea and Japan for the occupation forces. Returning to the United States in 1946, the *Hazard* was decommissioned and joined the reserve fleet. Stricken from the navy register in 1971, it was purchased by a group of Omaha businessmen and placed on public display. Painted in its original camouflage colors, the *Hazard* retains all its original equipment, with the exception of the minesweeping cable. The vessel is open to the public along with the submarine *Marlin* and an A-4 Skyhawk at Freedom Park on the Omaha waterfront. NR. NHL. [Greater Omaha Military Historical Society]

■ **USS Marlin (SST-2)**
2497 Freedom Park
1600 Abbott Drive
1953

The experimental submarine USS *Marlin* represents the U.S. Navy's continued refinement of diesel boat hulls that ultimately led to the hull forms used in the nuclear submarines of today's navy.

The U.S. Navy began a long and distinguished submarine tradition in 1898 when John P. Holland's 53-foot-long submersible, the *Holland*, was launched. From this tiny, 64-ton predecessor the navy ultimately built more than 1,000 undersea craft, culminating in the deep submergence nuclear submarine. The USS *Marlin*, built at the beginning of the age of the nuclear submarine, was in many ways a throwback to the beginning of the U.S. submarine tradition. The steel-hulled, 131-foot-long boat and its sister ship, the USS *Mackeral* (SST-1), were the smallest operational submarines built by the navy since 1911. The boat's cramped quarters accommodated two officers and 16 enlisted crew members (by comparison the nuclear *Los Angeles*–class submarines carry 127 crew members). Like its ancestors, the *Marlin* was

armed with a single torpedo tube. It also was diesel-electric powered—by 1953 a mode of propulsion about to disappear from the U.S. Navy.

The *Mackeral* and the *Marlin* were built as target submarines. Based at Key West, Florida, the *Marlin* was used to train crews on the navy's ships, planes, and helicopters as well as students at the navy's fleet sonar school who searched for the sounds of the target sub. The *Marlin* also helped train naval officers seeking to qualify on fleet ballistic missile submarines; a navy pamphlet for visitors proudly pointed to the fact that "many junior officers have received a basic working knowledge of submarine ship handling on *Marlin*."

Throughout its 25-year career the tiny submarine visited several Caribbean ports and participated in fleet exercises at Guantanamo Bay, Cuba. By the fall of 1972, however, the navy decided that the *Mackeral* and the *Marlin* were "well below the standards of a modern target submarine" and made plans to decommission the two boats. The *Marlin* made its last dive, its 3,045th, on October 27, 1972, and was decommissioned at Key West on January 1, 1973. Laid up, the tiny submarine was sent to Omaha at the request of local citizens to become a fixture of Freedom Park on the city's riverfront, where the minesweeper *Hazard* (AM-240), a Skyhawk carrier jet, and other naval artifacts are displayed. The submarine was dedicated and opened to the public in August 1974, less than two years after the navy's decision to dispose of it. The *Marlin* is a popular and well-visited attraction. NR. [Greater Omaha Military Historical Society]

■ ■ ■ ■ ■ ■   OKLAHOMA   ■ ■ ■ ■ ■ ■

MUSKOGEE

In an aggressive and active wartime career the USS *Batfish* (SS-310) set a record for the number of enemy submarines sunk and in doing so helped inspire the navy's postwar development of hunter-killer submarines. Launched from the Portsmouth Naval Shipyard into the Piscataqua River on May 5, 1943, the *Batfish* was commissioned in August. Sailing from New London, Connecticut, in October for the Pacific, it arrived at Pearl Harbor on November 19. On its first of six war patrols, in the enemy territory south of Honshu, Japan, the boat sank two Japanese ships. Subsequent patrols destroyed 12 other vessels totaling 37,080 tons of shipping. The *Batfish*'s moment of glory came during a three-day period in February 1945. On February 10 the submarine engaged a Japanese RO-class submarine off Luzon and sank it on the surface. The next day the *Batfish* sighted another enemy boat. According to the commanding officer, "Just as we were preparing to fire, the target dived. To avoid becoming a target ourselves, we ran until we heard him blowing his tanks.... We fired four torpedoes and the first three hit. There were continuous explosions for 15 minutes." The *Batfish*'s war duty ended on a seventh patrol off Japan to rescue downed American flyers.

■ **USS Batfish (SS-310)**
Muskogee War Memorial Park
One Port Place
Off the Muskogee Turnpike near
its intersection with U.S. 62
1943

Arriving at San Francisco in September 1946, the *Batfish* was decommissioned and held in reserve. Reactivated in 1952, the famous fleet boat sailed to Key West, Florida, to serve as a training submarine. Decommissioned again in 1957 and laid up at Charleston, South Carolina, the *Batfish* was hauled to New Orleans for use as a moored naval reserve training vessel until stricken from the U.S. Navy Register in 1969. Slated for disposal, perhaps by scrapping, the submarine was acquired by Oklahoma citizens and submarine veterans and hauled up the Arkansas River in 1971. Hauled ashore and opened to the public after confronting numerous political, financial, and operational problems, the *Batfish* is open to the public from May through October at Muskogee's War Memorial Park on the shores of the Arkansas River. [Muskogee War Memorial Park]

GREAT LAKES

The former flagship of the Cleveland Cliffs Steamship Company, the *William G. Mather* is one of the last surviving Great Lakes steam freighters.

CHICAGO

■ **U-505**
Museum of Science and Industry
57th Street and Lakeshore Drive
1941

The German submarine *U-505*, a World War II prize, was the first foreign warship captured on the high seas by the U.S. Navy since 1815. Damaged, boarded, and captured off Cape Blanco in French West Africa, the *U-505* was brought to the United States. Fleet Adm. Ernest J. King called this the "most unique and dramatic incident" of the U.S. antisubmarine war in the Atlantic. The *U-505*'s keel had been laid down at the Deutsches Werft Shipyards in Hamburg, Germany, on June 2, 1940. The future sea raider, given hull number 295, was

The German submarine *U-505*, captured during the antisubmarine war in the Atlantic, is now a permanent war memorial.

built as one of 156 Type IX C submarines. On its sixth war patrol the *U-505*, bound for Freetown, Sierra Leone, was tracked and captured by a U.S. Navy hunter-killer task group made up of the escort carrier USS *Guadalcanal* and the destroyer escorts USS *Chatelain*, *Flaherty*, *Pope*, and *Pillsbury*. On June 19, 1944, the task group arrived at Bermuda with their prize, the only Type IX captured by the Allies. The crew of the *U-505* was imprisoned there in a special camp, and all personnel of the task force were sworn to secrecy so that no news of the capture would leak out. The task group was awarded a Presidential Unit Citation for the meritorious conduct in the capture of the *U-505*, but the award remained classified until after the war.

The capture of the *U-505* yielded considerable information about the technology used in building U-boats as well as valuable intelligence information about German equipment and codes. Most important in the capture were the full set of charts and code books, an "Enigma" coding machine with extra parts, and copies of messages showing code groups on one side and deciphered copy on the other. This material provided a valuable check on earlier gathered intelligence and allowed the Allies to read coded German messages with confidence. While Allied technical experts in Bermuda and the United States studied the *U-505*, it was put in condition to operate under its own power. While not commissioned as a U.S. Navy vessel, it was operated as part of the Special Submarine Group at the submarine base in New London, Connecticut. When Germany surrendered, the *U-505* was taken on a tour of the Atlantic and Gulf coasts by an American crew to promote the selling of war bonds. Following the surrender of Japan, it was tied up at the Portsmouth Naval Shipyard and left there for nine years.

The Museum of Science and Industry in Chicago had been seeking a submarine for exhibit since 1926 and in 1948 began efforts to acquire the *U-505*. Considerable popular support led to congressional approval of the transfer. The submarine was made seaworthy and towed through the St. Lawrence River, Welland Canal, and the Great Lakes to Chicago in May and June 1954. On August 13, 1954, it was gently slid ashore, and on September 3, 1954, it was moved into its present position as a dry-berth exhibit outside the museum. During a ceremony on September 25, 1954, Adm. William H. ("Bull") Halsey gave the principal address dedicating the *U-505* to the 55,000 Americans who had lost their lives at sea in World War II. NR. NHL. [Museum of Science and Industry]

■ ■ ■ ■ ■ ■ ■ INDIANA ■ ■ ■ ■ ■ ■ ■

HAMMOND

The oldest American passenger steamship on the Great Lakes, the *Milwaukee Clipper* was built as the *Juniata* by the American Shipbuilding Company to carry passengers and freight for the Anchor Line of the Erie and Western Transportation Company, a subsidiary of the Pennsylvania Railroad. In 1940 new stringent rules of the Bureau of Marine Inspection and Navigation led to the vessel's being sold and rebuilt as the *Clipper*. Reconstructed to surpass not only safety rules but also standards of accommodation, the *Clipper* followed the "air-flow" streamlining of the Art Moderne style as did many trains, planes, and automobiles of the machine age. The entire ship, including the interior design and the aluminum furniture, reflected the new aesthetic. Many design elements introduced in the *Clipper* are still being included in modern ocean-going passenger ships.

The rebuilt *Milwaukee Clipper* served the route between Milwaukee, Wisconsin, and Muskegon, Michigan, from 1941 to 1970, carrying only automobiles as cargo. Contracts with

■ **Milwaukee Clipper**
East side of Hammond Marina
Off Lake Shore Drive
1904

Reconstructed in 1940 to surpass new safety rules and standards of accommodation and given a new appearance in the streamlined Art Moderne style, the *Milwaukee Clipper* served the route between Milwaukee, Wisconsin, and Muskegon, Michigan, from 1941 to 1970.

auto manufacturers to transport new cars during the winter months allowed the ship to operate at a profit without a full passenger load after most all-passenger vessels were forced into retirement. A number of new services were offered to passengers, including a casino, a 120-seat movie theater, a "marine lounge," a "harem lounge," and a children's nursery. Recently saved from being scrapped by the Port Authority of Hammond, Indiana, the vessel will be restored as a floating exhibit on Lake Michigan, opening to the public in 1993. In addition to exhibits interpreting the vessel, the *Clipper* will feature boutiques, a theater, dining in the former eating areas, dancing in the former dancehall, and bed-and-breakfast accommodations. The quadruple-expansion steam engine installed in 1905 is one of the few surviving examples of this important engine type. NR. NHL. [Hammond Port Authority]

■ ■ ■ ■ ■ ■ ■   **MICHIGAN**   ■ ■ ■ ■ ■ ■ ■

DETROIT

■ **Columbia**
■ **Ste. Claire**
Foot of Park Street
1902 and 1911

The *Columbia* represents the typical propeller-driven excursion steamer of the turn of the century.

The steamers *Columbia* and *Ste. Claire* are the last remaining classic excursion steamers designed by Frank E. Kirby, a noted naval architect. They are the last operating representatives of the typical propeller-driven excursion steamer of the turn of the century, a type once found in many parts of the country. The *Columbia* was built by the Detroit Shipbuilding Company of Wyandotte, Michigan, in 1902, and the *Ste. Claire* by the Toledo Shipbuilding Company of Toledo, Ohio, in 1911, both for the Detroit, Belle Isle, and Windsor Ferry Company. Both served Bois Blanc Island, a picnic and park area located near the mouth of the Detroit River in Canadian waters, popularly called "Boblo" because visitors were unable to pronounce Bois Blanc. Largely unaltered, both the *Columbia* and the *Ste. Claire* continue to travel between Canada and the United States, carrying visitors to the Boblo Island Amusement Park. NR. [International Shipping Company]

The oldest surviving railcar ferry in the United States, the *Lansdowne* is now a floating restaurant on the banks of the St. Claire River on the Detroit waterfront. Designed by Frank E. Kirby, the "father" of the Great Lakes car ferries, the *Lansdowne* was Kirby's first vessel of this type. Constructed at Detroit Dry Dock for the Grand Trunk Railroad, the iron-hulled ferry was launched on May 11, 1884. The ferry inherited the massive horizontal low-pressure steam engines of a predecessor, the *Michigan I* (1873). Although built in the United States, the ferry was registered in Canada. The *Lansdowne*, named for the Marquis of Lansdowne, then the governor-general of Canada, entered service in November 1884 and quickly established an excellent reputation as "a first class ice boat" in its rapid crossings of the frozen St. Claire. Two lines of track running fore and aft allowed the ferry to load railcars from the bow. The *Lansdowne* was damaged early in its career. Just after midnight on August 6, 1899, the steam barge *W. B. Morley*, proceeding upriver, rammed the *Lansdowne*, then crossing with 18 cars. The collision tore holes in both vessels and knocked cars off the tracks. The *Morley* sank off Detroit; the *Lansdowne* made it back to its slip at Windsor, on the Canadian side, but sank at its moorings at 3 a.m. Raised and repaired, it continued in service with the ferries *Great Western* and *Huron*. By 1906 the three carried an average of 540 railcars per day across the St. Claire. The *Great Western* was sold in 1923, and the *Huron* was held in reserve, making the *Lansdowne* the regular boat on the run. When it was retired, it was extensively remodeled. Its superstructure was removed and replaced, and one engine was scrapped before the Lansdowne Restaurant opened in 1983. The ornately furnished restaurant, complete with box cars, is now a popular Detroit riverfront attraction. [The Lansdowne Restaurant]

■ **Lansdowne**
Lansdowne Restaurant
201 West Atwater
1884

The last remaining paddle car ferry when taken out of service, the *Lansdowne* has been extensively modified as a restaurant.

DOUGLAS

■ **Keewatin**
■ **Reiss**
Blue Star Highway
and Union Street
Just south of the
Saugatuck-Douglas Bridge
1907 and 1913

The history of these two steam-powered vessels, displayed side by side at Harbour Village, reflects in part the passing of the steam age on the Great Lakes. Like the tugboat *Edna G.* on Lake Superior at Two Harbors, the *Reiss* is an excellent example of a lakes-built steam tugboat. Constructed by the Great Lakes Towing Company at Cleveland, Ohio, in 1913, the *Reiss* was originally named the *Q. A. Gillmore*. It ended its career working for the C. Reiss Coal Company of Milwaukee, Wisconsin, when it was reportedly the last operating steam tugboat on the Great Lakes. Since its retirement, it has been displayed with the Canadian Pacific Railroad (CPRR) passenger steamer *Keewatin*.

Built in 1907 at Glasgow, Scotland, the *Keewatin* steamed to Canada and was brought to the lakes through the Welland Canal. To navigate the canal the *Keewatin* had to be cut in half and riveted back together. Entering into service between Port McNicoll and Thunder Bay in Canadian waters, the *Keewatin* was an important link in the CPRR system—in the 1880s a transportation network served by steamships as well as trains. The first CPRR steamers were a trio of Scottish-built vessels—the *Athabaska*, the *Algoma*, and the *Alberta*—which began service in 1884. The *Algoma* was wrecked off Isle Royale on Lake Superior in November 1885 and was permanently replaced by the steamer *Manitoba* in 1889. These pioneering steamships were augmented and then replaced by two larger, more modern vessels in 1907—the *Keewatin* and its sister, the *Assiniboia*. Capable of carrying 288 passengers, 34 automobiles, and package freight, the *Keewatin* and the *Assiniboia* outlasted the *Athabaska* and the *Alberta*, which were relegated to freight service and ultimately scrapped, and the *Manitoba*, which was taken out of service. In 1965 the *Keewatin* and the *Assiniboia* were retired from passenger service. The *Assiniboia* remained in service carrying package freight, but the *Keewatin* was laid up. Since purchased in 1967 by the Peterson family of Douglas for their marina, now known as Harbour Village, the vintage "Kee" has been a prominent local landmark, and, along with the *Reiss*, is open to the public for tours. The *Keewatin* is now the last example afloat of an upper Great Lakes propeller steamer, a type built in both the United States and Canada. Little altered but with its boilers removed, the *Keewatin* is an outstanding example of naval architecture and marine engineering and one of a few steamers retaining a quadruple-expansion marine steam engine. [R. J. and Diane Peterson]

ELBERTA

■ **City of Milwaukee**
Marine Terminal Railyard,
East Slip
1931

It was essential for the economic development of the upper Midwest that railroad cargoes cross the waters of the Great Lakes. At first such cargoes were reloaded onto package freighters for forwarding to lake ports, there to be loaded aboard freight cars. Barges carried loaded train cars across the calm rivers that were part of the lakes system. In 1892 a bold experiment began at South Frankfort, Michigan, to transport loaded freight cars across the open water of the Great Lakes. The effort required a specialized craft able to load 24 train cars and work on the often stormy and ice-packed lakes. The experiment, a success, began a unique American maritime enterprise—the Great Lakes ferry fleet for train cars. Eventually, 39 vessels were built for this service, which continues today. At its peak the Great Lakes Car Ferry fleet used 14 vessels to transport 14 full freight trains a day across Lake Michigan alone. As many as 26 port cities around the Great Lakes were part of this rail link. The greatest annual mileage of any ship in the world is claimed by a Great Lakes ferry.

The *City of Milwaukee* was built in 1931 by the Manitowoc Shipbuilding Company for the Grand Trunk Railroad. The vessel ran between Grand Haven and Milwaukee (and later Muskegon). With the decline of cargo as the Depression deepened, the *Milwaukee* became a spare boat and was frequently leased out to other car ferry fleets, thus establishing a historical connection to each of the Great Lakes Car Ferry

The *City of Milwaukee*, the sole surviving example of a Great Lakes car ferry of the "classic" period before 1940.

fleets. In 1947 the coal-fired boilers were converted to oil burners. The Grand Trunk Western ceased car ferry operation in 1978. The *Milwaukee* was purchased by the state of Michigan for the Ann Arbor Railroad and remained in service until 1982. It was then sold to the city of Frankfort, which later turned over ownership to a nonprofit group that wanted to establish the *Milwaukee* as a museum ship.

The *City of Milwaukee* is the sole surviving example of a pre-1940 "classic" Great Lakes car ferry. In excellent and nearly original condition with only minor changes, the vessel embodies the distinctive characteristic of these specialized craft and possesses all the historic features associated with these vessels. Used in cross-lake train-car ferry service for all its working life, the *Milwaukee* is presently docked at the Marine Terminal Railyard of the Ann Arbor Railroad, where cross-lake ferry service began nearly 100 years ago. NR. NHL. [Society for the Preservation of Steamship City of Milwaukee]

GLEN HAVEN

The *Aloha*, built at Sturgeon Bay, Wisconsin, in 1937, and one of three historic fishing tugboats preserved on the Great Lakes, was retired after a long career and donated to the National Park Service for display at Sleeping Bear Dunes National Lakeshore in Michigan. This type of tugboat is a unique regional craft built to trawl the lake waters for trout, whitehead, and other fish. Short, stocky, and stout, the wood-hulled tugboats are completely enclosed vessels, usually less

■ **Aloha**
Sleeping Bear Dunes National Lakeshore
1937

The *Aloha*, a typical
example of a Great Lakes
fishing tugboat.

than 60 feet in length, and tow gill nets. Early tugboats were
steam-powered, but most built in the 1930s were gasoline-
or diesel-powered, usually with a small diesel engine manufactured by the Kahlenberg brothers of Two Rivers, Wisconsin, an important early firm that remains in business, now
manufacturing castings, propellers, whistles, and bells. As the
nets are hauled, workers at the stern gut, head, and split the
fish. When the tugboat docks, the fish are unloaded through
large side hatches.

Placed on the shore of the historic community of Glen
Haven, the *Aloha* is exhibited next to the park's excellent
small craft museum, which includes fishing, lifesaving, and
recreational craft. Nearby is the Sleeping Bear Point Lifesaving Station and maritime museum, which interprets the history of shipping and shipwrecks on Sleeping Bear Point.
[Sleeping Bear Dunes National Lakeshore]

MUSKEGON

■ **USS Silversides (SS-236)**
USS Silversides and
Maritime Museum
1322 Ruddiman Avenue
1941

Built at the Mare Island Navy Yard in Vallejo, California, the
Gato-class USS *Silversides* was commissioned into the U.S.
Navy just eight days after Japan's attack on Pearl Harbor. A
top-ranked World War II submarine, it served the Pacific
Fleet along Japan's coasts, in the East China Sea, and through
key enemy shipping routes around the Marianas, Carolines,
Bismarck Archipelago, and along the Solomons to Guadalcanal. Its mission was to stop raw materials and supplies—
oil, bauxite, rubber, coal, food, and iron ore—from reaching
Japan. The *Silversides* completed 14 war patrols and sank 23
ships, the third highest total of enemy ships sunk by a U.S.
submarine during World War II. The *Silversides* was also
assigned special missions such as mine laying and reconnaissance and served with the Submarine Lifeguard League, rescuing two American aviators downed in air strikes over Japan.

After the armistice the *Silversides* served as a reserve training boat near Chicago until decommissioned in 1969. Scheduled for scrapping in 1972, it was saved by the Combined
Great Lakes Navy Association, which was given title to the
vessel in July 1973. Moved to Muskegon Lake in 1987, the
Silversides is being restored to its World War II appearance.
Its diesel engines and most systems are now operable. The
submarine is open to the public seasonally. NR. NHL. [USS
Silversides and Maritime Museum]

The USS *Silversides* served the
Pacific Fleet by stopping raw
materials and supplies from
reaching Japan.

PORT HURON

Known by its last station designation of "Huron," the lightship *No. 103* is the only surviving example of a lightship built specifically for service on the Great Lakes. Its hull was designed and built for the particular wave conditions of the Great Lakes; below the waterline the vessel has finer lines and is perceptibly shorter than its ocean-going sisters to match the lakes' shorter wave periods. Launched in 1920, the *No. 103* served as the relief lightship for the 12th Lighthouse District, headquartered in Milwaukee, Wisconsin, from 1921 to 1923. In 1924 it was reassigned to Grays Reef on Lake Michigan for two years. In 1927 it once again became the "Relief," serving until 1934.

In 1934–35 the *No. 103* served at North Manitou Shoal on Lake Michigan before being reassigned in 1935 as the relief lightship for the 11th Lighthouse District, headquartered in

■ **Lightship No. 103** ("**Huron**")
Pine Grove Park
1921

Detroit. In 1936 the district reassigned the *No. 103* to Lake Huron, a station the vessel would retain for 34 years until its retirement in 1970. The Lake Huron station, perhaps the most significant lightship station on the Great Lakes, was at the south end of the lake off the entrance to the St. Clair River and marked the Corsica Shoals, also known as Northwest Shoal. The shoals marked by the station are six miles north of Port Huron and were the scene of numerous groundings in the late 19th century, which led to the establishment of the station in 1893. The station guided mariners into an 11-foot-deep dredged channel through the shoals.

The last lightship to serve the Lake Huron station as well as the last lightship on the Great Lakes, the *No. 103* was replaced by a lighted buoy in 1970. Decommissioned in 1971, it was transferred to the city of Port Huron. From 1973 to 1977 the local naval reserve maintained and used the lightship for training purposes. The *No. 103*, now an outdoor exhibit, is open to the public. NR. NHL. [City of Port Huron]

The *No. 103*, the last lightship to serve the Huron station.

SAULT STE. MARIE

■ **Valley Camp**
End of Portage Street
1917

One of a handful of historic "lakers," or boats that plied the Great Lakes, preserved as historic ship exhibits in the United States, the *Valley Camp* was built at Lorain, Ohio, in 1917 as the *Louis W. Hill* for the Producers Steamship Company of Cleveland. The 550-foot-long, 7,038-ton steamship was built with a classic laker profile. The elevated forecastle is surmounted by the pilothouse, and an elevated deckhouse aft at the stern accommodates the ship's crew quarters. The long expanse of the deck is broken by 32 hatches that open into the holds, which contained varied bulk cargoes throughout the steamer's career, including grain, stone, coal, and iron ore. In a 50-year career the veteran laker hauled more than 16 million tons of cargo more than three million miles. Unlike most other lakers, the *Valley Camp* was built with longitudinal framing alone, as opposed to the more common combination of transverse and longitudinal frames. The *Valley Camp* is the sole serving U.S. example of only 15 lakers built in this fashion, known as the "Isherwood system" after its British designer, Sir Joseph Isherwood. The ship retains its original triple-expansion marine steam engine, another classic feature now missing from many other historic lakers that remain in service. Sold to the National Steel Corporation in 1936, the steamer was acquired by the Wilson Transit Company in 1955 and its name was changed to the *Valley Camp*. In 1957 the Wilson Company sold it to the Republic Steel Corporation, which used it until 1968, when the corporation retired the old laker and sold it for its scrap value to Le Sault de Sainte Marie Historical Sites. Placed in a berth on the St. Mary's River just east of the Soo Locks, the *Valley Camp* is now a museum ship; its holds are filled with exhibits and five 1,200-gallon aquariums. The *Valley Camp* is open on a seasonal basis. NR. [Le Sault de Sainte Marie Historical Sites]

The *Valley Camp* carried iron ore, coal, stone, and grain for more than 50 years in the Great Lakes merchant trade.

SOUTH HAVEN

■ **Evelyn S.**
Lake Michigan
Maritime Museum
260 Dyckman Avenue
1939

One of three historic Great Lakes fishing tugboats preserved and on display, the *Evelyn S.* is a dry-berth exhibit. Built at Sturgeon Bay, Wisconsin, in 1939, it is nearly identical to the *Aloha* (1937) and the *Buddy O.* (1936), the other two preserved fishing tugboats. The three unique craft are significant examples of regionally built, almost vernacular craft, well adapted to the conditions of their trade; they are hardy, enclosed vessels that operated on the cold, often icy waters of the five Great Lakes. Owned by the Anderson Fish Company of Frankfort, Michigan, the *Evelyn S.* is 55 feet long with a

The *Evelyn S.*, a Great Lakes fishing tugboat preserved and on display.

white oak hull sheathed in iron. On occasion it served as an ice-breaker on Betsie Bay for the ports of Frankfort and Elberta. The decline of the commercial fishing industry on the lakes began in the 1940s, when the trout population began to shrink because of an attack by lamphrey eels. Sold in 1952 and relocated to Muskegon, where it was employed as a towboat, the *Evelyn S.* was acquired by the maritime museum in 1981 and placed on display as a representative of the changing technologies and "the migratory patterns of fish and people" on the Great Lakes. [Lake Michigan Maritime Museum]

■ ■ ■ ■ ■ ■   **MINNESOTA**   ■ ■ ■ ■ ■ ■

DULUTH

In 1893 the Duluth, Mesabi, and Northern Railway built the first dock for shipping iron ore in Duluth. By 1920 the harbor had 10 modern ore docks, and Duluth had become a major link in the transcontinental transportation of iron ore, coal, and grain. From 1901 to 1930 the majority of the nation's ore

■ **William A. Irvin**
Minnesota Slip
350 Harbor Drive
1938

supply was shipped from Minnesota, with the bulk leaving on boats from Duluth. The only survivor of four bulk ore carriers built in 1938, the *William A. Irvin*, named for the president of U.S. Steel from 1932 to 1938, was the flagship of U.S. Steel's Pittsburgh steamship fleet. Its design reflected several trend-setting innovations that represented the most

The *William A. Irvin* transported iron ore and coal around the Great Lakes until it was retired in 1978.

up-to-date technological advances in freighter construction following the Depression. In addition to transporting iron ore and coal around the Great Lakes, the *Irvin* was used for seven-day round-trip vacations as a way of entertaining U.S. Steel's guests and thanking its most loyal customers. Retired as a bulk ore carrier in 1978, the *Irvin* still operates and is open seasonally for public tours. NR. [Duluth Entertainment Convention Center]

MINNEAPOLIS

■ **Minnesota Centennial Showboat**
University of Minnesota campus
Next to University Hospital
1899

One of 49 stern-wheel towboats built for the U.S. Army Corps of Engineers between 1882 and 1940, the *General John Newton* was constructed at Dubuque, Iowa, by the Iowa Iron Works in 1899. The 175-foot-long, 211-ton steel-hulled stern-wheeler was built for the corps's New Orleans district as both a survey boat and a towboat. For nearly six decades the *Newton* remained with the New Orleans district, working upriver to survey, patrol, and carry freight, mail, and passengers to corps projects. During floods, the sturdy towboat also served as a rescue vessel, transporting emergency supplies and food to stricken areas and evacuating people threatened by rising waters. Retired in 1957, the *Newton* was given by the Corps of Engineers to the University of Minnesota's theater in 1958 to serve as a floating, operating showboat under the auspices of the university theater. Starting upriver on March 6, the towboat arrived at Minneapolis on April 3, 1958, where it was converted into a showboat. Since then, it has been the scene of the university theater's annual summer productions. In 1981 the New Orleans Steamboat Company purchased the showboat's steam engines for $35,000. Twenty tons of castings were removed, lightening the vessel, which was then further modified for its showboat career. Moored along the east bank of the Mississippi River at the university, the *Minnesota Centennial Showboat* little resembles the *General John Newton* but serves as a popular and active participant in the cultural life of the Twin Cities area. [University Theater, University of Minnesota]

TWO HARBORS

■ **Edna G.**
End of Waterfront Drive
1896

The *Edna G.* is an excellent example of a late 19th-century, steel-hulled, steam-powered harbor tugboat. Built at Cleveland, Ohio, by the noted Great Lakes firm, the Cleveland Ship Building Company, for the Duluth and Iron Range Railroad Company, the tugboat was named for the daughter of J. L. Greatsinger, the retiring president of the railroad company. For more than eight decades, with a brief interruption of service during World War I, when it was sent to Norfolk, Virginia, the *Edna G.* shuttled ore carriers to and from the docks at Two Harbors, 25 miles from Duluth on Lake Superior's northern shore. Even though confined to the waters of Agate Bay, the *Edna G.* operated 24 hours a day and was a vital part of the nationally important ore trade. The boat is particularly significant, however, because it has one of the last coal-fired marine steam engines in North America: the fore-and-aft compound condensing engine, installed in 1896, was never replaced. The boilers were replaced in 1948 but remained hand fired. The eight-hour, three-man shifts that

worked the tugboat throughout the season kept the *Edna G.* in excellent condition. Laid up since 1981, when it was the last steam-powered tugboat working in the United States, the *Edna G.* has been hauled ashore for display in a concrete-and rock-lined dry berth on the shoreline of Agate Bay, close to the docks where it worked for nearly 90 years. NR. [City of Two Harbors]

The *Edna G.* operated as a tugboat transporting ore carriers to and from docks at Two Harbors, Minnesota.

WAHKON

A launch used on Mille Lacs Lake to convey passengers and boats to fishing areas inaccessible by rowboat alone, the *Ellen Ruth* is associated with Guy Hill (1880–1948), a resort operator whose activities and promotional efforts were important in developing walleye and northern pike fishing and other recreational activities. Built in 1932 by the Joseph Dingle Boatworks in St. Paul, Minnesota, the *Ellen Ruth* has recently been restored as a dry-berth exhibit. NR. [City of Wahkon Civic Association]

■ **Ellen Ruth**
Intersection of U.S. 27 and Main Street
1932

■ ■ ■ ■ ■ ■ ■ NEW YORK ■ ■ ■ ■ ■ ■ ■

BUFFALO

The oldest operating fireboat in the United States, the *Edward M. Cotter* serves both as a floating fire-pumping station, supplying water to the city's high-pressure fire lines, and as a fire-fighting and ice-breaking ally of the port of Buffalo's shipping and waterfront industry. Built as the *William S. Grattan* for the nationally important port of Buffalo, the new fireboat augmented the city's two-vessel fireboat fleet as the new Welland Canal neared completion and the city prepared to greet the world at the upcoming Pan-American International Exposition. While conforming to the national fireboat type, the boat exemplifies features adapted to its use on the frequently frozen Great Lakes. The fireboat's career has been divided between fireboat duty and ice breaking, keeping

■ **Edward M. Cotter**
Michigan and Ohio Streets
1900

Buffalo's harbor open in the winter and keeping the city's water intake free of ice.

A combatant in every major conflagration in Buffalo since the turn of the century, the *Grattan* is the only fireboat in U.S. history known to have burned. In 1928 the boat was swept by flames while fighting a fire. Rebuilt as a more powerful vessel, the fireboat returned to service in 1930. Renamed the *Firefighter* in 1953, it was renamed again in 1954 as the *Edward M. Cotter*, in memory of the president of Fire Fighters Local 282, AFL-CIO. On October 7, 1960, it became the first U.S. fireboat to cross the international line to fight a fire in Colburne, Ontario, Canada. [City of Buffalo Fire Department]

An operating fireboat on the Great Lakes, the *Edward M. Cotter* has helped combat every major conflagration in Buffalo since the turn of the century.

■ **Americana**
Foot of Main Street
1926

Built as the *Fishers Island* by the Bethlehem Ship Building Company of Wilmington, Delaware, for the Fishers Island Navigation Company, this 685-passenger steamship was used as an interstate excursion ferry between New London, Connecticut, and its namesake in New York. Requisitioned by the U.S. Army to carry soldiers between New York City and Fort Wright during World War II, the vessel was renamed the *Colonel John E. Baxter* in 1941. Taken out of service after the war, it was purchased in 1959, converted from steam to diesel power, and renamed the *Block Island*. The vessel served the run between New London, Connecticut, and Block Island, Rhode Island, until laid up in 1986. Refurbished and renamed the *Americana* in 1988, it carries passengers on excursions in and around Buffalo, New York, during the summer months. [Lake Erie Boat Cruise Corporation]

■ **USS Croaker (SSK-246)**
Buffalo and Erie County Naval and Servicemen's Park
One Naval Park Cove
1942

Built as part of the effort to assemble a major submarine force just before and after the U.S. entry into World War II, the USS *Croaker* was launched by the Electric Boat Company in Groton, Connecticut. Commissioned as hull number SS-246 in 1944, the submarine was sent into the Pacific to wage a war of attrition against Japan's merchant marine and navy. The *Croaker* made six war patrols, attacking and sinking 11 ships weighing a total of 40,000 tons—a cruiser, four tankers, two freighters, an ammunition ship, two escort craft, and a minesweeper. The *Croaker*'s war career typifies the tremendous success of the submarine war against Japan.

At the end of the war the *Croaker* returned to Groton, where it was decommissioned and placed in reserve. Recommissioned in 1951, the submarine served as a school ship out of New London, Connecticut, until March 1953. Converted

to a hunter-killer submarine at the Portsmouth Naval Shipyard, it was reclassified as SSK-246. Returning to active duty in February 1954, the submarine participated in various submarine operations until stricken from the U.S. Navy Register in 1971. Displayed for years in Groton, it was moved to Buffalo in 1988. Now restored and open for tours, the *Croaker* is part of the historic fleet at the Naval and Servicemen's Park, which includes the guided missile cruiser *Little Rock* and the destroyer *The Sullivans*. [Buffalo and Erie County Naval and Servicemen's Park]

The USS *Little Rock* was originally built as part of the *Cleveland* class, whose 29 ships constituted the largest class of U.S. World War II cruisers. Although laid down during World War II on March 6, 1943, and launched on August 27, 1944, the *Little Rock* was not commissioned until June 17, 1945, after the war ended in Europe and was moving toward its inevitable conclusion in the Pacific. The cruiser saw no World War II combat; however, it served with distinction as

Above: The USS *Croaker*, constructed as part of the effort to build a major submarine force during World War II. Below: The USS *Little Rock*, representative of the most numerous of America's wartime cruisers and later modified to be a guided missile cruiser.

■ **USS Little Rock (CLG-4)**
Buffalo and Erie County Naval and Servicemen's Park
One Naval Park Cove
1945

From 1946 to 1989, the large harbor tugboat *Nash* served the lower Great Lakes region by assisting in harbor maintenance and construction projects.

a flagship for both the Second and Sixth fleets. In 1960 it was converted to a guided missile cruiser, capable of firing 30-foot-long Talos missiles. The Talos missile, one of the nation's heaviest shipborne attack weapons, could carry a conventional or nuclear warhead and had a range of more than 70 miles. The modernized cruiser made four cruises to the Mediterranean and two in the North Atlantic. The *Little Rock* was stricken from the U.S. Navy Register in 1976 and was acquired by the city of Buffalo in 1977. The ship is now a museum vessel on display at the Naval and Servicemen's Park, the nation's only inland naval park. [Buffalo and Erie County Naval and Servicemen's Park]

■ **Nash**
1176 Niagara Street
1943

The *Nash*, originally the large harbor tugboat *Major Elisha K. Henson*, was built in 1943 by the U.S. Army Corps of Engineers and is typical of large harbor tugboats built by the army during and after 1943 to a standard plan. It is the only known essentially unmodified example of this type left in the United States and is the only known surviving army vessel associated with the D-Day landings. Towing, hitherto a minor aspect of military logistics, became an important part of moving military cargoes during World War II. In response to the massive movement of cargoes and vessels on both coasts, on the lakes, and in the war theaters, the U.S. Army built a vast fleet of tugboats, numbering several thousand, as part of a massive small-craft program. The largest vessels, of which several hundred were built, were the large harbor tugboats (LTs). These were sent to every theater of war under their own power, although the majority were pressed into service to support amphibious landing operations and invasions. In particular, army towing operations were a significant aspect of the war in northern Europe, the southwest Pacific, and Alaska.

The standard design for a 114-foot-long LT was prepared by the New York naval architectural firm of Cox and Stevens in 1943. The first tugboats built to the new standard were LTs 1, 2, 3, 4, and 5, ordered from the Jakobsen Shipyard at Oyster Bay on Long Island, New York. The LTs were quickly built and prepared for service. LT-5, christened the *Major Elisha F. Henson*, was launched on November 22, 1943, and sailed for Great Britain in February 1944 to participate in Operation Overlord, the planned Allied invasion of Hitler's Europe. On June 6, 1944, the *Henson* sailed for Normandy with two barges. Under fire the tugboat ferried supplies to the landing beaches for the next month, in the process shooting down a German fighter aircraft on June 9. After remaining in service in Great Britain throughout the war, the *Henson* returned to the United States. Many of the army's tugboats were decommissioned, sold, or scrapped by the Army Transportation Corps. The *Henson*, however, was assigned to the Buffalo district of the Corps of Engineers in May 1946 and renamed the *John F. Nash* in honor of the Buffalo district's senior engineer and chief civilian assistant from 1932 to 1941. From 1946 to 1989 the *Nash* served the lower Great Lakes region by assisting in harbor maintenance and construction projects, including the St. Lawrence Seaway in the 1950s. Retired in 1989, the tugboat has been declared excess property by the corps and, while in its custody, is currently being offered for sale or transfer by the General Services Administration. [General Services Administration]

The USS *The Sullivans*, built by the Bethlehem Steel Company of San Francisco, was first called the *Putnam*, but its name was changed to *The Sullivans* in honor of the five Sullivan brothers—George, Francis, Joseph, Madison, and Albert—who lost their lives in the Battle of the Solomon Islands when their ship, the USS *Juneau*, sank on November 13, 1942. Launched on April 4, 1943, *The Sullivans* was christened by Mrs. Thomas F. Sullivan, mother of the five men. The destroyer was commissioned at San Francisco on September 30, 1943. *The Sullivans* is an excellent example of the *Fletcher* class, the largest and most important class of U.S. destroyers in World War II.

The Sullivans served with distinction in World War II, taking part in intense combat, rescuing downed aviators, and earning nine battle stars for its service. It served in the Marshalls, the Marianas, the Carolines, the Philippines, and the Ryukyus, screening carriers during air strikes against

■ **USS The Sullivans (DD-537)**
Buffalo and Erie County
Naval and Servicemen's Park
One Naval Park Cove
1943

Named for five brothers who lost their lives in the Battle of the Solomon Islands, the USS *The Sullivans* is an excellent example of a *Fletcher*-class destroyer.

Japanese forces. Other wartime duties included bombarding enemy positions on Iwo Jima. The destroyer sortied with three aircraft carriers now preserved as historic ship exhibits in the United States—the *Intrepid*, the *Cabot*, and the *Yorktown*. The destroyer's last combat action in the war was off Okinawa, when it joined other destroyers screening carriers during the invasion of that island fortress. The destroyers fought off harrowing kamikaze attacks, but enemy planes managed to hit and badly damaged the carriers *Enterprise* and *Bunker Hill*. Sent to Mare Island Navy Yard for an overhaul, *The Sullivans* missed the war's end. Decommissioned in 1946, it was reactivated for Korean War service in 1951. During that conflict *The Sullivans* again screened carriers and bombarded shore targets. After its Korean War deployment, which earned the destroyer two more battle stars, and various other peacetime activities, it supported the U.S. marine landings at Beirut, Lebanon, in 1958. It also served with NATO forces and was part of the support fleet for Project Mercury when Alan Shepard splashed down on May 5, 1961, in the Caribbean after his successful mission as the first American in space. Other 1960s assignments included blockading Cuba during the missile crisis of October 1962 and serving as a support vessel for the emergency investigation of the loss of the nuclear submarine *Thresher* in the deep ocean in April 1963. *The Sullivans* was laid up in 1965 and remained inactive until 1977, when it was donated to the city of Buffalo, arriving there in 1978. It underwent its last restoration in 1990 and now allows public access to many of the belowdeck compartments. NR. NHL. [Buffalo and Erie County Naval and Servicemen's Park]

OSWEGO

■ **Derrick Boat No. 8**
H. Lee White Marine Museum
Oswego Port Authority
East Side Dock
1925

Currently a dry-berth exhibit, the steel-hulled, 76-foot long *Derrick Boat No. 8* is the last steam-powered canal barge referred to as a floating derrick. Its engine was built by the Ames Boiler Works of Oswego, New York, and figures prominently in the museum's exhibit on steam power. [H. Lee White Marine Museum]

■ ■ ■ ■ ■ ■ ■ ■   OHIO   ■ ■ ■ ■ ■ ■ ■ ■

CINCINNATI

Between 1831 and the 1920s more than 50 showboats carried circuses and dramatic productions to large and small towns on the rivers of America. Showboats were perhaps the most unique American adaptation of barges. They evolved to become a theater on a large scow-form barge pushed by a separate towboat. Two preserved showboats—the *Majestic* and the *Goldenrod*—presently survive; however, only the *Majestic* retains its historic interior arrangement.

The *Majestic* was built in 1923 for showman Tom J. Reynolds to replace an earlier showboat of the same name. It served along with the small diesel stern-wheel towboat named the *Attaboy* on the Mississippi and Ohio rivers, and a number of tributary rivers, including the Muskingum, Monongahela, Kanawha, Green, Big Sandy, and Tennessee. The boats wintered at Point Pleasant, West Virginia, and set out each year with the spring rise in river water levels. The Reynolds family, augmented by a few actors hired for the season, crewed both boats and performed at night. A single advance man distributed posters on shore and obtained necessary licenses the morning before the show. As the showboat approached the landing, one Reynolds daughter played the calliope. The usual stay at a town allowed only a single 2½-hour performance in the evening; the next day the boat moved on to the next town.

During World War II the *Majestic* was laid up at Point Pleasant, West Virginia, only occasionally offering small shows. After the war several colleges leased the *Majestic* for summer performance seasons. Now owned by the city of Cincinnati, the *Majestic* is used as a floating theater, providing seasonal performances to the public. NR. NHL. [City of Cincinnati]

■ **Majestic**
Public Landing at
the end of Broadway
1923

Showboats such as the *Majestic* were unique adaptations of barges that carried circuses and dramatic productions to towns along the rivers of America between the 1830s and the 1920s.

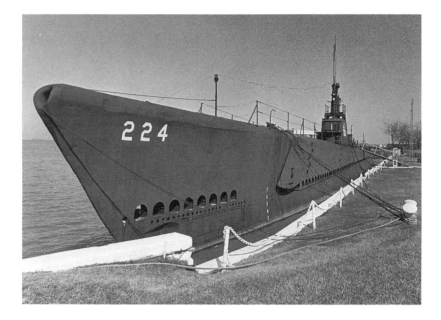

CLEVELAND

■ **USS Cod (SS-224)**
North Marginal Road
Between East 9th Street and
Burke Lakefront Airport
1943

The *Gato*-class submarine *Cod* is one of 236 fleet-type submarines built during World War II and the only one not altered to accommodate civilian visitor access. Access to the boat is by the hatches and ladders that once served the *Cod*'s crew. Launched by the Electric Boat Company of Groton, Connecticut, in March 1943, the *Cod* was commissioned on June 21. Sent to the western Pacific, it operated out of Australia and the Philippines. The submarine made seven war patrols, sinking 10 warships and 30 merchant ships and damaging seven vessels.

On its first patrol the *Cod* penetrated the South China Sea but made few contacts and launched only one attack with unobserved results. Later patrols were more successful. On its third patrol the *Cod* attacked a 32-ship convoy, sinking a destroyer and a merchant ship before being driven deep by enemy depth charges. Later, like other U.S. submarines, it patrolled the coast of Japan on "lifeguard" duty, rescuing aviators who bailed out or were shot down during the intense final aerial assault on Japan. The *Cod* also continued to attack Japanese shipping and on its sixth patrol attacked a convoy on April 24, 1945. The Japanese responded with the most severe depth-charge attack the *Cod* had received. It survived but was almost lost when the after-torpedo room caught fire; a torpedo in its tube was manually fired to save the submarine. On its final patrol, off the coast of Indochina, the *Cod* attacked and sank junks, barges, and sampans supplying cutoff Japanese forces at Singapore. The boat also came to the aid of the Dutch submarine *0-19*, which had run aground on a sandbar. Unable to tow the smaller ship to the safety of deep water, the *Cod* took its crew aboard and destroyed the Dutch ship with gunfire. The *Cod* received seven battle stars for its wartime service.

After the war the *Cod* was decommissioned in June 1946 and laid up until placed in active service during the Korean War.

It also participated in joint Canadian Fleet exercises. After operating with the Royal Canadian Navy for several years the vessel was again mothballed. In 1959 it was brought to Cleveland and served, while in reserve, as a training platform for submarine reservists. In January 1976 the boat was donated to the Cleveland Coordinating Committee for Cod and is now displayed on the Cleveland waterfront as a museum and memorial. NR. NHL. [Great Lakes Historical Society]

One of the few preserved lakers, the *William G. Mather* is an excellent example of the bulk freighters built on the Great Lakes during a shipbuilding boom that began after World War I and ended with the Depression. In that 10-year period 40 new vessels were launched from Great Lakes shipyards, among them the 8,662-ton, 600-foot-long *Mather*. Constructed in River Rouge, Michigan, at the Great Lakes Engineering Works yard, the *Mather* was named for William Gwin Mather, a prominent Cleveland mining and shipping magnate and president of the Cleveland-Cliffs Iron Company, whose subsidiary, the Cleveland-Cliffs Steamship Company, was the owner of the new steamer. The *Mather* carried iron ore to feed the needs of the American steel industry and was the flagship of Cleveland-Cliffs until 1952. It was repowered in 1954, when the original quadruple-expansion marine steam engine was replaced by a set of more efficient steam turbines; another important modification was the automation of the boiler controls in 1964, when the *Mather* was selected as the pilot ship in a U.S. Maritime Administration program to improve the efficiency of U.S. flag vessels. The *Mather* proved the worthiness of the system, and during the next five years many other companies followed suit. The declining steel industry forced the lay-up of the *Mather* in 1980. Cleveland-Cliffs gradually phased out its steamship line and sold its idle ships; by 1987 only the *Mather* remained. Awaiting probable scrapping, its aft cabins damaged by fire, the *Mather* was saved when Cleveland-Cliffs offered the freighter to the Great Lakes Historical Society. The society committed itself to retaining the ship as a floating museum on the Cleveland lakefront, and on October 8, 1988, the *Mather* returned home. The freighter has been restored and is open to the public. [Great Lakes Historical Society]

■ William G. Mather
East Ninth Street Pier
1925

GEORGETOWN

The stern-wheel river towboat *Donald B* is a working vessel on the Ohio River. Three steam-powered stern-wheel towboats exist in museums, and about 10 diesel-powered stern-wheel towboats have been converted for private recreational use, but the *Donald B* is the only known unchanged 1920s diesel stern-wheel towboat left in the United States.

The *Donald B* was built in 1923 by the Marietta Manufacturing Company of Point Pleasant, West Virginia, as the *Standard*, the first vessel on the Ohio River owned by Standard Oil of Ohio (SOHIO). The *Standard* initiated gasoline barge service to distribution points on the Ohio River, allowing economical automobile transportation in areas not

■ Donald B
3106 Old A and P Road
1923

A working vessel on the Ohio River, the *Donald B* is the only known unchanged 1920s diesel stern-wheel towboat in the United States.

reached by distribution points fed by railroads. The *Standard* delivered bulk oil products, primarily ethyl and Red Crown gasoline, to distribution terminals on the Ohio River. Its registered home port was Cincinnati, but it carried oil products from Standard's Ohio River plant at Marietta to bulk plants at New Matamoras, Clarington, Belpre, Long Bottom, Middleport, and McConnelsville. Products from these six plants were distributed by horse-drawn oil tank wagons. The river distribution system was a success, and the *Standard* was eventually joined by a fleet of 10 other towboats and more than 50 barges.

The *Standard* was built with a 60-horsepower horizontal gasoline engine (and thus used a SOHIO company product as fuel), and it drove the stern wheel using a sliding belt and chain drive. When the company added a second barge to the first, more power was needed than a gas engine could supply, so in 1930 the gasoline engine was replaced with a four-cylinder Fairbanks-Morse compression-ignition (diesel) engine capable of 100 horsepower. At the same time the drive was converted to the shaft, differential, and chain that now powers the boat.

Barge No. One, a specially fitted steel barge 96 feet long and 18 feet wide, was built to work with the *Standard*. Petroleum barges had not yet been perfected, and at first this barge used an ordinary scow-form hull with a number of cylindrical tanks, with expansion trunks atop, partially submerged in the hull. These tanks closely resembled a string of railroad tank cars set lengthwise into the middle of the barge. The tanks carried 23,000 gallons of gasoline and 4,800 gallons of refined oil. The full potential for carrying bulk fuel was realized in 1929, when the cylindrical tanks were removed from the barge, the hull was subdivided into compartments, and the entire hull interior was used for fuel cargo; in this way the hull tanks could carry about 100,000 gallons. As demand increased, another slightly longer barge was built to operate with the first. The *Standard* continued to serve the Ohio

River route into the late 1930s, carrying gasoline and oil to distribution points on the river banks. The vessel also performed emergency work of other kinds when needed. Under orders of the U.S. Army Corps of Engineers, the *Standard* carried relief supplies and medical personnel to isolated Ohio towns during the disastrous floods of 1937.

The 100-horsepower engine threw a rod through the side of the boat in 1939 at Maysville, Kentucky, and a fire lightly scorched much of the port side of the superstructure. SOHIO replaced the damaged boat with a larger, more powerful towboat, and the *Standard* was sold in 1940 to Ray Brookbank of Georgetown, Ohio, who renamed it the *Donald B* for his oldest son. Brookbank used the boat for general towing on the Ohio River and for fleeting operations near Georgetown. When Brookbank died in 1965, the boat's title went to his son Donald. The *Donald B* continues to work for the Brookbank towing firm. It has spent its entire career in general barge towing on the Ohio River and its tributaries and has been maintained in operating condition, requiring only minor modifications over time. NHL. [Brookbank River Transportation]

The *W. P. Snyder, Jr.* spent its entire career towing barges loaded with coal, iron ore, and finished steel products on the Ohio River and its tributaries.

MARIETTA

An important component of the American transportation system since the 1850s, towboats have been used to move barges on all the navigable waters of the western rivers. The *W. P. Snyder, Jr.* is one of only three steam-powered towboats and the only "pool type" boat—boats designed to pass under low bridges—remaining in the United States. It has spent its entire career towing barges loaded with coal, iron ore, and finished steel products on the Ohio River and its tributaries.

■ **W. P. Snyder, Jr.**
Ohio River Museum
601 Second Street
1918

A riveted-steel, stern-wheel–propelled towboat, the *Snyder* was built as the *W. H. Clingerman* in 1918 by James Rees and Sons of Pittsburgh for the Carnegie Steel Company. It was the first Carnegie towboat on the Ohio, Monongahela, and Mississippi rivers. The high cost of transporting coal by rail for steel-making purposes had encouraged the company to find a less expensive mode of transporting coal to its mills. Soon towboats became a vital part of America's steel industry and, because of the importance of steel in the country's industrial expansion, to the growth and well-being of the entire economy. Barges moved by towboats continue to be the most economical means of carrying such bulk cargoes. The *Clingerman* towed primarily coal barges from mines on the upper Monongahela River to the Carnegie mills in Clairton, Pennsylvania. The vessel also occasionally towed barges loaded with finished steel and made at least one trip to Memphis, Tennessee. The superstructure is wood, and the hull is supported by a hogging truss system in the traditional manner of western rivers steamboats. The boat's large stern-wheel is propelled by a cross-compound, noncondensing, reciprocating steam engine.

In 1938 the *Clingerman* was renamed *J. L. Perry*, a name the vessel kept until 1945, when it was renamed the *A-1*. The Crucible Steel Company of America bought the boat from Carnegie Steel later in 1945 and renamed it the *W. P. Snyder, Jr.*, in honor of the president of the company. With the advent of diesel towboats and their smaller crew requirements, steamboats soon were put out of business, and in 1954 the *Snyder* was laid up. In 1955 the Crucible Steel Company donated the boat to the Ohio Historical Society and the Sons and Daughters of Pioneer Rivermen. Now a museum vessel in an excellent state of preservation, the *Snyder* remains almost unchanged from its appearance and condition when built. NR. NHL. [Ohio Historical Society]

■ **Becky Thatcher**
237 Front Street
Off Interstate 77 to Pike/Green Street, exit 1
1927

A former U.S. Army Corps of Engineers stern-wheel river towboat and inspection steamboat, the *Mississippi III* is one of only a handful of surviving corps vessels built to control America's waterways and one of only two known remaining inspection boats. It was the best-known inspection steamer of the Mississippi River Commission on the western rivers. The commission was responsible for setting construction priorities and recommending levels of funding for river navigation and flood-control projects, and the *Mississippi III* carried commissioners on biannual inspection trips, at low water in the fall and high water in the spring, from St. Louis to New Orleans. Its wide-ranging travels, traditional appearance, and association with its two well-known predecessors made the vessel a favorite of river folk.

When the hull, engines, and boilers of the *Mississippi II* wore out in 1926, the old cabin was combined with a new hull and new machinery. Its entire superstructure was slid across scaffolding onto the new hull. The new boat had a broad flat bow that served to push barges when not on inspection trips. The *Mississippi III*'s dual life, as inspection steamer and towboat, took the vessel 200 miles up the upper Mississippi, over 100 miles up both the Missouri and Ohio rivers, over part of

the White River, part of the intracoastal waterway, and all of the Atchafalaya River.

A new diesel inspection boat replaced the 35-year-old *Mississippi III* in 1961, when it was decommissioned and sold. Its engines, boilers, and superstructure interiors were removed to become a floating restaurant and river museum named the *Becky Thatcher II* at St. Louis and Hannibal, Missouri. It was sold to Ohio Showboat Drama in 1975, and its main deck was converted in 1976 to a theater with a river showboat theme. The main deck continues to serve as a nonprofit community theater, while the upper decks are leased for use as a restaurant. The boat is moored on the Muskingum River, just upriver from where it enters the Ohio River at Marietta. NR. [Ohio Showboat Drama]

Now the *Becky Thatcher*, the *Mississippi III* originally was a U.S. Army Corps of Engineers' stern-wheel river towboat and inspection steamboat. Its main deck has been converted to a theater with a river showboat theme.

TOLEDO

An excellent example of an early 20th-century Great Lakes bulk freighter, the *Willis B. Boyer* was built as the *Col. James M. Schoonmaker* by the Great Lakes Engineering Works in Ecorse, Michigan. When built, the *Schoonmaker* was hailed as the largest freighter on the Great Lakes. Its capacity of 15,000 tons was a dramatic increase from previously built freighters, whose capacity ranged from 3,000 to 12,000 tons. For most of its career the *Schoonmaker* carried coal, iron ore, and other cargo from Duluth to Cleveland and various other ports for the Shenango Furnace Company. The vessel held a six-year Great Lakes cargo tonnage record before 1920. Sold to the Interlake Steamship Company in 1969, the *Schoonmaker* was renamed the *Willis B. Boyer*, in honor of the former chairman of the board. Sold again in 1971 to

■ **Willis B. Boyer**
International Park
26 Main Street
At the south end of Martin Luther King Bridge, connecting Cherry and Main Streets
1911

Below: Now a popular attraction, the *Willis B. Boyer* carried coal for most of its career. Bottom: One of the last of the *Gato*-class submarines, the USS *Cobia* sank 13 enemy vessels during World War II.

the Cleveland-Cliffs Iron Company, the *Boyer* was retired nine years later after 69 years of service. The *Boyer* was opened to the public as a floating exhibit on the Maumee River in July 1987. Concerts performed on deck bring thousands of people to the vessel and the adjoining park. During the summer the *Boyer* can be reached by shuttle boat from the portside area of Toledo's waterfront. [City of Toledo; Toledo-A-Float]

■ ■ ■ ■ ■ ■ ■   WISCONSIN   ■ ■ ■ ■ ■ ■ ■

MANITOWOC

One of the last representatives of the *Gato*-class submarines built, the USS *Cobia* was launched by the Electric Boat Company in Groton, Connecticut. Soon after its completion, the U.S. Navy switched to the newer, improved *Balao* design. During World War II the *Cobia* earned four battle stars and is credited with sinking 13 Japanese vessels totaling more than 18,000 tons and ranging from a small junk to a 7,800-ton cargo ship. Placed in the reserve fleet after the war, the *Cobia* was recommissioned from 1951 to 1954 and from 1959 to 1970 to serve as a training ship. In 1970 it was dedicated by the people of Wisconsin as an international memorial to submariners throughout the world and placed on display along the Manitowoc River at the Manitowoc Maritime Museum. Twenty-eight fleet boats were built by the Manitowoc Shipbuilding Company during the war; however, none survives unaltered. Although not built at Manitowoc, the *Cobia* is symbolic of the state's participation in winning World War II. NR. NHL. [Manitowoc Maritime Museum]

■ **USS Cobia (AGSS-245)**
Manitowoc Maritime Museum
75 Maritime Drive
1943

SUPERIOR

The U.S. Army Corps of Engineers built dozens of dredges to meet its responsibilities for harbor improvement and safe navigation during the last quarter of the 19th century and the first three decades of the 20th century. Many of these

■ **Col. D. D. Gaillard**
Barker's Island
Highway 2 or 53 from Superior
1916

dredges were large, steam-driven vessels, but a large number of small dredges was also built, including small "dipper" dredges used to excavate the harbor floors with a large iron or steel bucket that was hinged from a boom to dip down into the mud or sand, one scoop at a time. The only example of a dipper dredge preserved for public display is the tiny *Col. D. D. Gaillard*, named for David Dubose Gaillard, a career corps officer. Built in 1916 at Green Bay, Wisconsin, the *Gaillard* was an unpowered barge towed into position by tugboats. A tiny coal-fired boiler fed a steam engine that worked the dipper, which dropped the spoil into scows moored alongside. The *Gaillard* had a long career on the Great Lakes, working at the Superior Front Channel and at Detroit, Grand Marais, Marquette, and Presque Isle, Michigan, and on the St. Lawrence Seaway. Fitted with a new engine in 1933 and a new boiler in 1951, the veteran craft remained in active service until 1982, when the corps policy shifted to having work done by private contractors. After its retirement the *Gaillard* was donated to the Head of the Lakes Maritime Society; although not open to the public, it is displayed along with the society's whaleback *Meteor*. [Head of the Lakes Maritime Society]

■ **Meteor**
Barker's Island
Highway 2 or 53 from Superior
1896

The last surviving example of the whaleback carriers, the *Meteor* is a striking example of a unique type of ship designed to offer little resistance to wind and wave. Whaleback steamers were built with long, narrow steel hulls that were rounded fore and aft with tapered bows and sterns. The bottom was flat or occasionally spoon shaped, and the decks were rounded. Access to the hull was through deck-mounted turrets and watertight hatches that were sealed with tallowed rope gaskets and bolted down. The aft turret supported an elevated deckhouse that accommodated the pilothouse and crew's quarters. The engine room was beneath the aft turret, through which the ventilation and stack passed, while the forward turret contained the steam winches. The bow ended in a blunted, conoidal "snout," which gave the whaleback the more common nickname of "pigboat." Designed by Alexander McDougall of Duluth, Minnesota, the first whalebacks, a group of steel barges, were built in 1888. The first whaleback steamer, the *Colgate Hoyt*, was launched in 1890. The concept proved successful, and during the next decade nearly 50 whalebacks were built—half of them barges, half steamers. Thirty-nine whalebacks were constructed on the Great Lakes, while a few others were built on the East Coast and one was built in Great Britain. The most famous whaleback was a passenger steamer, the *Christopher Columbus*, built in 1892; other whalebacks were used to carry bulk cargoes. The design lost favor because the hull required reinforcing if it was more than 45 feet in breadth. In addition, the whalebacks could not be built large enough to accommodate the ever-increasing bulk cargoes generated by Great Lakes shipping. And the decks, constantly awash, made work dangerous, their rounded surfaces making it easy to spill both cargoes and crew. The last whalebacks were built before the end of the century, although a number of these amazingly hardy vessels persisted in

careers that lasted for several decades. In time all were victims of sinking and scrapping except the *Meteor*.

Built at Superior by the American Steel Barge Company and launched as the *Frank Rockefeller* on April 25, 1896, the whaleback *Meteor* originally carried iron ore. Sold and re-modeled in 1925 to carry sand, it was sold again in 1928 and renamed the *South Park*. Freighting grain and occasionally carrying automobiles on the deck with special rigging, the steamer was purchased by Cleveland Tankers and converted into a tanker. Renamed the *Meteor*, the veteran whaleback served on the lakes for another 26 years before being retired in 1969. Laid up for three years, the *Meteor* was donated to Superior by Cleveland Tankers in 1972. Beached on Barker's Island in Superior Harbor, within a few miles of where it was built, the last whaleback is now a popular exhibit. NR. [Head of Lakes Maritime Society]

The *Meteor* is the only surviving whaleback, the forerunner of the modern Great Lakes cargo carrier.

TWO RIVERS

Nearly identical to the 1937 fishing tugboat *Aloha*, the *Buddy O.* was a product of the same yard. Built at Sturgeon Bay, Wisconsin, for Ole Olsen of Frankfort, Michigan, the *Buddy O.* fished the waters of the Manitou Passage in consort with the fishing tugboat *Grace*. Olsen sold his catches, both fresh and smoked, at Frankfort. Later sold and moved to South Haven, Michigan, the *Buddy O.* ended its career in Wisconsin, where it was donated to the Rogers Street Fishing Village Museum. Hauled ashore, the fishing tugboat is displayed in the heart of French Side Fishing Village, a National Register historic district in Two Rivers. The *Buddy O.*, like the *Aloha* and the other preserved fishing tugboat, the *Evelyn S.*, was powered by a Kahlenberg diesel engine. The historic Kahlenberg company is located in Two Rivers, and a display of its products can be found at the Rogers Street Museum and at the nearby Manitowoc Maritime Museum. [Rogers Street Fishing Village Museum]

■ **Buddy O.**
Rogers Street Fishing Village Museum
2102 Jackson Street
1936

WEST

The *David S. Campbell*, an active fireboat on the Portland, Oregon, waterfront.

FAIRBANKS

■ **Nenana**
Alaskaland Park
Airport Road
1933

The *Nenana*, the only U.S. steamboat preserved in Alaska, is one of only five surviving western rivers steamboats. Built to be a passenger and freight packet for the Alaska Railroad, it was designed as a steamer rather than a diesel or diesel-electric boat, which could not operate as well in the harsh conditions of the Yukon River. The *Nenana*'s compound steam engines, the most efficient type that could be applied to a stern-wheeler, expanded steam twice to extract more energy from a given amount of steam. Unlike most other western rivers steamboats, the *Nenana* was built to use a condenser, which, like the compound engines, made the engine more efficient and had the added advantage of quiet operation.

The steamboat *Nenana* was built for the Alaska Railroad for service on the Yukon, Nenana, and Tanana rivers in Alaska.

Like other western rivers packets, the *Nenana* often pushed, or towed, up to six barges and could carry up to 100 tons of cargo on its main deck. The boat also had accommodations for 52 passengers who could take advantage of spacious staterooms equipped with hot and cold running water and electricity. Because airplane travel began to lure away ship passengers after World War I, tourists were sought from beyond the local region to augment low passenger revenues. Until 1941 the American Express Travel Department organized tours that included a riverboat excursion. The creation of new wood-burning stern-wheel–propelled steamboats was expected to make the older steamboats obsolete, but the *Nenana*'s cargo capacity generated revenues large enough to keep it running. From the middle of May to October 1 the *Nenana* made a 1,600-mile round trip to Marshall every two weeks, except for occasional trips beyond the Arctic Circle to Fort Yukon. The rest of the year the steamboat spent on a specially constructed platform grid high on the riverbank free of damaging ice floes.

The military buildup in Alaska during World War II kept the *Nenana* busy. It transported supplies to Galena Air Base, from which fighter aircraft were sent to the Soviet Union, and to a number of military establishments in Alaska's advance defense system. After the war ended the decline in passenger revenues, which had been arrested by the war, continued. The Alaska Railroad suspended all river passenger services after the 1949 season. At the close of the 1952 navigation season the *Nenana* was reconditioned at Whitehorse, Yukon Territory, but made only one more trip north for the Alaska Railroad. In 1954 Yutana Barge Lines, a newly formed company, leased the entire Alaska Railroad fleet and operated the *Nenana* to haul freight on rivers for one season but found it to be unprofitable.

In 1955 the *Nenana* was put up for public auction. All bids were rejected as too low until a group associated with the Chamber of Commerce formed to bring the boat to Fairbanks. This group, Greater Fairbanks Opportunities, purchased the steamboat, drove it up the Tanana and Chena rivers to Fairbanks, and opened it as a museum ship in 1957. For a time, during a severe shortage of rooms, the vessel also operated as a hotel. Weather, neglect, and souvenir hunters damaged the *Nenana* at its berth on the river, and in 1965 it was moved to a permanent protected dry berth where it could be preserved and interpreted. The *Nenana* became the centerpiece of Alaskaland, a historical park in Fairbanks. An extensive five-year program of restoration, begun by the Fairbanks Historical Preservation Foundation in 1987, is scheduled for completion in July 1992. NR. NHL. [Fairbanks North Star Borough; leased to Fairbanks Historical Preservation Foundation]

■ ■ ■ ■ ■ ■ ■   CALIFORNIA   ■ ■ ■ ■ ■ ■ ■

BURLINGAME

Built in 1922 for the U.S. Army's Quartermasters Corps at Charleston, West Virginia, the freight-supply steamer *General Frank M. Coxe* ferried troops, military passengers, mail, and supplies to the army's posts on Angel and Alcatraz islands in San Francisco Bay. The 150-foot-long, 900-ton steel vessel was a familiar sight on the bay. When the military prison on Alcatraz was closed in 1933 and the federal peni-

■ **Gen. Frank M. Coxe**
Pattaya Princess Restaurant
430 Airport Boulevard
1922

The *Gen. Frank M. Coxe* on San Francisco Bay in 1935 (below) and today stripped of its engines and bearing little resemblance to its historic appearance.

tentiary opened in 1934, the *Coxe* continued to make deliveries to the island. Retired at the end of World War II, the steamer retained its name and entered service as a harbor tour boat for the Red and White Fleet. Laid up by Red and White, the *Coxe* was converted into a floating restaurant that has shifted moorings and owners through the years. Now moored in the lee of Coyote Point near the San Francisco International Airport, the former quartermaster steamer is now the Pattaya Princess Restaurant. Stripped of its engines and extensively remodeled, with a false side wheel attached to the hull, the *Coxe* bears little resemblance to its historical appearance and scarcely reflects its rich military past. [Robert Sherman]

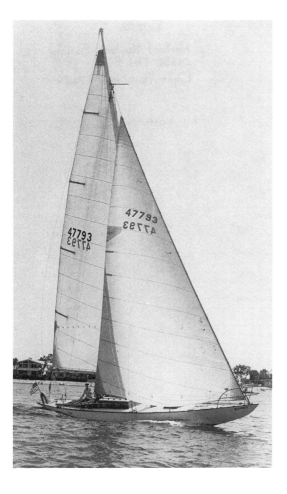

DANA POINT

The *Virginia* is an excellent example of the early 20th-century racing sloops designed by the noted naval architect William Gardner, whose work was influential in the development of American yachts. The *Virginia* is the last of Gardner's "Q-boat" yachts to survive. Constructed at the Wood and McClure shipyard on City Island, New York, the vessel was commissioned by the newspaper writer and artist Stuart Blackton of Seagate, Long Island. After a long racing career under many owners the sloop was given to the Nautical Heritage Society in 1984. The *Virginia* is used as a sail-training vessel, offering training for youths and adults in sailing, safety, navigation, and other sea-oriented activities. [Nautical Heritage Society]

■ **Virginia**
Dana Point Youth and
Group Facility
Ensenada Place
Off Dana Point Harbor Drive
1913

EUREKA

The passenger vessel *Madaket* has seen continuous service since being launched in 1910. Built as the *Nellie C.* in Fairhaven, California, the vessel was renamed in 1931 and served as a ferry in Humboldt Bay from 1910 to 1972, when it became a Humboldt cruise vessel. The Humboldt Bay Maritime Museum recently completed rebuilding the *Madaket* and relaunched it as a tour vessel on December 16, 1989. [Humboldt Bay Maritime Museum]

■ **Madaket**
Humboldt Bay
Maritime Museum
1410 Second Street
1910

LONG BEACH

■ **Queen Mary**
Pier J, Port of Long Beach
Off Long Beach Freeway,
Queen Mary exit
1936

One of the largest passenger liners built, the *Queen Mary* is the only remaining "superliner" of its vintage and size. Continuing a tradition of trans-Atlantic steam-passenger service between Britain and the United States that was nearly a century old, the *Queen Mary* set out on its maiden voyage in 1936. Designed for a regular passenger capacity of nearly 2,000, with an accompanying crew of nearly 1,200 and a cruising capacity of about 30 knots, the *Queen Mary* and the *Elizabeth I* were intended to take the place of several smaller vessels. Built by John Brown and Company in Clydebank, Scotland, for the steamship company Cunard White Line, the *Queen Mary* set a new speed record on its first voyage from Southampton to New York.

In 1939 the *Queen Mary* was stripped of its elegance and painted gray to serve as a transport vessel during World War II. As such, it logged 72 voyages, for a total of more than 569,000 miles during the war and its immediate aftermath. The *Queen Mary* carriedCommonwealth troops from Australia and India to North Africa in 1941. The next year the transport voyaged to Sydney from New York with its first American troops aboard. For the rest of the war the *Queen Mary* remained under American direction, carrying American troops to Britain for the eventual invasion of the European continent, dispatching prisoners of war to rear-area detention centers in South Africa, Australia, and the United States, transferring the wounded, conveying Winston Churchill and other military leaders to conferences, and returning troops home to America after the conclusion of the war.

The "superliner" *Queen Mary* serves as a floating exhibit and hotel along the Long Beach waterfront.

Refitted to its prewar standard, the *Queen Mary* resumed its New York–Southampton service in the summer of 1947. Because of the popularity of air travel starting in the late 1950s, travel by sea declined, and the *Queen Mary* was sold to the city of Long Beach in 1967. Made into a tourist attraction, the vessel is a floating exhibit and hotel along the Long Beach waterfront. [WCO Port Properties]

OAKLAND

Yard tugboats were designed for assisting in moving vessels and other tasks associated with shipyards. The yard tugboat *Hoga*, named after the Sioux Indian word for "fish," was built by the Consolidated Shipbuilding Corporation at Morris Heights, New York, for the U.S. Navy. The *Hoga*, a well-preserved, largely unaltered example of this once-common type of craft, is of exceptional significance in American history as the only known surviving yard craft present at Pearl Harbor during the Japanese attack on the U.S. Pacific Fleet on December 7, 1941.

The *Hoga* was moored with other yard service craft near the dry docks at 1010 Dock when Pearl Harbor was attacked by Japanese forces. With 10 of its 11-man crew aboard, the *Hoga* was underway within 10 minutes of the first strike. While not engaged in combating the enemy, the *Hoga* and other service craft performed heroic service, extinguishing fires on burning battleships and other vessels in the harbor and rescuing wounded sailors from the oily waters of Battle-

■ **City of Oakland**
FDR Memorial Pier
Jack London Square
1940

The *City of Oakland*, formerly the *Hoga*, bravely fought fires during the attack on Pearl Harbor.

ship Row. The *Hoga* distinguished itself particularly through its crew's actions in helping beach the burning, sinking USS *Nevada* at Hospital Point when its run for the open sea was aborted by Japanese bombers who intended to sink the vessel in the channel and block Pearl Harbor. Photographs of the *Nevada* show the *Hoga* off the battleship's port bow, pouring water onto the burning, partially sunken vessel. The *Hoga* also fought fires on Battleship Row for 48 hours, concentrating on the blazing hulk of the USS *Arizona*. In the weeks, months, and years following the attack the *Hoga* and its sister tugboats and support craft were worked hard assisting in the salvage, refitting, and repairing of damaged vessels and keeping Pearl Harbor active as a naval base as it expanded for a naval war in the Pacific. For its actions the *Hoga* was awarded with a meritorious citation.

Oakland, one of California's most active ports, was without municipal fireboat protection after the war until the *Hoga* arrived in 1948. Rechristened the *Port of Oakland* and later the *City of Oakland*, the vessel fought numerous shipboard fires and waterfront blazes, rescued people in the water, and served as a tour boat for President Jimmy Carter during its 42-year career as an Oakland fireboat. The decline of large wood warehouses and piers, improvements in shipboard fire control, and the crowding of the harbor with smaller pleasure craft have limited the fireboat's use, and the city of Oakland, like other major ports, is now considering a smaller, more maneuverable vessel to meet the needs of the 21st-century waterfront. Plans call for the *City of Oakland* to begin a new career as a museum vessel. NR. NHL. [Port of Oakland]

■ **Lightship WAL-605**
(**"Relief"**)
Oakland Estuary
1951

The importance of the Overfalls lightship station, established in 1898 off the south entrance to Delaware Bay, was reflected by the assignment of a modern Coast Guard–built lightship in 1951. The *WAL-605* and its sister ship the *WAL-604* were constructed at the Rice Brothers' yard at East Boothbay Harbor, Maine. The *WAL-605* served at Overfalls for the first

Now known by its last designation "Relief," the lightship *WAL-605* served the Blunts Reef station on the northern California coast from 1960 to 1969.

nine years of its career, the last lightship to be moored at that station. Following the discontinuation of the Overfalls station in 1960, the *WAL-605* was sent to the Pacific Coast to the Blunts Reef station off Cape Mendocino on the northern California coast. Serving as the "Blunts" from 1960 to 1969, the *WAL-605*, like all other Coast Guard lightships, was redesignated, becoming the *WLV-605*.

In 1969 the *WLV-605* was taken off the Blunts Reef station and assigned to be the "Relief" for all West Coast lightship stations. Whenever a lightship was pulled off a station to be overhauled, the *WLV-605* was placed in its stead. In its last years of service the lightship was stationed again at Blunts Reef as well as at the significant stations on the San Francisco and Columbia rivers. Decommissioned in 1976, the *WLV-605* was sold to the State Capital Museum Association of Olympia, Washington, for use as a floating museum ship. The museum plans proved unsuccessful, and the vessel was sold to a private owner who used it for fishing trips. Donated to the nonprofit United States Lighthouse Society in 1986, the vessel has been restored, and the society offers occasional public tours of the ship berthed on the San Francisco waterfront. NR. NHL. [U.S. Lighthouse Society]

Built in 1934 as the U.S. Coast Guard cutter *Electra*, the *Potomac* commenced its career patrolling the coast from its home port of Norfolk, Virginia, to as far north as Boston in search of rum-running vessels engaging in their illicit trade. The *Electra*'s coast guard career was short-lived, however, for in 1935 the vessel was transferred to the U.S. Navy for use as a presidential yacht. Commissioned in 1936, the USS *Potomac* (AG-25) entered into service for President Franklin Delano Roosevelt.

Roosevelt, an avid sailor and former assistant secretary of the navy, used the *Potomac* as his "floating White House"—there conducting state visits, such as that of the king and queen of Great Britain to the United States in 1939, and policy-setting meetings with his cabinet, senators, congressmen, and government officials. The *Potomac* took Roosevelt to significant meetings such as his rendezvous with Winston Churchill in 1940 to arrange the Atlantic Charter. Roosevelt also hosted one of his famous "fireside chats" from the *Potomac*'s radio room, and he frequently used the *Potomac* as a retreat, making day trips to reinfuse himself with the vigor required by the duties of his office.

■ **Potomac**
FDR Memorial Pier
66 Jack London Square
1934

Restored to its 1939 appearance as the presidential yacht for President Franklin Delano Roosevelt, the *Potomac* is a floating museum and Roosevelt memorial.

With the outbreak of World War II the *Potomac* was relegated to inland water cruises and used less and less by the president. When not in use, the *Potomac*, fitted with new sonar and hydrophone equipment, engaged in research for the naval research laboratory on Chesapeake Bay through the remainder of the war years. Following Roosevelt's death in 1945, President Harry S Truman replaced the *Potomac* with a larger vessel, the USS *Williamsburg*. The *Potomac* was decommissioned by the navy on November 18, 1945.

Sold to the state of Maryland, the *Potomac* was operated by the state's Tidewater Fisheries Commission to patrol the Chesapeake Bay, inspecting fisheries and making occasional cruises with the governor of Maryland. In 1960 the *Potomac* was sold to private owners who operated it as a passenger and freight vessel between Puerto Rico and the Virgin Islands. It then had a series of owners, including the entertainer Elvis Presley, until it ended up in San Francisco after being seized by the U.S. Customs service after a drug raid.

Laid up and partially submerged, the *Potomac* was raised by salvage divers and sold at auction to the port of Oakland. One of three surviving major vessels used as presidential yachts, the *Potomac* has been restored by the Association for the Preservation of the Presidential Yacht Potomac as a floating museum and Roosevelt memorial. It is operated on the San Francisco Bay as an educational vessel when not berthed at the FDR Memorial Pier on the Oakland Estuary. NR. NHL. [Port of Oakland]

REDWOOD CITY

■ **Warden Johnston**
Redwood City Municipal
Yacht Harbor
900 Chesapeake Drive
1945

Built at McNeil Island Federal Penitentiary by inmate shipwrights, the prison launch *Warden Johnston* is named for James Johnston, the first warden of the notorious U.S. Penitentiary at Alcatraz. The 275-ton, wood-hulled launch replaced army vessels that formerly called at the island prison, notably the quartermaster steamer *Gen. Frank M. Coxe.* The *Warden Johnston* made daily runs between the Alcatraz dock and a small pier at the foot of Van Ness Avenue, ferrying correctional officers to work, carrying to the city the wives and children of officers who lived on the island, and on occasion inmates, handcuffed and shackled for a short ride, going to court on the mainland or being transferred to the penitentiary. The *Warden Johnston* served the penitentiary until it closed in 1963. Deeded to the Sea Scouts by the government, the launch has been slightly modified for cruises. When not moored at the Redwood City yacht har-

The stern-wheel river steamboat *Delta King*, c. 1930.

bor, where it is open for tours, the *Warden Johnston* is frequently seen on the bay, occasionally calling at Alcatraz, now a unit of the National Park Service's Golden Gate National Recreation Area. [San Mateo County Council Boy Scouts]

SACRAMENTO

The stern-wheel river steamboat *Delta King*, sister of the *Delta Queen*, carried cargo and passengers between Sacramento and San Francisco until automobiles became a more popular mode of transportation. During World War II the vessel served as a hospital ship and quarters for crews handling the submarine nets guarding the entrance to San Francisco Bay. After the war the *Delta King* cruised on the Mississippi and tributary rivers as a passenger steamboat. Later sunk and raised from the San Francisco Bay, the *Delta King* was brought back to its Sacramento port and refitted as a floating attraction that includes a hotel, theater, and restaurant. NR. [River Boat Delta King]

■ **Delta King**
Old Town Sacramento
1000 Front Street
1926

SAN DIEGO

The ferry *Berkeley*, the oldest essentially unmodified passenger and car ferry in the United States, is the finest example of the three surviving propeller-driven ferries of the double-ended type, the best known American ferry type. (The other two double-ended propeller ferries are the modified *Maj. Gen. Wm. H. Hart* in New York and the dilapidated *San Mateo* in Seattle.) Of all American ferries the *Berkeley* alone

■ **Berkeley**
San Diego Maritime Museum
The Embarcadero
North Harbor Drive at Ash Street
1898

retains its original 19th-century steam system without modification and in working order, from the triple-expansion engine to the smallest fuel oil feed pumps—all the product, as was the hull, of the Union Iron Works of San Francisco, a nationally important shipbuilding and engine manufacturing firm. The *Berkeley*'s power system is an engineering landmark of now obsolete marine steam technology.

Along with the side-wheel ferry *Eureka*, the *Berkeley* exemplifies ferry service at the nationally significant port of San Francisco. It entered service on the Oakland–San Francisco run, carrying passengers across the bay in a 20-minute ride that connected San Francisco with the terminus of the transcontinental railroad at the Oakland Mole in the San Francisco Bay. The *Berkeley* operated this route until the completion of the Bay Bridge in 1939 made the operation of commuter ferries on the bay illegal. From 1939 to 1958 the *Berkeley* served as a "train boat," ferrying passengers from San Francisco to Oakland for the transcontinental railroad and meeting passengers disembarking from Southern Pacific trains at Oakland and carrying them to San Francisco. As such, the *Berkeley* became one of the last ferries to operate on San Francisco Bay.

Moored on the San Diego waterfront, the *Berkeley* serves as a floating repository for the San Diego Maritime Museum's collections. NR. NHL. [Maritime Museum Association of San Diego]

The *Berkeley* still maintains its 19th-century steam engine system, while its interior remains largely unmodified.

The smallest member of the San Diego Maritime Museum's fleet of historic vessels is the steam yacht *Medea*. Built in 1904 and launched in August, the iron-hulled, 140-foot-long steamer was a product of the yard of Alexander Stephens and Sons of Glasgow. Constructed for MacAllister Hall, the *Medea* carried him and his guests on hunting parties up the Scottish coast. A veteran of two world wars, the *Medea* made antisubmarine patrols for the French Navy during World War I, armed with a 75-millimeter gun and six depth charges and towing an observation balloon. Sold to private owners after the war, the *Medea* cruised in British and Mediterranean waters until the outbreak of World War II. Acquired by the Royal Navy, it towed a barrage balloon, a blimplike structure that served as a decoy during fleet actions, and later was assigned to the Free Norwegian Navy's submarine flotilla as a supply and accommodation vessel. Sold to private interests once again in 1946, the yacht passed through several hands. In 1971 it was sold to Paul Whittier of California, shipped to Long Beach on a container ship, and taken to British Columbia and restored. The yacht was donated to the San Diego Maritime Museum in July 1973 after steaming down under its own power. Moored alongside the ferry *Berkeley*, the *Medea* is a beautiful example of a classic steam yacht design, with teak, polished brass, and the gleaming steel of the twin-cylinder 254-horsepower compound engine. Open to the public with limited access below decks, the *Medea* occasionally operates on San Diego Bay. [Maritime Museum Association of San Diego]

■ **Medea**
San Diego Maritime Museum
The Embarcadero
North Harbor Drive at Ash Street
1904

Brought to San Diego to become a floating exhibit in 1973, the *Medea* occasionally operates on San Diego Bay.

The *Star of India*, the first square-rigger to be saved and preserved on the Pacific Coast, was built as the *Euterpe* in Ramsey, Isle of Man, Great Britain, in 1863 for Messrs. Wakefield, Nash and Company, East India merchants. Used first in the India trade, sailing from Liverpool to Calcutta on

■ **Star of India**
San Diego Maritime Museum
The Embarcadero
North Harbor Drive at Ash Street
1863

its maiden voyage, the *Euterpe* was sold in 1871 to Shaw and Savill and used by that firm for 35 years to carry immigrants and cargo from Great Britain to New Zealand and occasionally to Australia. From there, returning home, the *Euterpe* at times journeyed to the Americas. Sailing from the British Isles for the last time when it left Greenock, Scotland, on October 4, 1897, with a cargo of coal and bound for Honolulu, the *Euterpe* was sold there in 1898. It was purchased by the Pacific Colonial Ship Company of San Francisco and placed under Hawaiian registry. The Hawaiian registry was a clever ruse and one used by a number of shippers who thus replaced their older, worn-out American-built wood ships with staunch British iron and steel sailers. Foreign-built ships could not receive U.S. registries, but, anticipating the annexation of Hawaii by the United States, the shippers who bought foreign hulls registered them as Hawaiian and then received American registries after Hawaii became a U.S. territory on August 12, 1898. The Hawaiian Organic Act of 1900 granted American registry to Hawaiian ships by an act of Congress. A number of vessels became American in this fashion, among them the *Balclutha* and the *Falls of Clyde*. The *Euterpe*, once on the American registry, carried lumber from Puget Sound to Australia.

In 1901 the Alaska Packers Association of San Francisco acquired the *Euterpe* and changed its name to the *Star of India*. The association, a loose consortium of nearly 90 percent of Alaska's fish canneries, controlled between one half to three-quarters of Alaska's total salmon market each year,

A three-masted, iron-hulled vessel, the *Star of India* is the only extant Alaskan salmon vessel of its type. It was used to carry fishermen and cannery employees to the Alaskan fisheries.

producing more than a million cases. This enterprise required a large fleet of ships—as many as 30 ships each year to carry fishermen and cannery employees to and from the packers' Alaskan fisheries. The *Star of India* and the *Balclutha* are now the last surviving vessels of the association's great salmon fleet from 1891 to 1920.

Retired in 1923, the ship was purchased by James Wood Coffroth as the nucleus of a maritime museum in San Diego. The old iron ship suffered from neglect and the ignominy of having its masts cut down during the World War II by the navy to keep planes from hitting them, but after more than three decades of disrepair and abuse, it was restored in the 1960s in an effort spearheaded by Jerry MacMullen and others. By 1976 the *Star of India* once again was able to sail around the harbor in celebration of the nation's bicentennial, a feat made all the more amazing by the *Star of India*'s status as the oldest iron-hulled ship afloat. NR. NHL. [Maritime Museum Association of San Diego]

SAN FRANCISCO

The *Alma* is an excellent example of a once-common, vernacular working craft found on the major waterways of the United States from colonial times through the 20th century. Although built and operated on the San Francisco Bay, the *Alma* is in many ways indistinguishable from scows that were sailed on the Chesapeake Bay, the Gulf Coast, the Great Lakes, inland rivers, and other coastal waters of the United

■ **Alma**
San Francisco Maritime
National Historical Park
Hyde Street Pier
Hyde Street at Jefferson
1891

A scow schooner, the *Alma* represents a once-common craft found throughout the United States.

States. No scow schooner except the *Alma* is known to survive afloat in the United States.

From the time it was built until 1918 the *Alma* hauled freight under sail. It was converted to a barge and worked as such until 1926, when the vessel was refitted as an oyster dredger. By 1957 the *Alma* was the last San Francisco scow schooner in operation. That year the vessel was laid up until 1959, when it was sold once again to the California State

Division of Beaches and Parks. The *Alma*'s new owner pulled it off the mudflats and towed it to the San Francisco Maritime State Historical Park. Its dredging machinery and deckhouse were removed, and for several years it served as a floating work platform for other museum vessels. In 1964 the *Alma*'s initial restoration began and was completed in 1968, and the vessel was returned to the water. The following year the *Alma* received a new set of sails and began its program of interpreting the history of the working sail. NR. NHL. [National Park Service]

The *Balclutha* stopping in San Francisco on its maiden voyage, c. 1887.

■ Balclutha
San Francisco Maritime
National Historical Park
Hyde Street Pier
Hyde Street at Jefferson
1886

The *Balclutha* is the last square-rigged vessel afloat on San Francisco Bay and one of the only two American-owned square-riggers yet afloat on the West Coast. Built in 1886 near Glasgow, Scotland, the *Balclutha* sailed for San Francisco on its maiden voyage, leaving Cardiff with 2,650 tons of coal. In San Francisco the vessel was loaded with 59,179 centals of wheat and sailed for Fleetwood, England. In addition to the grain trade between England and California, the *Balclutha* carried other assorted cargoes, sailing to South America for nitrates and Australia for grain and to Montevideo, Calcutta, Antwerp, Rangoon, LeHavre, Cardiff, Plymouth, London, Cape Town, Naples, New Zealand, Callao, Rotterdam, Honolulu, Melbourne, and Puget Sound for various goods until 1899.

Sold in 1899, the *Balclutha* entered the lumber business, carrying lumber from Puget Sound ports to Australia and returning to San Francisco with coal from Newcastle. The vessel was given U.S. registration by a special act of Congress in 1901. In 1903 it was chartered by the Alaska Packers Association to carry fishermen and cannery crews to Karluk, Alaska. In 1904 it was wrecked at Sitkinak Island on the Alaskan coast. Purchased by the Alaska Packers Association (see p. 236), the vessel was rebuilt, renamed the *Star of Alaska*, and continued in the Alaskan salmon trade for the next three decades.

In 1925 the association bought its first steamship and began to take their sailing vessels out of service. The *Star of*

Alaska, the last, was laid up in 1930. Purchased by Frank Kissinger in 1933 and renamed the *Pacific Queen*, the vessel set sail for Los Angeles in 1934. While anchored off Catalina Island, it appeared as an extra in the motion picture *Mutiny on the Bounty*, starring Clark Gable and Charles Laughton. Beginning in 1935 the *Pacific Queen* was exhibited as a pirate ship in San Diego, and in 1939 it was towed back to San Francisco and displayed as an exhibit on Fisherman's Wharf until 1941. Laid up during the war, the *Pacific Queen* was again placed on display, this time at Long Beach.

In 1954 the *Pacific Queen* was sold to the San Francisco Maritime Museum. Its original name restored, the *Balclutha* was brought to Fisherman's Wharf and opened to the public. With the exception of a few alterations made during the course of its long career as a working vessel and as a museum ship, the *Balclutha* is essentially the same vessel that was launched in 1886. NR. NHL. [National Park Service]

The rich stands of redwood and Douglas fir along the West Coast sparked a busy lumber trade, supplying San Francisco and other growing urban coastal areas and eventually expanding to meet the lumber needs of the world. As early as the 1860s more than 300 mills operated in the redwood forests of northern California meeting a demand for building materials brought on not only by the population growth in northern and southern California, but also by fires, particularly the one that ravaged San Francisco in the aftermath of the April 1906 earthquake.

Throughout the active years of the lumber trade ships proved the least expensive and most efficient means of transporting lumber to markets. At first, ships built for purposes other than lumber transport were put to use, but by the 1870s West Coast shipyards had developed vessels to accommodate the special conditions of the coastal lumber trade. Large two- and three-masted schooners were built and rigged "bald-headed" (without topsails) to aid in driving north against prevailing winds. These schooners' simple rigs also allowed room for large deckloads of lumber and eased loading and unloading. Their shallow draft and heavily built hulls served well when crossing the wave-lashed sandbars that protected the coast's deep-water ports or when lying at anchor unprotected from the swell in numerous "dogholes"— the tiny anchorages dotting the coast where lumber was unloaded by chute or "under the wire" (timber and planks were slung by highwire from coastal cliffs down to a ship's

■ **C. A. Thayer**
San Francisco Maritime
National Historical Park
Hyde Street Pier
Hyde Street at Jefferson
1895

The *C. A. Thayer*, one of two surviving examples of the sailing schooners designed specifically for use in the 19th-century Pacific Coast lumber trade.

deck). By the 1880s the two-masted schooners of the lumber trade were giving way to larger, three-masted schooners. The *C. A. Thayer*, a product of the yard of Hans D. Bendixsen, one of the more prolific Pacific Coast shipbuilders, was built of locally available Douglas fir and launched in 1895.

The *C. A. Thayer* was named for the secretary of the E. K. Wood Lumber Company. A large three-masted schooner designed primarily for coastal work, it could carry 575,000 board feet of lumber while requiring only a small crew. An example of the most advanced economical coastal lumber carrier, the *Thayer* regularly sailed from the Hoquiam, Washington, mill of the E. K. Wood Company to its yard at San Francisco and occasionally made offshore passages to supply wood to Honolulu and Fiji.

After nearly sinking in heavy weather the *Thayer* was sold in 1912 for use as a transport for two Alaskan salmon salteries. From 1912 to 1924 it carried supplies north from San Francisco in the spring and returned the summer's pack of salmon to market in the fall. During World War I, because of the shortage of ships and consequent high freight rates, the *Thayer* made four winter voyages to Australia, twice with northwest fir and twice with Mendocina redwood. Returning, the schooner brought coal from Newcastle or copra and hardwood from Sydney. In 1925 the *Thayer* began work in the Bering Sea codfishing industry, where it remained until it was laid up in 1931. In 1942 the U.S. Army bought the decaying *Thayer* for use as a barge in British Columbia and southeastern Alaskan waters. Its masts were cut out, its stern was rebuilt, the deckhouse was removed, and the hatches were enlarged. Resold to its pre-war owner in 1946, the *Thayer* was made ready for another five voyages to the Bering Sea and its masts were replaced. When retired in 1950, the *Thayer* was the last operating commercial schooner on the Pacific Coast.

Repaired to seaworthy condition, the *Thayer* reached its new home at the San Francisco Maritime Museum under its own power in 1956. Restoration was completed in 1963. NR. NHL. [National Park Service]

■ **Eppleton Hall**
San Francisco Maritime National Historical Park
Hyde Street Pier
Hyde Street at Jefferson
1914

One of two surviving Tyne River coal tugboats, the *Eppleton Hall* retains a working "grasshopper" side-lever marine steam engine, a rare remnant of a now-vanished early 19th-century technology. The Tyne, a center of British shipbuilding and maritime activity, was once home to hundreds of steam tugboats that hauled barges loaded with coal and handled the square-riggers that sailed to river ports calling for coal. The first steam tugboat on the Tyne was named simply the *Tyne* and later renamed the *Perseverance*. Launched in 1814, it was followed by generations of wood-, iron-, and finally steel-hulled tugboats. A century later, in 1914, the South Shields yard of Hepple and Company Ltd. launched the *Eppleton Hall* into the Tyne to continue this hard-working tradition. One of the last of the Tyne coal tugboats, the "Eppie" towed coal barges for a variety of owners until 1968, when it was sold for scrap, partially gutted, and left to rest as a burned-out, rusted, water-filled hulk.

Discovered in 1969 by the San Francisco Maritime Museum Association, the *Eppleton Hall* was acquired for resto-

ration as an example of tugboats with similar engines that had worked on San Francisco's harbor during the California gold rush. In 1970 it was partially rebuilt and strengthened, but it retained many of its original fittings and, most important, the engine. The *Eppleton Hall*, now converted to diesel-burning boilers, steamed across the Atlantic in an epic voyage that lasted six months. Moored at San Francisco next to the British square-rigger *Balclutha*, the tugboat remained in operational condition for many years. Transferred to the National Park Service with the other historic ships in San Francisco, the now dilapidated *Eppleton Hall* awaits restoration once again while displayed pierside. [National Park Service]

The last of the famed British paddleboats, the *Eppleton Hall* served all its working years towing coal-laden barges on the River Tyne in Great Britain.

The last intact wood-hulled side-wheel steam ferry afloat in the continental United States and the oldest surviving San Francisco Bay ferry, the *Eureka* was built as the ferryboat *Ukiah* to serve as a combination passenger and railcar ferry running primarily between Tiburon, on the Marin peninsula north of the Golden Gate Bridge, and San Francisco. Rebuilt in 1922, the *Ukiah* was torn down to the weather deck and rebuilt as an automobile and passenger ferry. Renamed the *Eureka*, it could carry 120 automobiles and 2,300 passengers. Operating from San Francisco's ferry building and the Northwestern Pacific Railroad station in Sausalito, the *Eureka* continued to link Marin with the city well after the Golden Gate Bridge was completed. After disembarking, passengers transferred to electric intra-urban trams that whisked them to their destinations in the Marin County suburbs.

When ferry service was finally discontinued after the construction of the Bay and Golden Gate bridges, the *Eureka*

■ **Eureka**
San Francisco Maritime
National Historical Park
Hyde Street Pier
Hyde Street at Jefferson
1890

The last intact wooden-hulled side-wheel steamer afloat in the continental United States, the *Eureka* was built as a combination passenger and railcar ferry running primarily between Tiburon and San Francisco. Right: The *Eureka* houses a collection of antique automobiles dating from its years of service.

was taken over by Southern Pacific Railroad in 1941. It served the only remaining ferry route connecting San Francisco with Southern Pacific passenger trains in Oakland until that route was discontinued in 1958. Then laid up because of a snapped crank pin, the ferry was donated by Southern Pacific to the newly created San Francisco Maritime State Historical Park. The state of California restored the vessel and opened it for display in 1963. In 1977 the park was deeded to the National Park Service. The *Eureka* remains on display; on its lower deck is a collection of antique automobiles from its years of service. Its 1890 "walking beam" marine steam engine is operable and is occasionally driven by an electric motor. This engine is one of only two left in American steamers; the other is in the National Historic Landmark steamboat *Ticonderoga*. The *Eureka*'s engine is the only operating example and the only one of the two survivors left afloat in North America of this once-common mid-19th century marine engine type. NR. NHL. [National Park Service]

■ **Hercules**
San Francisco Maritime
National Historical Park
Fort Mason Center
Pier 1
Intersection of
Marina Boulevard
and Beach Street
1907

The last remaining, largely unaltered example of an early 20th-century oceangoing steam tugboat, the *Hercules* broke many towing records, beginning with its maiden voyage through the Straits of Magellan towing its sister ship, the *Goliath*. Its cargoes included logs, sailing vessels, and other large disabled ships. Built in Camden, New Jersey, the vessel worked along the West Coast; one significant job included towing the canal locks constructed in San Francisco to the site of the Panama Canal. In 1924 the *Hercules* was sold to the Western Pacific Railroad and after minor modifications was used to shuttle railroad car floats across San Francisco Bay. Its wartime duty included bringing the battleship *California* from Hawaii to San Francisco.

Retired in 1962, the *Hercules* was acquired by the California State Park Foundation for the San Francisco Maritime State Historical Park for use as a floating exhibit with occasional operation. After a careful restoration the *Hercules* again steams the waters of the San Francisco Bay. NR. NHL. [National Park Service]

The *Hercules* towing a disabled vessel early in its career and docked at Fort Mason Center today.

One of two surviving Liberty ships preserved in the United States, the *Jeremiah O'Brien* is the only unaltered example. The ship is a product of a World War II emergency ship-building program that resulted in the construction of 2,751 Liberty ships. Designed as cheap, quickly built, simple cargo steamers, the Liberty ships formed the backbone of a massive sealift of troops, arms, materiel, and ordnance to every

■ **Jeremiah O'Brien**
Fort Mason Center
Pier 3
Intersection of Marina Boulevard and Beach Street
1943

theater of war. Built rapidly, with prefabricated sections, the Liberty ships were a triumph of mass production. Based on a British design, plans for the Liberty ships were drawn up by the New York naval architectural firm of Gibbs and Cox. In early 1941 the final design was submitted to President Franklin D. Roosevelt, who approved the efficiency of the design but said he thought the ship was a "real ugly duckling." The nickname stuck.

The Liberty ship *Jeremiah O'Brien* has been preserved as a memorial to those who built, sailed, defended, repaired, and supplied Liberty ships during World War II.

The first Liberty ship, the SS *Patrick Henry*, took 245 days to build and was launched on September 27, 1941. The pace of construction picked up after the United States entered World War II, averaging two months from keel laying to sea trials. The record time, however, was eight days, set by Kaiser Industry's Richmond, California, shipyard in building the

SS *Robert E. Peary.* Eventually 18 shipyards across the United States were building the welded-steel ugly ducklings. In one of the more significant achievements of the war, large numbers of African American and women workers joined the shipyard labor force.

During the war more than 80 steamship companies operated Liberty ships crewed by merchant seamen. Armed with three- or five-inch deck guns and smaller caliber anti-aircraft guns, the Liberty ships also carried armed-guard crews from the navy or the coast guard. More than 200 Liberty ships were lost during the war, and the merchant marines suffered more casualties during the conflict than any other branch of service except the U.S. Marine Corps. After the war the Liberty ships, although designed for temporary emergency use, formed the backbone of a post-war merchant fleet that helped rebuild Europe and Asia. Although some were held in reserve for future national emergencies, many Liberty ships were sold to shipping lines. Others were recalled to military service during the Korean and Vietnam wars. By the 1970s, however, the heyday of the Liberty ship had passed.

The SS *Jeremiah O'Brien* was laid down as Maritime Commission hull number 806 at South Portland, Maine, by the New England Shipbuilding Corporation. Built in 56 days and launched on June 19, 1943, the ship was named for the first American naval hero of the Revolutionary War. The *O'Brien* made wartime voyages between the United States' and Canada's eastern shores and the United Kingdom as well as to South America, Australia, and the Philippines. From June until December 1944 it made 11 trips between the United Kingdom and Normandy in support of the D-Day invasion, including a trip from Belfast, Ireland, to Normandy with troops from General Patton's Fifth Division.

Laid up in 1946 in the National Defense Reserve Fleet on Suisun Bay in California, the *O'Brien* was set aside by the U.S. Maritime Administration in 1966 as the Liberty ship to be saved for future preservation. The National Liberty Ship

Routine maintenance aboard the *Jeremiah O'Brien.*

Memorial, a nonprofit group, was formed to restore, preserve, and operate the *Jeremiah O'Brien.* In 1949 the ship was restored to operating condition, primarily by World War II veterans of the merchant service. The vessel is displayed at the former San Francisco Port of Embarkation at Fort Mason as a museum vessel. Fort Mason is an appropriate berth, for from its piers sailed millions of tons of supplies and troops to the Pacific theater during World War II. The *O'Brien* makes an annual Seamen's Cruise each Memorial Day and has steamed on other occasions. The success of the *Jeremiah O'Brien* spurred efforts to save and restore the Liberty ship *John W. Brown* in Baltimore and the Victory ship *Lane Victory* in San Pedro. NR. NHL. ASME. [National Liberty Ship Memorial]

■ **Lewis Ark**
San Francisco Maritime National
Historical Park
Hyde Street Pier
Hyde Street at Jefferson
1905

First introduced to the waters of San Francisco Bay in the 1880s, locally built houseboats were called "arks" by their owners, who reportedly built them to conform to the shape of the "one Noah built." The owners of these floating summer cottages called themselves the "descendants of Noah." In an article in the *Strand* in 1899, Laura Starr wrote enthusiastically about the "indescribable charm of the life" aboard an ark:

> One has the pleasures of boating combined with the comforts of home; sea baths are at one's very threshold; fish are caught and cooked while you wait, in the manner that would give pleasure to any disciple of Izaak Walton.... There are neighbors, thirty or forty families of them, within easy reaching distance if one can pull a stroke, for there is always a following of rowboats resting upon the water in the wake of each ark.

Hundreds of these flat-bottomed craft once dotted San Francisco Bay, clustered at Belvedere, Berkeley, Oakland, and San Francisco's southern reaches. The *Lewis Ark*, a 50-by-20-foot barge with a single-story superstructure divided into six rooms, is surrounded by a roofed veranda. Painted white with green trim, the simple and yet ornately furnished structure was built in 1906 and was moored off Belvedere, the last haven for the arks after their decline in popularity in

The *Lewis Ark* is the last surviving example of the hundreds of "arks," or houseboats, that once dotted the backwaters of San Francisco Bay.

the first decade of the 20th century. Belvedere, an island linked by a bridge to the mainland at Tiburon, on the Marin County shore opposite San Francisco, sheltered the arks in its lee during the winter months. In the summer the bridge was raised to let the arks out. In 1939 the bridge right-of-way was filled in to make a paved causeway, trapping the last of the arks in the shallow lagoon, where many were either pulled ashore or left to rot in the water. The *Lewis Ark* was brought ashore and set up on pilings, where it remained until 1968, when it was donated to the state of California for display at Hyde Street Pier with the state's collection of historic ships. In 1979 the ark, along with the ships *C. A. Thayer*, *Eureka*, *Alma*, *Hercules*, and *Wapama*, was transferred to the National Park Service. Preserved in a dry-berth exhibit near the entrance to the San Francisco Maritime National Historical Park, the *Lewis Ark* is the last surviving example of the San Francisco Bay houseboat. NR. [National Park Service]

One of the best-restored World War II fleet boats, the *Pampanito* was built at the Portsmouth Naval Shipyard on the Piscataqua River between Maine and New Hampshire. A *Balao*-class submarine, it earned six battle stars for its World War II service in the Pacific, sinking five vessels with a total tonnage of 27,332. The *Pampanito*'s biggest day came on September 12, 1944, during its third patrol in the South China Sea. The *Pampanito* and two other submarines, the USS *Growler* and the USS *Sealion*, surprised an 11-ship Japanese convoy carrying war production materials of oil and raw rubber and sank seven vessels. Although they were not marked with a red cross, indicating the presence of prisoners, two of the transports were packed with nearly 2,200 Australian and British prisoners of war, loaded aboard at Singapore just six days earlier. Suffering from malaria and malnutrition, these weary and emaciated men were the "fit" survivors of 61,000 prisoners the Japanese had forced to build the Burma-Thailand jungle railroad, including a bridge across the River Kwai. After a year of atrocities, the prisoners were headed for Japan to serve as slave labor. On September 11 the first ships of the convoy were hit by the American submarines. As the Japanese crew abandoned the transport *Rakuyo Maru*, which took 12 hours to sink, they left 1,518 prisoners behind to fend for themselves in the open ocean. The next day, 50 miles away, the transport *Kachidoki Maru*, with 900 prisoners, was torpedoed and sank in 15 minutes. Three hundred prisoners drowned in the wreck, but another 600 made it into the water. Ultimately, the Japanese "rescued" 656 survivors from both ships and took them to Japan, where they worked—and many died—under horrible conditions until the war's end.

Four days after the sinkings, the *Pampanito*, hunting for more ships, came across scattered rafts filled with thirsty, sunburned, oil-soaked, and dying men. The submarine stopped its search for the enemy and began to pick up survivors, summoning the other submarines to come and assist. In all, 159 men from both ships were plucked from the sea, 73 by the *Pampanito*, although seven of the former prisoners died after their rescue. The pursuit of the convoy was forgotten. As one submarine commander noted, the "measure of saving one Allied life against sinking a Jap ship is one which leaves no question, once experienced."

The *Pampanito* went on to make three more patrols in the Pacific during the war before being retired from active ser-

■ **USS Pampanito**
Fisherman's Wharf
Pier 45
1943

vice. Following the war, the submarine was decommissioned until 1960, when it was assigned to naval reserve training at Mare Island. In 1976 it was acquired by the National Maritime Museum Association and in 1982 opened to the public as a floating exhibit on San Francisco's Fisherman's Wharf. NR. NHL. [National Maritime Museum Association]

SAN PEDRO

■ **Lane Victory**
Berth 52
End of Harbor Street
1945

In 1943 the Victory ship was introduced. An improved design to replace the emergency-fleet Liberty ships, the Victory ship was faster, with a more modern steam system, better trim and stability, stronger hulls, and more efficient, electrically driven winches and windlasses.

From 1943 until the end of the war the Federal Maritime Commission built 414 Victory ships and 117 Victory ship attack transports—a total of 531 ships. The Victory ships entered the war at an important juncture, ferrying supplies and troops to the European and Pacific theaters, including the climactic actions in the Pacific at Okinawa and Iwo Jima. Vital partners of the Liberty ships, the Victory ships were indispensable to the war effort. After the war many of the ships remained in service, ferrying troops home and helping rebuild ravaged Europe, the South Pacific, and Asia. Victory ships were recalled to war service during the Korean and Vietnam wars, and some were modified as support ships for the burgeoning American space program in the 1960s. Now retired from service, all but 60 Victory ships have been scrapped, with the other 59 irrevocably slated for sale or scrapping within the next 10 years. Only the SS *Lane Victory* will be saved, for this vessel, like the Liberty ship *Jeremiah O'Brien*, was singled out for preservation as the only unaltered Victory ship and the one in the best condition.

As the last Victory ship to retain the integrity of the original design and as the best representative of its class, the *Lane Victory* has been designated a memorial to the Merchant Marine veterans of World War II.

The *Lane Victory*, Maritime Commission hull number V-794, was built under contract by the California Shipbuilding Corporation of Los Angeles at Terminal Island. The ship was

named for Lane College, established at Jackson, Tennessee, in 1882 as a high school for African American youths by Isaac Lane, a bishop in the Methodist Episcopal Church. During its career the *Lane Victory* saw action at the end of the war in the Pacific, departing on its first voyage on June 27, 1945, under the auspices of the American President Lines, which was under contract to the War Shipping Administration. During the Korean War the *Lane Victory*'s moment of glory came in December 1950 during the evacuation of Korean civilians and United Nations personnel from Wonsan. As the cruiser *St. Paul* and the destroyers *Charles S. Sperry* and *Zellars* laid down a covering fire, the *Lane Victory* unloaded 3,834 troops, 1,146 vehicles, and 10,013 bulk tons of cargo, and then, on December 7, 1950, evacuated 7,009 Korean civilians, many of them women and children.

In 1970 the unmodified ship was returned to the U.S. Maritime Administration, painted, overhauled, and dry docked at the Ready Reserve Fleet on Suisun Bay, north of San Francisco. Because of the ship's excellent and unaltered condition, the Maritime Administration set it aside for preservation. The U.S. Merchant Marine Veterans of World War II, a national organization established in southern California in 1982, wanted to acquire a surplus wartime emergency cargo ship as a floating memorial and a sailing museum. After petitioning the Maritime Administration, the group was granted the *Lane Victory* on October 18, 1987. The formal conveyance took place a year later on October 18, 1988, when President Ronald Reagan signed into law H.R. 2032, authorizing the transfer of the ship to the Merchant Marine Veterans. The *Lane Victory* was readied for sea and on June 12, 1989, was towed from San Francisco to San Pedro. The ship is now berthed opposite Terminal Island, where it was built.

Now undergoing refurbishing and being made fully operational, the *Lane Victory* will serve as a floating, working museum dedicated to the maritime trades. In addition, it will be a "living ship memorial museum," passing on to succeeding generations knowledge of the heroic role of the men and women who served in the Merchant Marine NR. NHL. [U.S. Merchant Marine Veterans of World War II]

■ **Ocean Waif**
Los Angeles Maritime Museum
Berth 84
End of 6th Street
1927

A typical sailing yacht of the 1920s, the *Ocean Waif* exemplifies the recreational craft that continue to ply Los Angeles Harbor and the southern California coast. Built for racing and recreation, the vessel was constructed at the Wilmington Boat Works of Wilmington, California. Forty-two feet long, with decks made of teak and a hull made of fir, it is an operating exhibit. [Los Angeles Maritime Museum]

■ **Ralph J. Scott**
Berth 85
Adjacent to the Los Angeles
Maritime Museum
1925

The 1925 fireboat *Ralph J. Scott* is the fourth oldest fireboat remaining in the United States. Although altered and modified to continue fire fighting, the vessel basically retains its original 1925 configuration and is an excellent example of the 1920s high-speed, shallow-draft American fireboat, a type of fireboat now largely phased out of service after decades of use in the nation's ports.

The *Ralph J. Scott* was built as the *L. A. City No. 2* in response to the need for a modern fireboat with sufficient

The *Ralph J. Scott* when it was the *L. A. City No. 2* in 1925 (above) and today. It continues to operate as a fireboat for the Los Angeles Fire Department.

capacity to battle major waterfront fires in the Port of Los Angeles at San Pedro, the nation's second largest port and an important petroleum trade harbor. Two notable disasters fought by the fireboat included the explosion and burning of the tanker *Markay* in June 1947, one of the nation's greatest waterfront disasters, and the burning of the tanker *Sansinena* in December 1976. In 1965 the fireboat was renamed in honor of Ralph J. Scott, the fire chief responsible for its construction 40 years previously. Modified in 1969, the fireboat continues to operate from its temporary station adjacent to the Los Angeles Maritime Museum. NR. NHL. [City of Los Angeles Fire Department]

SAUSALITO

The *Wapama* is the last surviving example afloat of some 225 steam schooners specially designed for use in the 19th- and 20th-century Pacific Coast lumber trade and coastal service. These vessels formed the backbone of maritime trade and commerce on the coast, ferrying lumber, general cargo, and passengers to and from urban centers and smaller coastal settlements. The *Wapama* was built by the St. Helens Ship Building Company of St. Helens, Oregon. The shipbuilding company was part of a conglomerate of lumber industries owned by the magnate Charles R. McCormick. Originally the owner of a small mill on the Columbia River, McCormick got into the shipping business in 1904 in order to carry his own products to market. The *Wapama*, when launched into the Columbia River in 1915, joined the McCormick fleet of 12 vessels. By 1945 McCormick's interests included several companies and many retail lumber yards, with offices in New York, San Francisco, and South America.

The *Wapama* was towed by the steam schooner *Multnomah* to San Francisco, where its engines were installed in early 1915. The 951-ton wood steamer's maiden voyage was to northern California and Oregon ports; it returned to San Francisco in early May with 60 passengers, a full freight list, and one million board feet of lumber. In 1930 McCormick sold the *Wapama* to Albert E. Gillespie of Los Angeles, who placed it and the steam schooner *Celilo* in his White Flyer Line of steamers. The *Wapama* ran between Los Angeles and San Francisco for Gillespie and after 1932 for Erik Krag. The *Wapama* was sold again in 1937 to the Alaska Transportation Company. Renamed the *Tongass*, the steam schoo-

■ **Wapama**
Bay Model Visitor Center
1915

Because the *Wapama*'s keel was badly warped and its timbers riddled with dry rot, the vessel was pulled from the water in 1979 and placed on a steel barge for easier preservation.

ner carried freight and mail from Seattle to dozens of small, obscure cannery ports in southeastern Alaska.

The Alaska Transportation Company suspended operations in 1947, and in 1949 the *Tongass* was sold to a scrap yard. Very little was removed, and it was left to rot on Puget Sound. In 1958 the vessel, once again named the *Wapama*, was acquired by the San Francisco State Maritime Park and towed to San Francisco. Restoration work begun in the late 1950s continues to this day. Built of Douglas fir, the *Wapama* was so badly deformed and riddled with dry rot that it was pulled from the water in 1979 and placed on a steel barge to prevent its further deterioration. NR. NHL. [National Park Service]

HONOLULU

■ **USS Arizona (BB-39)**
USS Arizona Memorial
One Arizona Memorial Drive
Off Kamehameha Boulevard
1915

Unsalvaged and resting in the silt of Pearl Harbor, the USS *Arizona* is a partially frozen moment of time, its death wounds still visible and its intact hulk still holding most of the battleship's crew. The battle-scarred and submerged remains are the focal point of a shrine erected by the United States to honor and commemorate American servicemen killed on December 7, 1941, particularly those of the *Arizona*'s crew. The *Arizona*'s burning bridge and listing masts and superstructure—photographed after its attack and sinking and emblazoned on the front pages of newspapers across the land—epitomized to the nation the words "Pearl Harbor." The *Arizona* and the modern memorial that straddles it have become the major shrine and point of remembrance not only for the lost battleship but also for the entire attack and are visited annually by thousands of people.

Built at the New York Navy Yard, the USS *Arizona* was named for the former territory, which had become the 48th state on February 14, 1912. Commissioned on October 17, 1916, the battleship, the second and last of the *Pennsylvania* class, joined the U.S. Atlantic Fleet but did not see action in World War I. Used in training on Chesapeake Bay, the battleship was ordered to British waters following the cessation of hostilities in 1918 to be part of the escort for President Woodrow Wilson as he sailed to Brest, France. Following this duty, the *Arizona* was sent to the Mediterranean on a few months' cruise and then served an uneventful career with the Atlantic Fleet. In 1921 the battleship joined the U.S. Pacific Fleet, with a three-year break in service when it returned to the Atlantic coast to undergo modernization under the naval appropriations of 1929–31. Before rejoining the Pacific Fleet in 1931, the *Arizona* carried President Herbert C. Hoover on a cruise to the West Indies. It moved with the Pacific Fleet to Pearl Harbor on Oahu when the fleet's home port shifted from San Diego.

On December 7, 1941, the USS *Arizona* was moored at berth F-7 with the repair ship USS *Vestal* moored alongside. The battleship suffered hits from several bombs, was strafed, and then, around 8:10 a.m., was dealt a deathblow. Petty Officer Noburo Kanai, a crack bombadier in a high-altitude bomber, was credited with dropping the bomb that sank the *Arizona*. The 1,760-pound projectile hurtled through the air, reportedly striking near the second turret and penetrating deep into the battleship's interior before exploding near the forward magazine. The fury of the tremendous blast blew up the ship, killing most of those aboard instantly, including Rear Adm. I. C. Kidd and Capt. F. Van Valkenburgh, both of whom were posthumously awarded the Medal of Honor for their actions aboard the ship. The blast blew people off the decks of surrounding ships and threw tons of debris all over the harbor. The *Arizona* reportedly received eight bomb hits as it sank and was abandoned at 10:32 a.m. When the attack was finally over, the American losses totaled at least eight battleships, three light cruisers, three destroyers, and four auxiliary craft either sunk, capsized, or damaged, 188 aircraft lost and 159 damaged, and 2,403 troops killed or missing and 1,178 wounded. About half the dead were from the *Arizona*; of the approximately 1,177 men aboard the vessel, fewer than 200 survived.

In the aftermath of the Pearl Harbor attack the U.S. Navy began repair and salvage work and succeeded in raising all the sunken vessels with the exception of the *Arizona* and the *Utah*. Of the vessels raised the USS *Oklahoma* was the only one not salvaged and returned to duty. This crippled ship sat in dry dock through the war, was sold for scrap, and sank while under tow in 1947. The *Arizona* was investigated and surveyed, but wartime priorities precluded any work

except removing its topsides, which stuck above the water, and salvaging its armament. In 1942 a new battleship berth was constructed on the *Arizona*'s hulk. The steel and concrete quays also were used for memorial services and as landings by navy crews who came to raise and lower the U.S. flag flying from a pole welded to the severed stub of the battleship's mainmast.

The need for a larger, more fitting memorial became apparent in 1958. In 1961 appropriations for the new memorial were approved, and the structure was completed in 1962. By the late 1970s the number of visitors to the memorial had increased tremendously. Following 1980 legislation authorizing the National Park Service to operate the new USS Arizona Memorial, the National Park Service and the U.S. Navy worked cooperatively to preserve and interpret the story of the *Arizona*, the *Utah*, the Pearl Harbor attack, and the Pacific forces' wartime actions through the Battle of Midway in 1942. A modern visitor center, managed by the National Park Service, houses major exhibits, including attack artifacts, and models and graphics of the battleship as it was and as it sits now beneath the arched memorial's gleaming white walls on the oil-stained waters of Pearl Harbor. [U.S. Navy]

A shrine erected above the wreck of the USS *Arizona* by the people of the United States honors and commemorates all American service personnel killed during the attack on Pearl Harbor, December 7, 1941.

The submarine USS *Bowfin*, shown above at Bowfin Park, completed nine war patrols in two years of wartime duty. A manned torpedo known as a *kaiten*, built as part of an unsuccessful attempt by the Japanese to turn the war back to their advantage, is also displayed in Bowfin Park. Below: The *Falls of Clyde* began its career in the lucrative grain trade.

■ USS Bowfin (SS-287)
Bowfin Park
11 Arizona Memorial Drive
Next to the Ford Island Ferry
1943

Launched at Portsmouth, New Hampshire, on the first anniversary of Pearl Harbor, the *Bowfin* was a *Balao*-class submarine whose hull was reinforced with high-tensile steel for operation at depths of more than 400 feet. Because the Japanese could set depth charges only as deep as 300 feet at the beginning of World War II, the deeper diving *Bowfin* provided an extra margin of safety. The *Bowfin* completed nine war patrols in two years of wartime duty. One of the top-scoring U.S. submarines of World War II, the *Bowfin* is credited with sinking 16 Japanese vessels with a total of 67,882 tons. On a noteworthy patrol in November 1943 for which it received the Presidential Unit Citation, the *Bowfin* sank 12 vessels, only five of which were officially credited to the boat. Rear Adm. Ralph W. Christie, commander of the U.S. submarine forces in the Southwest Pacific, lauded the *Bowfin* crew's achievement: "They fought the war from the beginning to the end of the patrol." The *Bowfin* was the boat selected by Admiral Christie for a war patrol, thus becoming the only U.S. flag officer to be aboard a submarine during combat. The boat late was awarded the Navy Unit Commendation and eight battle stars for its wartime service, which included sinking a record number of ships, laying mines, rescuing downed aviators, and supplying Philippine guerilla troops.

At the war's end the *Bowfin* left Pearl Harbor for active duty with the Atlantic Fleet. In reserve from 1947 to 1951 the submarine again served with the Atlantic Fleet until its final decommissioning in 1971. In 1979 it was transferred to the Pacific Fleet Submarine Memorial Association. The only World War II submarine berthed at Pearl Harbor, it represents the aggressive and successful U.S. submarine war against Japan that was waged from Pearl Harbor. Moored at Bowfin Park it is displayed next to a new facility that includes memorabilia from the Pacific Fleet's submarine force. The *Bowfin* also serves as a memorial to the 52 U.S. submarines and 3,505 submariners lost during the war. NR. NHL. [Pacific Fleet Submarine Memorial Association]

■ Falls of Clyde
Hawaii Maritime Center
Pier 7
Off Ala Moana Boulevard
1878

The *Falls of Clyde* is the world's only surviving four-masted, full-rigged ship. The boat was built in Port Glasgow, Scotland, while Great Britain was experiencing a shipbuilding boom inspired in part by increased trade with the United States. The *Falls of Clyde*, specifically designed to carry bulk cargoes quickly and cheaply, was used principally in trade between Britain and India to carry cargoes such as cement, jute, iron, grain, and general merchandise.

The *Falls of Clyde* made 10 voyages to American ports while under the British flag. Sailing to San Francisco and Portland, Oregon, the ship took part in one of the most significant U.S.–Great Britain maritime trades—the California grain trade. The U.S. merchant fleet boomed in response to the trade, with the construction of hundreds of large wood sailing ships, called "downeasters" because they were built in New England shipyards, for sailing around Cape Horn to California. The largest number of vessels, however, came from Great Britain, 14,000 nautical miles away. The British medium clippers of the 1870s and 1880s served the trade best with their iron, and later steel, hulls, small crews, large storage capacity, and speed and economy of handling.

Making its last journey in 1898 under the British flag to San Francisco, the *Falls of Clyde* was sold to American owners that same year and gained American registry by a special act of Congress in 1900. Henceforth the vessel participated in the nationally important Hawaiian trans-Pacific sugar trade for the Matson Navigation Company, a shipping firm of international scope and significance that continues in business. The ninth vessel acquired by William Matson, the *Falls of Clyde* is the oldest surviving member of the Matson fleet. Usually sailing on a monthly schedule, it carried assorted freight, livestock, and small numbers of passengers between San Francisco and Hilo, Hawaii, returning to San Francisco laden with sugar and passengers.

After 1907 the *Falls of Clyde* entered another significant maritime trade—transporting petroleum as a sailing oil tanker. Refitted for the petroleum trade as a bulk cargo carrier, it is the oldest surviving American tanker and the only surviving sailing oil tanker left afloat in the world. After the ship was laid up in 1959, several efforts were made to save it from being scuttled as a breakwater. In 1963 a group of civic-minded Hawaiians purchased the *Clyde* and had it towed to Hawaii. Restoration of the vessel was completed, and it was opened to the public in 1968. Remasted in 1970 and subsequently rerigged, the *Falls of Clyde* was operated at Pier 5 by the Bernice P. Bishop Memorial Museum. Recently turned over to the new Hawaii Maritime Center, it is now the centerpiece of that maritime museum. NR. NHL. [Hawaii Maritime Center]

■ **USS Utah** (BB-31, AG-16)
USS Arizona Memorial
One Arizona Memorial Drive
Off Kamehameha Boulevard
1909

Although battle-scarred and partially submerged, the USS *Utah* is one of only two early American dreadnoughts that are on view and also the only unaltered pre–World War II target ship. The remains of this ship are the centerpiece of a shrine erected by the people of the United States to honor the *Utah*'s crew, some of whom lost their lives while trying to save their torpedoed ship during the Japanese attack on the U.S. Pacific Fleet at Pearl Harbor. Like the submerged hulk of the USS *Arizona* on the other side of Ford Island, the *Utah* is frozen in time, lying much as it did immediately after the Pearl Harbor attack. Although Pearl Harbor and its surrounding bases were repaired and ultimately modernized after the Japanese attack, the *Utah*, like the *Arizona*, was not. The intact battleship's hull, armed with then state-of-the-art weapons, is a unique, well-preserved entity with considerable architectural integrity.

The USS *Utah* was built as part of an early 20th-century arms race when military supremacy was determined by control of the seas. One of the first of the *Florida* class, the *Utah* was laid down on March 6, 1909, at the Camden, New Jersey, yard of the New York Shipbuilding Company. Completed just nine months later, the *Utah* was launched on December 23, 1909. It was assigned to the Atlantic Fleet in March 1912, and for the next two years the battleship performed regular duties in the Atlantic Fleet, drilling and engaging in training cruises.

In 1914 the *Utah* intervened for the United States in Mexico, then torn by civil war. Twice it was deployed at Veracruz: in February–April, when it anchored off shore to transfer refugees to nearby Tampico, and again in late April–June, when it joined other American ships in an attempt to contravene the landing of arms shipped from Germany to Mexican General and President Victoriano Huerta, who had succeeded Francisco I. Madero, the assassinated legal president. Between 1914 and 1917 the *Utah* trained and cruised the Atlantic seaboard and the Caribbean. Following the United States' entry into World War I in April 1917, the battleship served as a gunnery and engineering training ship on the Chesapeake Bay until August 1918, when it was dispatched with other battleships to Ireland to protect and support convoys to Great Britain. The *Utah* served as flagship for this group of American dreadnoughts until the armistice. Along with the *Arizona*, the *Utah* served as an honor escort for the *George Washington* when it carried President Woodrow W. Wilson to France. Returning to the United States at the end of 1918, the *Utah* served in a variety of missions, including a stint as flagship for the U.S. Navy's European Squadron in 1921 and diplomatic missions to South America.

Meanwhile the naval arms race had resulted in negotiations to limit warship production. The Washington Naval Treaty of 1922 limited the United States to 18 battleships; several older vessels were scrapped, and two battleships, the USS *Wyoming* and the *Utah*, were to be converted into target ships. Awaiting conversion, the *Utah* continued its regular duties, including transporting President-elect Herbert C. Hoover from South America to the United States between December 1928 and January 1929. Finally decommissioned in 1931, the *Utah* was converted to a target ship at Norfolk Navy Yard in 1932 and redesignated an AG-16. Transferred to the Pacific Fleet in June 1932, the *Utah* spent the remainder of its career as a target ship and a mobile platform for testing new weapons, particularly antiaircraft guns.

The *Utah* was one of the first vessels attacked on December 7, 1941. The attack's planners had ordered their pilots to ignore the *Utah*, a noncombat ship, but eager pilots aimed two torpedoes at it and the nearby light cruiser *Raleigh*. One torpedo slammed into the *Utah*'s side at 8:01 a.m. as its crew was raising the flag on the fantail. As the second torpedo detonated on the port side, the ship rolled onto its beam ends, trapping many men below decks. Moreover, the heavy timbers laid on the decks to protect the crew from the practice bombs shifted and blocked hatches and filled the water with crushing, deadly debris. The senior officer aboard, engineering officer Lt. Cmdr. Solomon S. Isquith, worked to save his men, plunging below decks and barely escaping with his own life. Other heroes included fireman John B. Vaessen, who remained at his post in the dynamo room, keeping the lights on to aid escapees, and chief watertender Peter Tomich, who also stayed at his post, securing the boilers and making sure his men had escaped. Both Vaessen and Tomich, along with many other men, were trapped when the *Utah* capsized. While under attack from strafing Japanese planes, crew members cut into the hull freeing 10 men, including Vaessen but not Tomich, who remains entombed in the ship. For his heroic actions Tomich posthumously received the Medal of Honor. The *Utah* had 64 casualties—six officers and 58 crew members—most of whom remain inside their ship.

After the attack on Pearl Harbor the *Utah* was pulled partly upright but slid in the mud and stuck. Light salvage yielded only a few guns, and the *Utah* was abandoned. National attention focused on the USS *Arizona*'s remains and plans for a major memorial to span its hulk. Veterans of the *Utah* and other Pearl Harbor survivors argued that the *Utah* not be neglected, and in 1971, after extensive lobbying, a memorial was dedicated on the shore of Ford Island overlooking the exposed portions of the "forgotten" casualty of the December 7, 1941, attack. NR. NHL. [U.S. Navy]

■ ■ ■ ■ ■ ■ ■ ■ IDAHO ■ ■ ■ ■ ■ ■ ■ ■

LEWISTON

■ **Jean**
Hells Gate State Park
1938

The *Jean* participated in maritime commerce of the Pacific Northwest, specifically the Columbia River system, where river towboats transported large cargoes. Although stern-wheelers had been common for decades, a unique feature of the *Jean* was the use of twin, independently operated stern wheels, designed so that one could turn in reverse while the other turned forward, allowing it greater maneuverability than other stern-wheelers. The vessel, built by Commercial Iron Works in Portland, Oregon, also sported the latest technology—all-steel construction. The *Jean* operated on the Columbia and Willamette rivers for the Western Transportation Company, primarily towing large log rafts measuring 60 by 720 feet to a paper mill at Camas. Other cargoes included hog fuels, paper products, and oil. Because it could no longer compete with the new diesel-powered workboats, the *Jean* was retired from towing in 1957. It served as a floating machine shop and maintenance vessel until donated to the Luna House Historical Society in 1976. Ownership was transferred to the state of Idaho in 1979, and the *Jean* is now moored on the Snake River, several miles south of Lewiston. NR. [State of Idaho]

One of the *Jean*'s unique features—its independently operated twin stern wheels.

■ ■ ■ ■ ■ ■ ■ ■ MONTANA ■ ■ ■ ■ ■ ■ ■ ■

POLSON

■ **Paul Bunyan**
Miracle of America Story Museum
58176 Highway 93
1926

In the late 19th and early 20th centuries the Flathead Valley area of Montana boomed as a result of its rich stands of timber. A number of large logging operations worked in the forests through the winter. During the spring floods logs were floated down the various rivers and streams and caught by log booms at the river mouths on Flathead Lake. There large rafts of logs were towed to the mill at Somers, a community of 350 established in 1901 at the end of the lake. The Somers Lumber Company produced railroad ties, lumber, sash, doors, and boxes for nearly five decades. At its peak in 1937 the mill produced 60 million feet of lumber and employed 375 workers. A number of towboats were built for use on Flathead Lake between 1901 and 1926. The only survivor of some 25 to 30 steamers and motor vessels operated on the lake is the *Paul Bunyan*, built by and for the Somers Lumber Company in 1926. Powered by a 180-horsepower diesel engine, the *Bunyan* towed up to 750,000 board feet of lumber on each trip to the mill. When the mill closed in 1947 the vessel was laid up, and by 1957 it had been hauled ashore, placed on a cradle, and converted to a residence with the engine removed and additions built alongside the hull. Acquired by the Miracle of America Story Museum in 1987, the former towboat is now an onshore exhibit. [Miracle of America Story Museum]

■ ■ ■ ■ ■ ■ ■   OREGON   ■ ■ ■ ■ ■ ■ ■

ASTORIA

The lightship *WAL-604* and its sister lightship *WAL-605* are the best representatives of the last class of lightships built under the auspices of the U.S. Coast Guard. Although these vessels closely resembled earlier lightships their construction was innovative. The *WAL-604* (redesignated the *WLV-604* in 1965) was the fourth lightship assigned to the

■ **Lightship WAL-604**
("**Columbia**")
Columbia River Maritime Museum
1792 Marine Drive
1950

station off the Columbia River bar, which it serviced its entire career. The 16 crew members worked 28-day shifts, taking 14 days off in rotation so that two-thirds of the crew were aboard at any given time. The routine of service was largely uneventful: rescues in 1952 and 1960, being blown off station in 1962, and being sideswiped by a hit-and-run vessel in 1964 were the chief events of note in the *WAL-604*'s history. Retired in 1979 as the last "Columbia" lightship as well as the last lightship on the Pacific Coast, the *WAL-604* is a public exhibit maintained by the Columbia River Maritime Museum on the Columbia River waterfront. NR. NHL. [Columbia River Maritime Museum]

Retired as the last "Columbia" lightship in 1979, the *WAL-604* was towed to its permanent berth in 1980.

PORTLAND

■ **David S. Campbell**
Fireboat Headquarters
3660 Northwest Front Avenue
1927

An active fireboat on the Portland waterfront, the *David S. Campbell* is named for Portland's most famous fireman, who, while chief of the bureau, was killed in a major fire in 1911. The *Campbell*, operated by the Portland Bureau of Fire, Rescue, and Emergencies Services, exemplifies a 1920s American fireboat. Permission to view the vessel can be obtained by calling the station. [Bureau of Fire, Rescue, and Emergency Services]

RIVER QUEEN

■ **River Queen Restaurant**
1300 Northwest Front
1922

Built by the Bethlehem Steel Company in San Francisco for the Southern Pacific Company, the automobile ferry *Shasta* crossed San Francisco Bay between Oakland and San Francisco. Capable of carrying 62 automobiles and 2,200 passengers, the *Shasta* and its sister ships, the *Yosemite* and the *San Mateo*, ran until 1939 when the completion of the Bay and Golden Gate bridges ended their careers. Sold to the Black Ball Line for Puget Sound service, the ferry was sold with the rest of the Black Ball fleet to the state of Washington in 1951. Sold again in 1959, the ferry was towed to Portland, renamed, and remodeled into a floating restaurant on the Columbia River. [River Queen Restaurant]

■ ■ ■ ■ ■ ■   WASHINGTON   ■ ■ ■ ■ ■ ■

ANACORTES

■ **La Merced (hulk)**
On the waterfront
Off Oakes Avenue
1917

The four-masted schooner *La Merced* lies on the shore of Fidalgo Island, between Cap Sante and Shannon Point in the Guemes Channel and opposite Guemes Island. Beached and used as a breakwater in the shipyard of Anton Lovric, the *La Merced* is surrounded by rock and dredge spoil but is not submerged. This once-common vessel type formerly navigated all coasts of the United States and even sailed into international waters. The *La Merced*'s hull form and rig are typical of hundreds of other four-masted schooners built on Chesapeake Bay, in Maine and throughout New England, and on the Gulf Coast from 1880 through the end of World War I. Although the shattered wrecks of several four-masters lie where they were lost on North Carolina beaches or where they were laid up in Maine coves and ports, only three of these vessels survive as intact entities. Of these the *La Merced* is the best-preserved example. Built in Benicia, California, the *La Merced* was engaged in a variety of maritime trades of the Pacific coastal region, including the petroleum trade, the passenger trade, and fishing and canning operations in Alaska. NR. [Anton Lovric]

■ **W. T. Preston**
R Avenue at 7th Street
1939

Built at the Lake Union Drydock on Lake Union in the heart of Seattle in the summer of 1939, the steel-hulled snagboat *W. T. Preston* continued the tradition of receiving hand-me-down machinery, including the engines originally installed in the *Swinomish* in 1914. The *Preston* also received the whistle from the *Skagit* (1884), preserving a tradition

The U.S. Army Corps of Engineers' snagboat *W. T. Preston* worked nearly 11 months each year removing debris and waterlogged pilings and logs, as well as derelict or abandoned boats, ships, and airplanes.

and providing a link to the first snagboat to work in the region. Commissioned on January 19, 1940, the *Preston* built nets to protect the Lake Washington Ship Canal dam and locks from floating bombs sent downstream during World War II. Laid up in 1943 for the duration of the war, the boat resumed service in 1946.

After the war, as the region's population and marine traffic increased, the snagboat's area of operation was enlarged to include Lake Washington, the lower reaches of Puget Sound to Tacoma and Olympia, and former ports of call farther north such as Anacortes and environs. With a 14-member crew living aboard the vessel, the *Preston* worked nearly 11 months of each year removing large pieces of drift, waterlogged pilings and logs, and derelict boats, ships, airplanes, and debris. Floating items were snagged with wires, hooked or grabbed by the clamshell bucket, and loaded into a barge towed alongside the boat. Originally this debris was burned, but in later years the U.S. Army Corps of Engineers contracted with private commercial firms to dispose of it by means of landfill, salvage, recycling, and controlled burning.

By the 1960s the *Preston* was the last stern-wheeler operating on Puget Sound and became a showpiece as well as a working vessel. In its last two decades of operation the *Preston* participated in many civic events and celebrations on the sound. Costly to operate, the snagboat was retired on October 22, 1981.

Laid up at the Corps of Engineers' facilities at Hiram Chittenden Locks on the Lake Washington Ship Canal, the *Preston* was transferred to the city of Anacortes, a former port of call, in 1983. Moved ashore into a dry berth, the vessel is open to the public as a museum vessel. NR. NHL. [City of Anacortes]

SEATTLE

The schooner yacht and pilot *Adventuress* is a significant example of the "fisherman profile" yacht design created by Bowdoin B. Crowninshield, a noted early 20th-century American naval architect whose work influenced the development of American yachts and fishing schooners. Commissioned by a private owner for Arctic exploration and hunting, the *Adventuress* made one voyage to Alaska before

■ **Adventuress**
Various ports in Puget Sound
1913

it was bought by the San Francisco Bar Pilots Association in 1914. The schooner was the 19th pilot boat acquired by the pilots, who guided traffic across the treacherous San Francisco bar marking the entrance to the busy port of San Francisco. The *Adventuress* worked with two other schooners that served as station ships, alternating their sea patrol—five days out and five days in—while the *Adventuress* shuttled back and forth, taking pilots out and bringing them in as well as carrying supplies and equipment. Retired and sold in 1952, the *Adventuress* passed through several owners before being acquired by Youth Adventure, which operates the vessel as a sailing school, offering training for youths and adults in sailing, safety, and other sea-oriented activities. The *Adventuress* sails in and out of ports all over Puget Sound. For the schooner's current location call (206) 232-4024. NR. NHL. [Youth Adventure]

The *Adventuress*, rigged out as a pilot boat.

■ Arthur Foss
Maritime Heritage Center
1002 Valley Street
1889

The *Arthur Foss* is the only known wood-hulled 19th-century tugboat left afloat and in operating condition in the United States. Built as the *Wallowa*, it began its career towing lumber and grain-laden square-rigged ships across the treacherous Columbia River bar. After working on the bar for nine years it played an important role in transporting people and goods to Alaska during the Klondike gold rush. In 1904 it was given a new engine and for the next 25 years towed log rafts around Puget Sound and the Washington coast. Sold in 1929 to the Foss Launch and Tug Company of Seattle, the *Wallowa* boosted the Foss Fleet to 36 tugboats and 80 scows (barges), making it the largest such fleet on the Pacific Coast at that time. In 1933 the tugboat was used as a set in filming *Tugboat Annie*, the MGM film that epitomized tugboats and tugboating for a generation of Americans. Renamed the *Arthur Foss* in 1934, the vessel continued in service to the Foss Company until 1970, except for service in the U.S. Navy during World War II. While under charter to the U.S. Navy, it was the last vessel to escape from Wake Island in January 1942 before Japanese forces attacked and captured that Pacific outpost. In 1970 the boat was transferred to Save Our Ships, an organization that became the present-day Northwest Seaport. After being operated by the museum for a short period, the tugboat was laid up and deteriorated. Restored to operating condition in 1981 by a dedicated group of volunteers, the *Arthur Foss* approaches the end of its first century in good shape, operating on Puget Sound and ranging north to Alaska and British Columbia as a goodwill ambassador for the state of Washington. Northwest Seaport plans to open the tugboat to the public as a floating exhibit at South Lake Union. NR. NHL. [Northwest Seaport]

The *Arthur Foss* towed lumber and grain-laden square-rigged ships across the treacherous Columbia River bar.

The fireboat *Duwamish*, owned and maintained by the Seattle Fire Department, is an excellent example of fireboats typically found in major American port cities during much of the 20th century. Although earlier tugboats modified for fireboat use and used as auxiliary fireboats may exist, the *Duwamish* is the second-oldest surviving fireboat in the United States built specifically as a fire-fighting vessel.

When it went into service in 1909, the *Duwamish* was claimed to be the world's most powerful fireboat because of the amount of water it could discharge. In 1927 it was joined by a new, smaller gasoline-powered fireboat, the *Alki*. The U.S. Coast Guard took over the *Duwamish* during World War II, returning it to the Seattle Fire Department in 1946. The fireboat was modernized in 1949, when diesel-electric engines were installed, and remained in service on the Seattle waterfront until 1985, when it was replaced by a new fireboat with an aluminum and fiberglass hull. Laid up and maintained in excellent condition by the fire department, the *Duwamish*, a City of Seattle Historic Landmark, awaits a permanent berth as a museum vessel. NR. NHL. [Seattle Fire Department]

■ **Duwamish**
Lake Washington Ship Canal
Chittenden Locks
1909

Built as part of a five-vessel contract, the *No. 83* and its surviving sister ship, the *No. 84*, are the earliest surviving examples of American lightships, but only the *No. 83* has retained its original marine steam engine and machinery. Constructed and launched in 1904 as the "Blunts Reef" lightship, the *No. 83* arrived in San Francisco in 1905 with the *No. 76*, which was to serve as relief. With orders to remain at station despite the severity of storms, the *No. 83* was subjected to fierce weather and was blown off station six times in 1906 and 1907. Rammed by the steam schooner *Del Norte* in 1910, the *No. 83* was heavily damaged and retired to San Francisco for repairs. On another occasion 155 survivors from the stranded coastal steamer *Bear* rowed through heavy seas and thick fog to find refuge in the *No. 83*.

The *No. 83* remained on station at Blunts Reef until 1930, when it was replaced by a new diesel electric vessel, the *No. 100*, the first of a new class of lightships. Transferred to the San Francisco bar station, the *No. 83* served as guide to the entrance to the busy port of San Francisco Bay. Modernized in its new role as the "San Francisco" lightship in the early 1930s, the *No. 83* was redesignated the *WAL-508* in 1939,

■ **Lightship No. 83 ("Relief")**
Maritime Heritage Center
1002 Valley Street
1904

The lightship *No. 83* served to guide mariners to the port of San Francisco from 1930 to 1951.

when the U.S. Lighthouse Establishment was absorbed into the U.S. Coast Guard. Manned by coast guard crews, the *No. 83* took on a more direct military role in 1942, when it served as a patrol and guard boat for the navy at the entrance to San Francisco Bay following the United States' entry into World War II.

Replaced in 1951 by a new coast guard–built lightship, the *WAL-612*, the old *No. 83* was sent north as a relief lightship. Again redesignated the "Relief," the vessel served as such at the Columbia River bar, Umatilla Reef, and Swiftsure Bank, at the latter marking the approach to Puget Sound and its active ports. The 56-year career of the *No. 83* ended on July 18, 1960, when the vessel was decommissioned at Seattle. Acquired later by Save Our Ships, a Seattle-based organization that later became Northwest Seaport, the ship awaits final restoration as a floating exhibit. NR. NHL. [Northwest Seaport]

■ **Virginia V**
4455 Shilshole Avenue, N.W.
1922

This 115-foot-long wood boat is the last of Puget Sound's "mosquito fleet." Built in 1922 at Maplewood, Washington, by Matthew Anderson for the West Pass Transportation Company, the *Virginia V* joined the ranks of the "mosquito fleet"—the large number of small, unlicensed steamers that flitted around like mosquitoes in Puget Sound and other inland waters in the Pacific Northwest since the mid-19th century. In time the term came to denote all small steamers working on coastal inland waters. In 1932 the *Marine Digest* reported that the U.S. Bureau of Navigation and Steamboat Inspection had issued identifying numbers to the members of the mosquito fleet. The number of small steamers had increased by 2,500 in just six months' time, so that by the end of June 1932 there were 260,983 known members of the mosquito fleet. Now there are only two—the *Virginia V* on the Pacific Coast and the *Sabino* on the East Coast.

The *Virginia V* was built to run from Seattle to Tacoma, a steamboat route inaugurated in 1890. The fifth steamer of the West Pass Transportation Company to bear the name *Virginia*, the "Five" made its maiden voyage on June 11, 1922, commencing a daily run past Vashon Island to connect the two great cities on Puget Sound with the numerous small communities between them. For 16 years the *Virginia*

V carried passengers, mail, and groceries, averaging 125,000 miles each year. This service was terminated in 1939, and in 1940 the *Virginia V* began working as an excursion boat. After the ship had passed through several owners, the Northwest Steamship Company—formed by steamship enthusiasts—acquired the aging steamer in 1968. Along with the Virginia V Foundation, the company campaigned to save the vessel, which was listed in the National Register of Historic Places in 1973 and received grant funds for restoration in 1978. The restored *Virginia V* reentered excursion service in 1980, when it was purchased by the foundation. Operating and earning its keep, the steamer is also supported by dedicated volunteers. The *Virginia V* retains its original triple-expansion marine steam engine, manufactured in 1904 and first in-stalled in the *Virginia IV*. NR. [Virginia V Foundation]

The *Wawona* is one of only three surviving three-masted schooners in the United States, one of which, the *C. A. Thayer*, is a sister ship. The *Wawona* is particularly noted for its association with Ralph ("Matt") Peasley, the hero of Peter B. Kyne's seafaring saga *Cappy Ricks; or the Subjugation of Matt Peasley*. Because of the book, Peasley, the skipper of the *Wawona* from 1900 to 1906, became one of the most famous of the Pacific Coast's lumber schooner masters. Constructed of Douglas fir at Fairhaven, California, the *Wawona* was one of 113 sturdy vessels built by Hans D. Bendixsen in his 32-year shipbuilding career. Built for the Dolbeer and Carson Lumber Company of San Francisco for service in the booming Pacific Coast lumber trade, the *Wawona* called at tiny lumber ports up and down the coast, often loading cargo "under the wire" from coastal cliffs. Dolbeer and Carson worked the schooner until 1914, when, like many other coastal schooners, including the *Thayer*, it entered the fishing trade. Purchased by Robinson Fisheries of Anacortes, Washington, the schooner worked the fisheries off the Alaska coast in the Bering Sea. Laden with 25 dories and 300 tons of rock salt, the *Wawona* would anchor in the middle of the codfish grounds. The dory fishermen, working with hand lines, would come back to the schooner laden to the gun-

■ **Wawona**
Maritime Heritage Center
1002 Valley Street
1897

Built for the Pacific Coast lumber trade, the *Wawona* later served as a Bering Sea codfisher.

wales. The cod were pitched onto the *Wawona*'s deck, where they were headed, gutted, and then packed in salt in the schooner's large, open hold for the trip back to port and market.

World War II interrupted the *Wawona*'s fishing career, and the schooner, chartered to the U.S. Army, was cut down to a barge. Now known as the BCL-710, the dismasted schooner was towed around Puget Sound with lumber until the end of 1945, when it was returned to its owners. New masts were installed, and in 1946 the *Wawona* returned to fishing, but its career ended after a disastrous season in 1947. Bought by private owners for cruising, the *Wawona* was laid up on Seattle's Lake Union. Meanwhile, Save Our Ships (SOS)—formed to preserve the maritime heritage of the Pacific Northwest—purchased the *Wawona* in 1964 and opened it that same year as a maritime museum on the lake. The fleet of SOS vessels grew to incorporate other historic ships—the *Arthur Foss*, the ferry *San Mateo*, and the lightship *No. 83* ("Relief")—and SOS became Northwest Seaport. The seaport, still located on Lake Union, is raising funds to preserve and restore the *Wawona*, which suffers from dry rot. In 1985 the National Park Service's Historic American Buildings Survey and the Historic American Engineering Record, working with Northwest Seaport and the National Trust for Historic Preservation, recorded the ship's plan, measuring and drawing all the vessel's essential features and construction details. This event marked the first time a ship has been recorded since the 1930s. Such drawings are deposited with the Library of Congress as a record for all time and for use in any possible restoration or reconstruction. NR. [Northwest Seaport]

■ **Zodiac**
Lake Union Drydock
1515 Fairview East
1924

Built as a luxury sailing yacht by the Hodgdon Brothers Shipyard in East Boothbay, Maine, the *Zodiac* was the largest vessel designed by William Hand, Jr., a renowned naval architect. The *Zodiac* was his concept of the perfect "racing fisherman," a schooner type favored by the codfishing fleet because of the ship's speedy journey back to market. After several years of cruising and racing, the *Zodiac* was sold in 1931 to the San Francisco Bar Pilots Association. Renamed the *California*, the vessel transferred pilots onto incoming and outgoing ships so that the pilots could guide the ships safely in and out of port. The *California* was the last American schooner pilot in service when the San Francisco Bar

The *Zodiac*, designed as a "racing fisherman."

Pilots replaced it with a smaller power vessel in 1972. The Zodiac Corporation acquired the vessel in the late 1970s and reinstated its original name in 1984. Restored as a working ship, the *Zodiac* offers sailing and safety training as well as public service cruises. When not at sea, the *Zodiac* is moored at the southend of Lake Union. NR. [The Vessel Zodiac Corporation]

The *Fireboat No. 1* steams out on a demonstration cruise in 1929.

TACOMA

The *Fireboat No. 1* is owned and maintained by the city of Tacoma as a historic monument and museum. Although built and operated only on Puget Sound, this well-preserved vessel is representative of most fireboats throughout the United States built before World War II. The *Fireboat No. 1*, one of only 10 specifically designed fireboats older than 50 years left in the United States, is the least modified and has not undergone extensive modernization.

The *Fireboat No. 1* was launched in 1929 to protect the shores of Puget Sound as well as the 38-mile waterfront of Tacoma, a busy port lined with sawmills and lumber yards. During the *Fireboat No. 1*'s 53-year career it responded to every major waterfront fire as well as emergencies ranging from pumping sinking vessels to rescuing people in the water. It was estimated that the fireboat rather than the U.S. Coast Guard responded to 80 percent of emergency calls received in Tacoma. The *Fireboat No. 1* also served a special role in waterfront and marine events, welcoming naval vessels and pumping displays for parades and patriotic celebrations.

Fireboat No. 1 was retired from service in 1982 following the purchase of two new fireboats in 1981. To preserve the vessel the Tacoma Fireboat Marine Museum Foundation, a non-profit group, was formed in 1982. In 1986 the fireboat was hauled out of the water, painted, and moved ashore to its present location. NR. NHL. [City of Tacoma Fire Department]

■ **Fireboat No. 1**
Marine Park
Ruston Way
1929

EPILOGUE:
LOST SHIPS AND LOSING BATTLES

P reserving the remnants of America's maritime past, particularly historic vessels, has always posed special challenges and problems. Ships were built to last for a few decades and then, if not wrecked on the ocean floor, were torn apart by ship-breaking crews using sledges, axes, or cutting torches. Ships that have survived are often exposed to tides, storms, and the corrosive salt air of the marine environment. Wood hulls have been ravaged by marine organisms or dry rot. Even in fresh water ships suffer from dry rot, rust, and the occasional fury of lake gales and ice or the flooding and snags in rain-swollen rivers. Ships removed from the water face a host of preservation problems– dry rot, insect infestation, and fire, which in the 1970s claimed two historic Alaska riverboats, the *Casca* and the *Whitehorse*.

In the past ships were often saved by people who simply loved old vessels and nautical lore, actions perhaps rooted in a love of history, pride in achievements past, or the ancestral tie to the sea. A few pragmatic business owners acquired old ships for excursions or for floating restaurants, hoping to capitalize on the fascination with ships; then, when the vessel was worn out or needed major repair, it was cast aside or left to sink. Nonetheless, the romantic appeal of saving ships has resulted in the preservation of more than a hundred vessels as museum exhibits, afloat and ashore, and nearly a hundred more that operate or have been converted to commercial uses that maintain the ship's integrity as a historic vessel. Major collections of ships now exist at several maritime and naval museums throughout the United States.

Even these institutions have had problems in caring for their collections. Despite the best intentions and the best application of funds and energy, many have lost ships or have had to transfer vessels to other institutions: the tugboat *Mathilda* was sent to the Hudson River Maritime Center from South Street Seaport, which was unable to maintain the tug, while the Maine Maritime Academy now maintains the schooner *Bowdoin*, once at Mystic Seaport. The National Park Service, which in 1974 acquired the San Francisco Maritime State Historical Park's collection of ships, had to pull the National Historic Landmark steam schooner *Wapama* from the water in 1979 for fear of losing it. The vessel, dried out and showing severe dry rot, remains on a steel barge. The dry rot is now halted, thanks to the application of water-soluble wood preservative, but the *Wapama* cannot be refloated without a costly, and almost complete, rebuilding. In 1977 the Maine Maritime Museum began a long, expensive restoration of the 1884 steam tugboat *Seguin* in 1977. Ten years and $440,000 later with the ship not yet restored or in the water, the project was halted, a panel of experts was convened, and the decision was made to document the tugboat and dismantle it. After a $25,000 documentation project, the *Seguin* was scrapped in March 1988. Northwest Seaport is discussing using the same strategy with the ferryboat *San Mateo* in Seattle.

The steamer *Princess Louise* was in the process of being repaired when it capsized in September 1989.

The *Wapama*, a National Historic Landmark steam schooner, awaits further restoration on its steel barge.

Many historic ships preserved in the United States are privately owned; often these ships were saved by people who might not otherwise identify themselves as preservationists. Even those who are preservationists, professional curators, historical architects, historians, or cultural resource managers are hard pressed at times to translate land-based experience into action to save historic ships. Compounding the problem is the fact that ships were built to work, requiring the constant attention of a crew to keep them working; as idle, wharf-bound, inanimate structures they are difficult to maintain. These include working vessels, such as the skipjacks of the Chesapeake Bay, a nationally significant fleet of oyster-dredging vessels that date to the 19th century. Among those unique and important craft listed in the National Register of Historic Places, a fair number have been abandoned, laid up on mudflats, or put on the market, victims of a declining industry and their intense need, as wood ships, for maintenance and costly repair.

The majority of preserved historic vessel projects have been and continue to be single ship endeavors, the result of local campaigns by cities, institutions, organizations, or individuals. Because of the lack of substantial public, corporate, or government support, and sometimes even with it, ships that should have been saved have been lost. The last clipper ship built by Donald McKay, the *Glory of the Seas*, was lost

Evidence of dry rot on the *Wapama*. Dry rot has been halted, thanks to an application of a water-soluble wood preservative, but the vessel cannot be put back on the water without a costly rebuilding.

The 1906 skipjack *Ida May* lies abandoned in 1990 in Chance, Maryland. Although listed in the National Register of Historic Places, a fair number of skipjacks have been abandoned on mudflats, victims of a declining industry and the costliness of maintaining and repairing wood ships.

in the 1920s. Having survived the demise of the clippers and the end of the age of deep-water sailing, the *Glory* was put ashore on Puget Sound. In an open letter urging that the clipper be saved, Cornelius Vanderbilt IV appealed to local and national sentiment as well as "pride, honor and patriotism," but it was too late. The *New York Times* noted on October 24, 1922, that while from a practical view the ship was "only so much junk," nonetheless "the junk in this case is ennobled by a fine national sentiment.... She is one of the humbler national monuments, it is true, as compared with 'Old Ironsides,' or the sword of Washington, or the home of Lincoln, but she embodies much that is worthwhile and she will live long in our maritime history." The *Glory of the Seas* was burned for scrap on May 13, 1923. In more recent times other ships, such as the square-rigger *Champigny* or the bark *Kaiulani*, were lost to the exigencies of funding. The failure to save the *Kaiulani* was a national tragedy. The sole survivor of the handful of American-built iron-and-steel sailing vessels, the 1899 Maine-built bark had weathered a career in a variety of trades, was accepted by President Lyndon Johnson in trust for the people of the United States in 1964, and then left to rust and be scrapped in the Philippines; only fragments eventually returned home. Another tragic maritime loss was the scuttling of the downeaster *Benjamin Packard* in 1939. The loss of the bark, once the effort of a campaign to save it, and the subsequent

loss of the downeaster *St. Paul* on the West Coast, forever closed the book on the last great wood square-rigged ships of the United States.

Despite the popularity of naval vessels as the centerpieces of preservation efforts, historic naval ships either languished, as did the USS *Hartford*, or were scrapped after being "saved," as was the USS *Oregon*. Other significant naval vessels that should have been saved but were laid up after World War II were ultimately denied preservation. The veteran battleship USS *New York* sailed from its namesake city in January 1946 for use as an atomic bomb target in the Pacific. As citizens groups and the state chamber of commerce lobbied to save the battleship, the *New York Times* wrote that "New York may lose forever its most useful and fitting war memorial unless something is done to prevent destruction of our century's Old Ironsides.... This ship should be permanently on display in New York...." The *New York* was sent anyway and was scuttled as a highly contaminated hulk after surviving two nuclear detonations. The nation's most historic surviving aircraft carrier, the USS *Enterprise* (CV-6), was described in late 1945 by Secretary of the Navy James Forrestal as "the one ship that most nearly symbolizes the history of the United States in World War II." Congress passed legislation authorizing the preservation of the "Big E" on the Potomac near the Washington Monument; however, the responsibility for financing the project was left in private hands, and funding efforts failed. The *Enterprise* was scrapped in 1959. The carrier's fate is reflected in the recent U.S. Navy decision to scrap the last World War II *Essex*-class carriers held in reserve. The *Bon Homme Richard*, the *Bennington*, and the *Hornet*, laid up at Bremerton, are about to be disposed of, despite efforts to save the *Hornet*, a veteran of several World War II campaigns, the Korean and Vietnam wars, and the space program. The *Hornet* recovered the crew of Apollo 11, the first men to walk on the moon, when they splashed down in 1969 after their historic mission.

In 1984 the National Park Service's newly established National Maritime Initiative began to develop a national

The veteran battleship USS *New York* sailed from its namesake city in January 1946 for use as an atomic bomb target in the Pacific.

One of the last *Essex*-class carriers, the USS *Hornet* recovered the crew of Apollo II when it splashed down in 1969.

inventory of preserved historic ships in the United States. In the seven years since the inventory began, nearly two dozen ships were dropped from the inventory because they had burned, had sunk, or were scrapped or because preservation efforts had been abandoned. These most recent losses underscore the fact that historic ships are fragile, endangered resources. Of the 242 vessels documented by the Historic American Merchant Marine Survey during the Depression, only one survives today. That vessel, the *Gjoa*, languished and was saved only when it was moved back to its native land, Norway, for preservation and display. A new list of more than 300 historic ships has now been compiled. The stories that follow describe a few of the losses since the inventory was started, highlight the problems faced in historic ship preservation, and reinforce the need to prevent more lost battles and difficult choices.

■ ■ ■ ■ ■ ■ CHIEF WAWATAM ■ ■ ■ ■ ■ ■

Built in 1911, the Great Lakes car ferry and icebreaker *Chief Wawatam* was cut down to a barge in 1988 in Canada. Thus ended a long career and a campaign by steam aficionados and the city of Mackinaw Straits, Michigan, where the ferry had been laid up, to save it. The oldest surviving Great Lakes car ferry, the *Chief Wawatam* linked rail service on Michigan's lower and upper peninsulas for the Michigan Central Railroad for more than 70 years. The 7¾-mile run across the Straits of Mackinac was always a money-losing proposition but was subsidized by the railroad. The ferry, built with a passenger lounge and dining room, carried freight and passenger cars. The Lake Superior Limited ceased operation in 1955, thus ending the last passenger train–ferry operation in the United States. The car ferry continued to work for another 30 years until it was finally taken out of service.

Plans to save the *Chief Wawatam* insisted on preserving the ferry's hull and steam engine. Designed by noted naval architect Frank Kirby, the boat inaugurated the modern era of ice breaking with its new design: the spoon bow rode up on the ice, while a bow propeller sucked away the supporting water from beneath it. In this fashion the *Chief Wawatam* was able to break ice two feet thick. The completely unmodified *Chief Wawatam* was Kirby's last ice breaker when the hull was cut down to a barge. The triple-expansion marine steam engine in the ferry was powered by six Scotch boilers, all handfired with coal. The *Chief Wawatam* was the last working "hand bomber" in the country outside of museum vessels. Efforts to preserve the car ferry as a museum, with revenue coming from restaurants or shops on the car deck, were dashed when the Michigan Department of Transportation rejected pleas to save *Chief Wawatam* and sold it; its only concession to preservation interests was to set aside machinery parts and fittings for museum display. Thus vanished an important vessel, one of only two unmodified historic Great Lakes car ferries. The future of the other, the *City of Milwaukee*, is at this time uncertain, despite the fact that it is a National Historic Landmark. A permanent home for the vessel has yet to be found.

■ ■ ■ ■ ■ CHAUNCEY M. DEPEW ■ ■ ■ ■ ■ ■

Built by the Bath Iron Works in 1913 as the *Rangeley*, the steamer *Chauncey M. Depew* ended its days as a floating restaurant in Secaucus, New Jersey. The 185-foot-long steel vessel, constructed for the Maine Central Railroad, had worked for more than 50 years in Maine, New York, and Bermuda and by 1988 was one of a handful of early 20th-century excursion steamers left in the United States. Sunk in 1971, the derelict *Depew* was raised and converted to a restaurant in 1977. Plans to restore the *Depew* to operating condition came to naught, despite the formation of the Rangeley Foundation, a spirited effort to acquire a historic steam engine to reinstall in the vessel, and the assistance of the National Trust's maritime preservation department. The *Depew* sank at its mooring on the Hackensack River in December 1987, effectively ending the preservation effort. Half submerged, the ill-fated steamer is gradually disintegrating while discussions about removing and scrapping it continue among city officials, the state, and the U.S. Army Corps of Engineers.

■ ■ ■ ■ ■   G. A. BOECKLING   ■ ■ ■ ■ ■

The excursion steam ferry *G. A. Boeckling* was built in 1909 by the Great Lakes Engineering Works to run across Sandusky Bay between Sandusky, Ohio, to Cedar Point Amusement Park. The *Boeckling* served from 1909 until it was retired in 1951, becoming in the process an important part of Sandusky's heritage. Purchased by Peterson Boat Builders of Sturgeon Bay, Wisconsin, the boarded-up *Boeckling* served as a floating warehouse for the next 30 years. In 1980 the Friends of the Boeckling, a nonprofit group with 600 members, formed to acquire and restore the ferry as a Sandusky attraction. In 1982 the steamer was brought back to Sandusky, and work was begun to survey and restore it. The group spent more than a half million dollars on the project, but on June 21, 1989, an early morning fire of suspicious origin swept through the ferry, destroying the wood superstructure and causing the steel main deck and the hull to buckle. The Friends of the Boeckling, disheartened by the long and difficult task of raising funds and working to save the ship, ended its efforts and did not attempt to rebuild it from its few remnants.

■ ■ ■ ■ ■ ■   MARGARET EMILIE   ■ ■ ■ ■ ■ ■

The two-masted schooner *Margaret Emilie*, built in 1912 as the *Dorothy Hilzheim*, was dismantled in 1989. It was then the last known Biloxi schooner, a type of shallow-draft, clip-per-bowed oyster and fishing schooner built to work in the Gulf's nationally important seafood industry. Between the 1870s and 1930s hundreds of these hardy shoal draft-vessels were built, many in Biloxi. After a long career working the oyster beds of the Mississippi Sound and conversion to a motor vessel around 1930, the *Margaret Emilie* was washed ashore by Hurricane Betsy in 1965. The derelict hulk's title passed to Biloxi residents interested in saving the city's and the region's rapidly vanishing maritime past. Displayed on shore for more than 20 years, the dismasted hulk, despite some restoration work, began to rot. Although listed in the National Register of Historic Places, the schooner was deter-mined to be unsalvageable and was dismantled and hauled away in the first week of January 1989. The loss of the schoo-ner is typical of the oft-repeated failure of well-meaning local efforts that successfully save a vessel and then let it slowly decay when the initial burst of enthusiasm wears off and funding becomes hard to find.

■ ■ ■ ■ ■ ■ ■   LUNA   ■ ■ ■ ■ ■ ■ ■

One of the nation's few surviving wood-hulled tugboats, the *Luna* was the first diesel-electric vessel in the world built for a commercial tugboat company. The successful operation of the *Luna* was a major influence on tugboat propulsion de-signs in the United States and abroad as the new, more reli-able diesel-electric system was adopted. The *Luna* worked in Boston Harbor for 41 years before being retired in 1971. Used as a floating residence by a succession of private owners, it was acquired for restoration by the Terra-Mare Research and Education Society in 1979. In the hope of spurring res-toration efforts, the *Luna* was designated a National Historic Landmark in 1988, but the tugboat sank at its mooring on the Charles River in Boston in 1990. Leaking fuel oil and slowly rotting, the half-sunk hulk will probably be scrapped in the immediate future.

■ ■ ■ ■ ■ ■   PRINCESS LOUISE   ■ ■ ■ ■ ■ ■

Built at North Vancouver, British Columbia, for the Cana-dian Pacific Railway in 1921, the *Princess Louise* ran between Vancouver and Alaska, calling at ports on the inside pas-sage; among the more famous ports of call were Ketchikan, Juneau, Sitka, and Skagway. Carrying passengers and freight to and from the Yukon to Canada's principal Pacific port, the *Princess Louise* remained in service until it was retired in 1962. Laid up in North Vancouver, the steamer was sold to American interests and brought to Los Angeles in 1966, where it was adapted as a restaurant. During the next two decades, the ship slowly deteriorated despite periodic renovation and repair. The restaurant closed in 1988, after filing for bankruptcy. Acquired by the Bank of San Pedro, the *Princess Louise* was in the process of being repaired for sale at auction when it capsized at the shipyard in September 1989. For the next few months efforts were made to refloat the ship while the hulk was stripped of more than $50,000 worth of fittings and antiques. Purchased by a salvage firm, the *Princess Louise* was proposed for use as a sunken fishing reef and diving attraction despite the pleas of preservationists. The owner refloated the steamer in late 1990 and was towing it to sea when the weakened hull gave way and the vessel sank outside the harbor near San Pedro. The problems of the *Princess Louise* highlight the dilemma faced by a number of historic vessels purchased for use as restaurants and other commercial uses. Commercial adaptive use is a viable solution for preservation and has saved many vessels that otherwise would have been lost, and many owners are committed to preserving the ships' historic integrity and keeping them afloat. Unfortunately, others who do not have the resources or the desire to expend the large amounts required to keep a ship afloat or to maintain it in a historic manner once the costs of preservation escalate have sold, scuttled, or scrapped their vessels. As a result, the majority of historic vessels that have been converted to other uses, although initially saved, have ultimately, like the *Princess Louise*, been lost.

■ ■ ■ ■ ■ ■   THE SKIPJACK FLEET   ■ ■ ■ ■ ■ ■

Maryland and Virginia's large fleet of historic skipjacks, working on the Chesapeake Bay as one of the nation's last two commercial sailing fleets (the other is the windjammer fleet of passenger vessels in Maine), has attracted considerable attention and interest. The skipjack is the official state vessel of Maryland, which has worked diligently to save the dwindling number of these sailing oyster boats. After a regional inventory most of the fleet was listed in the National Register of Historic Places, and a recent effort funded by the National Trust proposed a management plan for the fleet. Several Chesapeake Bay institutions and museums have arranged for tourist cruises and summer displays of skipjacks after the oyster season. However, the dwindling trade and the considerable needs of an aged wood fleet have whittled away the number of these unique, nationally important vessels. Within recent years several skipjacks have been laid up or in some cases abandoned on mudflats. These include the *Ruby G. Ford* (1891), the *Susan May* (1901), the *Bernice J.* (1904), the *Reliance* (1904), and the *Ida May* (1906). Other skipjacks are in poor repair, and the fleet's rapid decline and loss means the extinction of a maritime tradition, the loss of the skills of that tradition, and the preservation of only a handful of skipjacks in Chesapeake Bay museums from the dozens that exist now. The impending loss of the skipjack fleet is one of the most compelling issues in maritime preservation, and the tragedy engendered by their extinction would rival the loss of an individually significant ship such as the *Constitution*.

Top: The presidential yacht *Sequoia*, rescued from oblivion and beautifully restored, is now laid up in a Norfolk shipyard, awaiting monies to pay off its debt and provide a maintenance endowment. Right: The U.S. Army Corps of Engineers inspection launch *Suisun*, restored to its 1914 splendor, was badly damaged in an engine-room fire and explosion and must undergo substantial reconstruction and restoration.

HIGH HOPES, GRIM REALITIES, AND MODERATE GAINS: PRESERVING SHIPS TODAY

The difficulties of maritime preservation become evident when looking at the nation's historic ships in toto. Since 1985 several historic vessels have been lost. Some vessel owners have sold or are in the process of selling their vessels. The Harry Lundeberg School sold most of its fleet of historic vessels, including the lightship *No. 84*, the *Dauntless*, and the *Capt. James Cook*. The *No. 84*, in Yonkers, New York, is reportedly for sale again. The presidential yacht *Sequoia*, rescued from oblivion and beautifully restored, is now laid up in a Norfolk shipyard, its future uncertain since not enough money has been raised to pay off the ship's debts and provide for a maintenance endowment, requirements before it again enters presidential service.

Other vessels face major preservation needs. The U.S. Army Corps of Engineers' inspection launch *Suisun*, recently restored to its 1914 splendor, was badly damaged in an engine-room fire and explosion and must undergo substantial reconstruction and restoration. The fleet of historic ships at San Francisco Maritime National Historical Park requires a major restoration effort estimated at $16 million or more.

While the grim realities of maritime preservation are apparent, so are many notable successes. More historic vessels have been recognized as national treasures. As part of the National Maritime Initiative, the Historic American

Buildings Survey–Historic American Engineering Record revived the Historic American Merchant Marine Survey to prepare detailed drawings and photographic records of vessels. At the beginning of 1991 eight vessels had been documented through both drawings and photographs, while an additional six had been documented through photographs. The National Trust for Historic Preservation financed a preservation plan for Maryland's endangered historic skipjack fleet, working closely with the state.

The successes are best seen in touring the nation's historic ships. Some are spectacular and well known, such as the reconstruction and relaunching of the brig *Niagara* or the $5 million restoration of the battleship USS *Texas*. Many gains are more moderate, important projects that have involved considerable community efforts. The forecastle deck of the four-masted ship *Falls of Clyde* was recently rebuilt; the U.S. Army Corps of Engineers' inspection steamer *Sergeant Floyd* was restored and opened to the public in a new waterfront park in Sioux City, Iowa; and Tacoma, Washington, citizens saved and restored their historic 1929 *Fireboat No. 1.* The South Street Seaport Museum received a $250,000 grant from the state of New York to begin restoration of the schooner *Lettie G. Howard*, and Ray Williamson, the new owner of the schooner *Grace Bailey*, had it restored in 1990 in Rockland, Maine. At the San Francisco Maritime National Historical Park, not only has the steam schooner *Wapama*'s dry rot apparently been halted, but the steam tugboat *Hercules* is operational again.

The restoration of the presidential yacht *Potomac* in Oakland, California, was another major success. The riverboat *Delta King*, now a floating attraction in Sacramento, California, was a half-sunk rotting hulk only a few years ago. Other historic ships are being acquired and saved. The

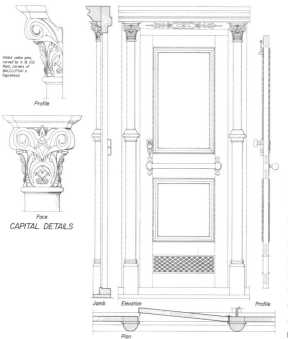

Gilded yellow pine, carved by A. & D.G. Reid, carvers of BALCLUTHA's figurehead.

Profile

Face
CAPITAL DETAILS

Jamb   Elevation   Profile

Plan

The Historic American Buildings Survey and Historic American Engineering Record revived the Historic American Merchant Marine Survey to prepare detailed drawings and photographic records of vessels. Shown are drawings of the details of a saloon door of the *Balclutha*.

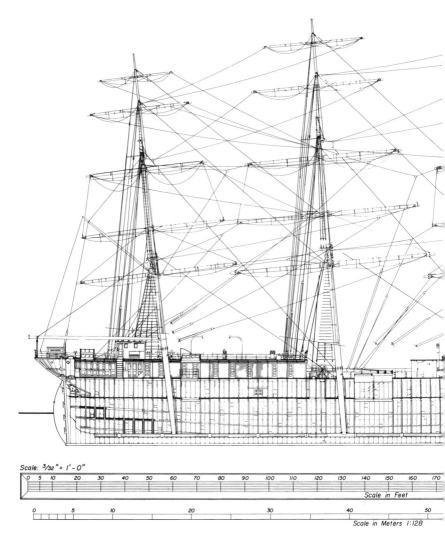

Scale: ³/₃₂ " = 1' - 0"

| 0 | 5 | 10 | 20 | 30 | 40 | 50 | 60 | 70 | 80 | 90 | 100 | 110 | 120 | 130 | 140 | 150 | 160 | 170 |

Scale in Feet

| 0 | 5 | 10 | 20 | 30 | 40 | 50 |

Scale in Meters 1:128

Shown above is a detailed drawing of the ship's overall profile of the *Balclutha*.

World War II aircraft carrier *Cabot* will form the core of a new naval museum in New Orleans; Patriot's Point, near Charleston, has acquired the historic U.S. Coast Guard cutter *Ingham*; and the submarine *Croaker* was rescued and restored by the Naval and Servicemen's Park in Buffalo, New York.

What does all this mean? Preservationists and citizens alike must resolve that the last examples and survivors of a long, rich maritime past will be preserved so that future generations can experience a whaler, a dreadnought, a fireboat, a lightship, an excursion steamer, a skipjack, or a fishing tugboat. The grim realities will always be a part of maritime preservation. The drama and the beauty of ships and the seafaring tradition, however, sustain the high hopes of the ship savers, and the gains, balanced against the failures, are moderate when assessed individually but significant and telling when viewed nationally. Historic ship preservation, with encouragement and the conscientious and consistent application of money and effort, could ultimately save the nation's historic ships for future generations to enjoy and appreciate. The passage will be stormy, marked by uncharted shoals and rocks, and safe haven in port not always certain. The ship savers, however, must stay the course.

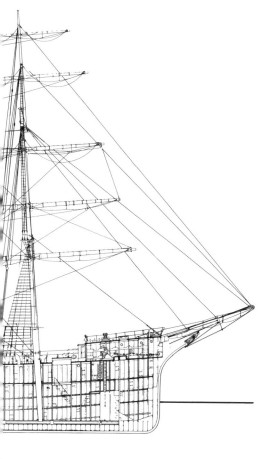

Below: In 1989 the battleship *Texas* visited Todd Shipyard, Galveston, Texas, as part of its restoration.

■ ■ ■ ■ ■ ■ ■ ■ ■ ■ ■ ■ ■ ■ ■ ■ ■ ■ ■ ■

VESSELS IN THE NATIONAL REGISTER

Listed below are all vessels more than 40 feet in length included in the National Register of Historic Places. Those indicated only by name and date are discussed elsewhere in *Great American Ships*. Others, not part of any regional list, include brief information regarding type, location, and original and current uses.

Adventure (1926) See page 92.

Adventuress (1913) See page 261.

USS *Alabama* (1942) See page 154.

USS *Albacore* (1953) See page 96.

Alma (1891) See page 237.

Alvin Clark (1846)
Vessel type: Schooner
Current location: Menominee, Mich.
Original use: Great Lakes general carrying trade
Current use: Laid up, for sale

Arkansas II (1940)
Vessel type: Snagboat
Current location: North Little Rock, Ark.
Original use: Snag removal
Current use: Laid up, awaiting restoration

Arthur Foss (1889)
See page 262 .

Balclutha (1886) See page 238.

Becky Thatcher (1927) See page 216.

USS *Becuna* (1944) See page 134.

Belle of Louisville (1914) See page 184.

Berkeley (1898) See page 233.

Bernice J. (1904)
Vessel type: Skipjack
Current location: Chestertown, Md.
Original use: Oyster dredging
Current use: Laid up on land

Binghamton (1905) See page 116.

Bowdoin (1921) See page 72.

USS *Bowfin* (1943) See page 254.

Brilliant See page 58.

C. A. Thayer (1895) See page 239.

USS *Cabot* (1943) See page 162.

Captain Meriwether Lewis (1932) See page 189.

USS *Cassin Young* (1943) See page 83.

Charles W. Morgan (1841) See page 62.

City of Milwaukee (1931) See page 198.

City of Oakland (1940) See page 229.

USS *Clamagore* (1945) See page 145.

Clarence Crockett (1908)
Vessel type: Skipjack
Current location: Deal Island, Md.
Original use: Oyster dredging
Current use: Under restoration for dredging

Claude W. Somers (1911)
Vessel type: Skipjack
Current location:
   Tilghman, Md.
Original use: Oyster dredging
Current use: Under restoration
   for dredging

USS *Cobia* (1943) See page 218.

USS *Cod* (1943) See page 212.

Columbia (1902) See page 196.

Commander (1917) See
page 131.

USF *Constellation* (1797) See
page 107.

USS *Constitution* (1797) See
page 84.

Delta King (1926) See page 232.

Delta Queen (1926) See
page 163.

Deluge (1923) See page 164.

Donald B (1923) See page 213.

USS *Drum* (1942) See page 157.

Duwamish (1909) See page 263.

E. C. Collier (1910) See
page 112.

Edna E. Lockwood (1889) See
page 113.

Edna G. (1896) See page 204.

USS *Edson* (1958) See
page 119.

Elf (1888)
Vessel type: Yacht
Current location:
   Earleville, Md.
Original use: Racing yacht
Current use: Yacht

Elissa (1877) See page 172.

Ellen Ruth (1932) See page 205.

Elsworth (1901)
Vessel type: Skipjack
Current location:
   Chestertown, Md.
Original use: Oyster dredging
Current use: Education,
   oyster dredging

Emma C. Berry (1866) See
page 63.

Equator (1888)
Vessel type: Schooner
Current location:
   Everett, Wash.
Original use: Cargo
Current use: Laid up

Ernestina (1894) See page 94.

Eureka (1890) See page 241.

F. C. Lewis, Jr. (1907)
Vessel type: Skipjack
Current location: Wewona, Md.
Original use: Oyster dredging
Current use: Under restora-
   tion for dredging

Falls of Clyde (1878) See
page 255.

Fannie L. Daugherty (1904)
Vessel type: Skipjack
Current location: Wewona, Md.
Original use: Oyster dredging
Current use: Oyster dredging

Fireboat No. 1 (1929) See
page 267.

Fire Fighter (1938) See
page 120.

Florence See page 64.

G. A. Boeckling (1909)
Vessel type: Ferry
Current location:
   Sandusky, Ohio
Original use: Passenger ferry
Current use: Destroyed by fire

Geo. M. Verity (1927) See
page 180.

George N. Cretekos (1941)
Vessel type: Sponge diving
   boat
Current location: Tarpon
   Springs, Fla.
Original use: Sponge fishing
Current use: Sponge fishing

Goldenrod (1910) See page 186.

Grace Bailey (1882) See
page 69.

HA-19 (1938) See page 169.

USS *Hazard* (1944) See page 189.

Helianthus III (1921)
Vessel type: Yacht
Current location: Annapolis, Md.
Original use: Cruising
Current use: Cruising, residence

Hercules (1907) See page 242.

Hilda M. Willing (1905)
Vessel type: Skipjack
Current location: Tilghman, Md.
Original use: Oyster dredging
Current use: Oyster dredging

Howard (1909)
Vessel type: Skipjack
Current location: Wewona, Md.
Original use: Oyster dredging
Current use: Oyster dredging

Ida May (1906)
Vessel type: Skipjack
Current location: Chance, Md.
Original use: Oyster dredging
Current use: Laid up, abandoned

USS *Inaugural* (1944) See page 188.

USS *Intrepid* (1943) See page 122.

Island Belle (1916)
Vessel type: Motor vessel
Current location: Smith Island, Md.
Original use: Passengers, mail, freight
Current use: Laid up

Jean (1938) See page 258.

Jeremiah O'Brien (1943) See page 243.

John W. Brown (1942) See page 245.

Joseph Conrad (1882) See page 64.

USS *Joseph P. Kennedy Jr.* (1945) See page 87.

Katahdin (1914) See page 75.

Katheryn M. Lee (1912)
Vessel type: Schooner
Current location: Dover, Del.
Original use: Oyster dredging
Current use: Oyster dredging

Kathryn (1901)
Vessel type: Skipjack
Current location: Tilghman, Md.
Original use: Oyster dredging
Current use: Oyster dredging

Kestrel (1892)
Vessel type: Yacht
Current location: Toms River, N.J.
Original use: Yacht
Current use: Laid up, under rehabilitation

USS *Kidd* (1943) See page 160.

L. A. Dunton (1921). See page 65.

USS *Laffey* (1944) See page 146.

Lane Victory (1945) See page 248.

Lehigh Valley Railroad Barge No. 79 (1914) See page 117.

Lettie G. Howard (1893) See page 124.

Lewis Ark (1905) See page 246.

Lightship *No. 79* ("Barnegat") (1904) See page 137.

Lightship *No. 83* ("Relief") (1904) See page 263.

Lightship *No. 87* ("Ambrose") (1907) See page 125.

Lightship *No. 101* ("Portsmouth") (1915) See page 153.

Lightship *No. 103* ("Huron") (1921) See page 201.

Lightship *No. 112* ("Nantucket") (1936) See page 76.

Lightship *No. 114* ("New Bedford") (1930) See page 95.

Lightship *No. 116* ("Chesapeake") (1930) See page 108.

Lightship *No. 118* ("Overfalls") (1938) See page 102.

Lightship *No. WAL-604* ("Columbia") (1950) See page 259.

Lightship *No. WAL-605* ("Relief") (1951) See page 230.

USS *Ling* (1943) See page 117.

USS *Lionfish* (1944) See page 87.

Little Jennie (1884) See page 118.

Lone Star (1868) See page 181.

Lotus (1908)
Vessel type: Motor vessel
Current location: Olympia, Wash.
Original use: Houseboat
Current use: Houseboat

Luna (1930)
Vessel type: Tugboat
Current location: Boston
Original use: Tugboat
Current use: Partially submerged

Maggie Lee (1903)
Vessel type: Skipjack
Current location: Tilghman, Md.
Original use: Oyster dredging
Current use: Laid up, for sale

Maggie S. Myers (1893)
Vessel type: Schooner
Current location: Dover, Del.
Original use: Oyster dredging
Current use: Crabbing

Majestic (1923) See page 211.

Mamie S. Barrett (1921)
Vessel type: River towboat
Current location: Unknown
Original use: Flagship
Current use: Unknown

Margaret Emilie (1912)
Vessel type: Schooner
Current location: Biloxi, Miss.
Original use: Oyster dredging
Current use: Dismantled

Marlin (1953) See page 190.

Mary D. Hume (1881)
Vessel type: Steam schooner
Current location: Gold Beach, Ore.
Original use: Steam schooner
Current use: Partially submerged

Mary W. Somers (1904)
Vessel type: Skipjack
Current location: Havre de Grace, Md.
Original use: Oyster dredging
Current use: Laid up in dry berth

USS *Massachusetts* (1942) See page 88.

Mayor Andrew Broaddus (1929) See page 185.

Mercantile (1916) See page 70.

Meteor (1896) See page 220.

Mike Fink (1936) See page 184.

Milwaukee Clipper (1904) See page 195.

Minnie V. (1906) See page 109.

Montgomery (1926) See page 156.

Mustang (1907) See page 114.

N. K. Symi (1935)
Vessel type: Sponge diving boat
Current location: Tarpon Springs, Fla.
Original use: Sponge fishing
Current use: Sponge fishing

USS *Nautilus* (1954) See page 61.

Nellie L. Byrd (1911)
Vessel type: Skipjack
Current location: Tilghman, Md.
Original use: Oyster dredging
Current use: Oyster dredging

Nenana (1933) See page 224.

New Way (1939)
Vessel type: Schooner
Current location: Philadelphia
Original use: Cable tender
Current use: Youth training

USB *Niagara* (1813) See page 133.

Niagara (1897)
Vessel type: Freighter
Current location: Erie, Pa.
Original use: Great Lakes general carrying trade
Current use: Proposed museum

Nobska (1925) See page 90.

USS *North Carolina* (1941) See page 143.

USS *Olympia* (1895) See page 137.

USS *Pampanito* (1943) See page 247.

Philadelphia (1776) See page 105.

Piasa (1921)
Vessel type: Towboat
Current location: Unknown
Original use: Towboat
Current use: Unknown

Potomac (1934) See page 231.

President (1924) See page 178.

PT 617 (1945) See page 91.

PT 796 (1945) See page 91.

Ralph J. Scott (1925) See page 249.

Ralph T. Webster (1905)
Vessel type: Skipjack
Current location: Tilghman, Md.
Original use: Oyster dredging
Current use: Laid up, abandoned

Rebecca T. Ruark (1886)
Vessel type: Skipjack
Current location: Tilghman, Md.
Original use: Oyster dredging
Current use: Oyster dredging

Ruby G. Ford (1891)
Vessel type: Skipjack
Current location: Tilghman, Md.
Original use: Oyster dredging
Current use: Laid up on land, abandoned

Sabino See page 66.

San Mateo (1922)
Vessel type: Ferry
Current location: Seattle
Original use: Ferry
Current use: Laid up

Santa Rosa (1926)
Vessel type: Ferry
Current location: Unknown
Original use: Ferry
Current use: Unknown

NS *Savannah* (1959) See page 148.

Sea Gull (1924)
Vessel type: Skipjack
Current location: Oriole, Md.
Original use: Oyster dredging
Current use: Laid up

Sequoia (1925)
Vessel type: Yacht
Current location: Norfolk, Va.
Original use: Yacht
Current use: In storage

Sergeant Floyd (1932) See page 182.

Sigsbee (1901)
Vessel type: Skipjack
Current location: Rock Hall, Md.
Original use: Oyster dredging
Current use: Laid up

USS *Silversides* (1941) See page 200.

St. Nicholas III (1939) See page 160.

St. Nicholas VI (1927)
Vessel type: Sponge diving boat
Current location: Tarpon
 Springs, Fla.
Original use: Sponge fishing
Current use: Laid up

Stanley Norman (1902) See
page 105.

Star of India (1863) See
page 235.

Ste. Claire (1911) See page 196.

Stephen Taber (1871) See
page 80.

Susan May (1901)
Vessel type: Skipjack
Current location: Wewona, Md.
Original use: Oyster dredging
Current use: Laid up,
 abandoned

USCGC *Taney* (1936) See
page 110.

USS *Texas* (1914) See page 174.

USS *The Sullivans* (1943) See
page 209.

Thomas W. Clyde (1911)
Vessel type: Skipjack
Current location: Wewona, Md.
Original use: Oyster dredging
Current use: For sale

Ticonderoga (1906) See
page 99.

USS *Torsk* (1944) See page 111.

U-505 (1941) See page 194.

Valley Camp (1917) See page
202.

Vashon (1930)
Vessel type: Ferry
Current location: Seattle
Original use: Ferry
Current use: Sunk

Vayu (1905)
Vessel type: Yacht
Current location:
 New London, Conn.
Original use: Yacht
Current use: Laid up, for sale

Virginia V (1922) See page 264.

Virginia W (1904)
Vessel type: Skipjack
Current location:
 Tilghman, Md.
Original use: Oyster dredging
Current use: Oyster dredging

W. P. Snyder, Jr. (1918) See
page 215.

W. T. Preston (1939) See
page 260.

Wapama (1915) See page 251.

Wavertree (1885) See page 130.

Wawona (1897) See page 265.

William A. Irvin (1938) See
page 203.

William M. Black (1934) See
page 179.

William S. Mitchell (1934) See
page 183.

Wm. B. Tennison (1899) See
page 112.

USS *Yorktown* (1943) See
page 149.

Zodiac (1924) See page 266.

FURTHER READING

Alden, John D. *The Fleet Submarine in the U.S. Navy.* Annapolis, Md.: U.S. Naval Institute Press, 1979.

_____. "Olympian Legacy." Reprint from *United States Naval Institute Proceedings.* Annapolis, Md.: U.S. Naval Institute Press, 1976.

Allen, Everett S. *Arctic Odyssey: The Life of Rear Admiral Donald B. MacMillan.* New York: Dodd, Mead & Co., 1962.

Ambler, Charles Henry. *A History of Transportation in the Ohio Valley.* 1931. Reprint. Westport, Conn.: Greenwood Press, 1970.

Anderson, William R. *Nautilus 90 North.* New York: New American Library, 1959.

Ansel, Willits D. *Restoration of the Smack Emma C. Berry at Mystic Seaport 1969–1971.* Mystic, Conn.: Marine Historical Association, 1973.

"Auxiliary Schooner *Adventuress.*" *The Rudder* (October 1913).

Baker, William Avery. *A Maritime History of Bath, Maine, and the Kennebec River Region.* 2 vols. Bath: Marine Research Society of Bath, 1973.

_____. *Sloops and Shallops.* Barre, Mass.: Barre Publishing Company, 1966.

Baldwin, Leland D. *The Keelboat Age on Western Waters.* Pittsburgh: University of Pittsburgh Press, 1980.

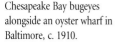

Chesapeake Bay bugeyes alongside an oyster wharf in Baltimore, c. 1910.

Bates, Alan L. *The Western Rivers Steamboat Cyclopoedium.* Leonia, N.J.: Hustle Press, 1968.

Bauer, K. Jack. *A Maritime History of the United States: The Role of America's Seas and Waterways.* Columbia: University of South Carolina Press, 1988.

Bearss, Edwin C. *Hardluck Ironclad: The Sinking and Salvage of the Cairo.* Baton Rouge: Louisiana State University Press, 1966.

Becton, F. Julian, and Joseph Morschauser. *The Ship That Would Not Die.* Missoula, Mont.: Pictorial Histories Publishing Co., 1980.

Bell, James D. "USS *Texas*: Planning the Restoration." *Sea History* 31 (Spring 1984).

Blair, Joan, and Clay Blair, Jr. *Return to the River Kwai.* New York: Simon and Schuster, 1979.

Booth, Russell. "USS *Pampanito*: The Last Three War Patrols." *Sea Letter* 37 (Spring 1987).

Brewington, Marion V. *Chesapeake Bay: A Pictorial Maritime History.* Cambridge, Md.: Cornell Maritime Press, 1953.

Brouwer, Norman J. *International Register of Historic Ships.* Annapolis, Md.: U.S. Naval Institute Press, 1985.

Bulkley, Robert J., Jr. *At Close Quarters: PT Boats in the United States Navy.* Washington, D.C.: Naval History Division, Department of the Navy, 1962.

Burgess, Robert H. *Chesapeake Sailing Craft, Part I.* Cambridge, Md.: Tidewater Publishers, 1975.

Butowsky, Harry A. *Warships Associated with World War II in the Pacific: National Historic Landmark Theme Study.* Washington, D.C.: National Park Service, 1985.

Carpenter, Dorr, and Norman Polmar. *Submarines of the Imperial Japanese Navy.* Annapolis, Md.: U.S. Naval Institute Press, 1986.

Chapelle, Howard I. *The American Fishing Schooners 1825–1935.* New York: W. W. Norton & Co., 1973.

_____. *American Small Sailing Craft: Their Design, Development, and Construction.* New York: W. W. Norton & Co., 1951.

_____. *The History of American Sailing Ships.* New York: Bonanza Books, 1985.

_____. *The National Watercraft Collection.* Washington, D.C.: National Museum of American History, 1960.

Chapelle, Howard I., and Leon D. Polland. *The Constellation Question.* Washington, D.C.: Smithsonian Institution Press, 1970.

Chesnau, Roger, ed. *Conway's All the World's Fighting Ships, 1922–1946.* New York: Mayflower Books, 1980.

Colton, J. Ferrell. *Windjammers Significant.* Flagstaff, Ariz.: J. F. Colton & Co., 1954.

Davis, Charles G. *American Sailing Ships: Their Plans and History.* New York: Dover Books, 1984.

Day, Jane, ed. *The Schooner Roseway: History and Log.* Camden, Maine: Yankee Schooner Cruises, n.d.

Delgado, James P. "*Berkeley*: Hard Worked in a Rough Service." *Sea Letter* 42 (Spring–Summer 1990).

DeLong, Harriet Tracy. *Pacific Schooner Wawona.* Bellevue, Wash.: Documentary Book Publishers Corp., 1985.

Dirksen, Louise. "*Jeremiah O'Brien*: A Ship That Wouldn't Quit." *Naval History* 4, no. 1 (Winter 1990).

Ditzel, Paul. *Fireboats: A Complete History of the Develop-ment of Fireboats in America.* New Albany, Ind.: Fire Buff House of Conway Enterprises, 1989.

Dulin, Robert O., Jr., William H. Garzke, Jr., and Robert F. Sumrall. *Battleships: United States Battleships in World War II.* Annapolis, Md.: U.S. Naval Institute Press, 1976.

Eifert, Virginia S. *Delta Queen: The Story of a Steamboat.* New York: Dodd, Mead & Co., 1960.

Elve, Steven D. *Rails Across the Water.* Rockford, Mich.: P. M. Service, 1984.

Ewing, Steve. *American Cruisers of World War II, A Pictorial Essay.* Missoula, Mont.: Pictorial Histories Publishing Co., 1984.

_____. *Memories and Memorials: The World War II U.S. Navy 40 Years After Victory.* Missoula, Mont.: Pictorial Histories Publishing Co., 1986.

Fahey, James C. *The Ships and Aircraft of the United States Fleet.* Falls Church, Va.: Ships and Aircraft, 1958.

Fairburn, William A. *Merchant Sail.* Center Lovell, Maine: Fairburn Marine Educational Foundation, 1944–55.

Flexner, James Thomas. *Steamboats Come True.* Boston: Little, Brown and Co., 1978.

Flint, Willard. *Lightships of the United States Government: Reference Notes.* Washington, D.C.: U.S. Coast Guard, 1989.

Fox, William A. *Always Good Ships: Histories of Newport News Ships.* Norfolk, Va.: Donning Co., 1986.

Square riggers lined up at South Street, New York City, c. 1885, with the Brooklyn Bridge in the background.

_____. *Dorothy: Hull Number One Comes Home.* Newport News, Va.: Society of Naval Architects and Marine Engineers, 1976.

Friedman, Norman. *The Postwar Naval Revolution.* Annapolis, Md.: U.S. Naval Institute Press, 1986.

_____. *U.S. Aircraft Carriers: An Illustrated Design History.* Annapolis, Md.: U.S. Naval Institute Press, 1983.

_____. *U.S. Destroyers: An Illustrated Design History.* Annapolis, Md.: U.S. Naval Institute Press, 1982.

_____. *U.S. Small Combatants, Including PT-Boats, Subchasers, and the Brown Water Navy: An Illustrated Design History.* Annapolis, Md.: U.S. Naval Institute Press, 1987.

Friedman, Norman, Arthur D. Baker, Arnold S. Lott, and Robert F. Sumrall. *USS Arizona Ship's Data: A Photographic History.* Honolulu: Fleet Reserve Association, 1978.

Friedman, Norman, Arnold S. Lott, and Robert S. Sumrall. *USS Mass. BB 59 Ship's Data.* Fall River, Mass.: USS Massachusetts Memorial Committee, 1985.

Gallery, Daniel V. *U-505.* New York: Warner Books, 1956.

Garland, Joseph E. *Down to the Sea: The Fishing Schooners of Gloucester.* Boston: David R. Godine, 1983.

Garland, Joseph E., and Captain Jim Sharp. *Adventure: Queen of the Windjammers.* Camden, Maine: Down East Books, 1985.

Gillen, Michael. "The *John W. Brown*." *Sea History* 41 (Autumn 1986).

Graham, Philip. *Showboats: The History of an American Institution.* Austin: University of Texas Press, 1951.

Grant, Gordon. *Sail Ho! Windjammer Sketches Alow and Aloft.* New York: William Farquher-Payson, 1926.

Greene, Letha C. *Long Live the Delta Queen.* New York: Hastings House Publishers, 1973.

Greenhill, Basil. *The Evolution of the Wooden Ship.* New York: Facts on File, 1988.

Grover, David H. *U.S. Army Ships and Watercraft of World War II.* Annapolis, Md.: U.S. Naval Institute Press, 1987.

Haas, Irvin. *America's Historic Ships: Replicas and Restorations.* New York: Arco Publishing Company, 1975.

Hall, Henry. *Report on the Shipbuilding Industry of the United States.* Washington, D.C.: Government Printing Office, 1882.

Hardy, A. C. *American Ship Types.* New York: D. Van Nostrand Co., 1927.

Harlan, George H. *San Francisco Bay Ferryboat.* Berkeley, Calif.: Howell-North Books, 1967.

Harrington, Joseph D. *Suicide Submarine: The Story of Japan's Submarine "Kamikaze" of Manned Torpedoes.* New York: Ballantine Books, 1962.

The double-ended fishing sloop *Viola* at anchor in Port Townsend, Washington, during the early 1900s.

Hawkins, Sam M. "The San Francisco Pilot Boats." *Pacific Motor Boat* (March 1936).

Hawkins, Van. Dorothy *and the Shipbuilders of Newport News*. Norfolk, Va.: Donning Co., 1976.

Hill, Ralph Nading, and Jerry P. Williams. *Lake Champlain Ferryboats*. Burlington, Vt.: Lake Champlain Transportation Co., 1990.

Hilton, George W. *The Great Lakes Car Ferries*. Berkeley, Calif.: Howell-North, 1962.

Hiscock, Barbara A. *Wawona: The Heritage of Sailing in the North Pacific*. Seattle: Save Our Ships, n.d.

Holland, F. Ross. *Great American Lighthouses*. Washington, D.C.: Preservation Press, 1989.

Holly, H. H. *Sparrow-Hawk: A Seventeenth Century Vessel in Twentieth-Century America*. Boston: Nimrod Press, 1969.

Hoyt, Edwin P. *Bowfin*. New York: Van Nostrand Reinhold Co., 1983.

Hudson, J. Ed. *The History of USS Cabot CVL-28: A Fast Carrier in World War II*. N.p., 1986.

Hulbert, Archer B. *The Paths of Inland Commerce*. New Haven, Conn.: Yale University Press, 1920.

Huycke, Harold. "The Ship *Pacific Queen*." *American Neptune* 4, no. 3 (July 1944).

Jentschura, Hansgeorg, Dieter Jung, and Peter Mickel. *Warships of the Imperial Japanese Navy, 1869–1945.* Annapolis, Md.: U.S. Naval Institute Press, 1986.

Johnson, Irving. *The Peking Battles Cape Horn.* Rev. ed. New York: National Maritime Historical Society, 1977.

Klegingat, Fred K. "Falls of Clyde." *Oceans* 5, no. 5 (September–October 1972).

Kline, M. S. *Steamboat Virginia V.* Bellevue, Wash.: Documentary Book Publishers Corporation, 1985.

Kline, M. S., and G. A. Bayless. *Ferryboats: A Legend on Puget Sound.* Seattle: Bayless Books, 1983.

Kochiss, John M. *Oystering from New York to Boston.* Middletown, Conn.: Wesleyan University Press, 1974.

Lang, Steven, and Peter H. Spectre. *On the Hawser: A Tugboat Album.* Camden, Maine: Down East Books, 1980.

Leavitt, John F. *Wake of the Coasters.* Middletown, Conn.: Wesleyan University Press, 1970.

_____. *The Charles W. Morgan.* Mystic, Conn.: Marine Historical Association, 1973.

Wood schooner under construction in Portland, Oregon, 1918. Contributing to the shipbuilding boom of World War I, wood schooners were much in demand for use as cargo ships during the war.

Lenihan, Daniel J., ed. *Submerged Cultural Resources Study: USS Arizona Memorial and Pearl Harbor National Historic Landmark.* Santa Fe, N.M.: Southwest Cultural Resources Center, National Park Service, 1989.

Levingston, Steve E. *Historic Ships of San Francisco.* San Francisco: Chronicle Books, 1984.

Lott, Arnold S., and Robert F. Sumrall. *Ship's Data: USS Texas BB35.* Annapolis, Md.: Leeward Publications, 1976.

Lowder, Hughston E., and Jack Scott. *Batfish: The Champion "Submarine-Killer" of World War II.* Englewood Cliffs, N.J.: Prentice-Hall, 1980.

Lubbock, Basil. *The Last of the Windjammers.* Vols. 1 and 2. Glasgow, Scotland: Brown, Son & Ferguson, 1975.

MacMullen, Jerry. *Star of India: The Log of an Iron Ship.* Berkeley, Calif.: Howell-North, 1961.

Marestier, Jean Baptiste. *Memoir on Steamboats of the United States of America.* Mystic, Conn.: Marine Historical Association, 1957.

Martin, Tyrone G.. *A Most Fortunate Ship.* Chester, Conn.: Globe Pequot Press, 1980.

Marvil, James E. *Sailing Rams: A History of Sailing Ships Built in and Near Sussex County, Delaware.* Laurel, Del.: Author, 1961.

Matteson, George. "A Centennial History of the Pioneer." *Seaport* 19, no. 2 (Summer 1985).

McNairn, Jack, and Jerry MacMullen. *Ships of the Redwood Coast.* Palo Alto, Calif.: Stanford University Press, 1945.

Merriman, David D., Jr. "USS *Albacore*: Forerunner of Today's Submarines." *Sea Classics* 13, no. 1 (January 1980).

Morris, E. P. *The Fore-and-Aft Rig in America.* New Haven, Conn.: Yale University Press, 1927.

Morris, Paul C. *American Sailing Coasters of the North Atlantic.* New York: Bonanza Books, 1979.

Morris, Paul C., and Joseph E. Morin. *The Island Steamers: A Chronology of Steam Transportation to and from the Offshore Islands of Martha's Vineyard and Nantucket.* Nantucket, Mass.: Nantucket Nautical Publications, 1977.

Morrison, John H. *History of American Steam Navigation.* New York: Stephen Daye Press, 1958.

Neill, Peter, ed. *Maritime America: Art and Artifacts from America's Great Nautical Collections.* New York: Balsem Press, Harry N. Abrams, 1988.

Newell, Gordon, and Joe Williamson. *Pacific Lumber Ships.* Seattle: Superior Publishing Co., 1960.

Newhall, Scott. *The Eppleton Hall.* Berkeley, Calif.: Howell North, 1971.

Olmstead, Roger. *C. A. Thayer & the Pacific Lumber Schooners.* San Francisco: Ward Ritchie Press, 1972.

_____. "The Square-Toed Packets of San Francisco Bay." *California Historical Society Quarterly* 51, no. 1 (Spring 1971).

Perry, Milton F. *Infernal Machines: The Story of Confederate Submarine and Mine Warfare.* Baton Rouge: Louisiana State University Press, 1985.

Petersen, William J. *Steamboating on the Upper Mississippi.* Iowa City: State Historical Society of Iowa, 1968.

Polmar, Norman. *The American Submarine.* Annapolis, Md.: Nautical and Aviation Publishing Co. of America, 1981.

"Propeller Ferryboat *Berkeley* in Service in San Francisco Bay." *Marine Engineering* 4, no. 2 (August 1989).

Putnam, George R. *Lighthouses and Lightships of the United States.* Boston and New York: Houghton Mifflin Co., 1917.

Putz, George. *Eagle, America's Sailing Square-Rigger.* Chester, Conn.: Globe-Pequot Press, 1986.

Raven, Alan. *Fletcher-Class Destroyers.* Annapolis, Md.: U.S. Naval Institute Press, 1986.

Steam ferry, "Boone No. 4 of Cincinnati," on the Ohio River around the turn of the century.

_____. *Essex-Class Carriers.* Annapolis, Md.: U.S. Naval Institute Press, 1988.

Reynolds, Clark G. *The Fighting Lady: The New Yorktown in the Pacific War.* Missoula, Mont.: Pictorial Histories Publishing Co., 1986.

Rhodes, Thomas G., and Harley E. Scott. *Steamboats Today: A Pictorial Directory of North American Vessels.* New York: Cayuga Creek Historical Press, 1986.

Roberts, John. *Anatomy of the Ship: The Aircraft Carrier Intrepid.* Annapolis, Md.: U.S. Naval Institute Press, 1982.

Robinson, Bill. *The Great American Yacht Designers.* New York: Alfred A. Knopf, 1974.

Rosenberg, Max. *The Building of Perry's Fleet on Lake Erie 1812–1813.* Harrisburg, Pa.: Pennsylvania Historical and Museum Commission, 1987.

Ross, Al. *Anatomy of the Ship: The Destroyer The Sullivans.* Annapolis, Md.: U.S. Naval Institute Press, 1988.

Rybka, Walter. "*Elissa* Sails: The Ship Is Now Real and Beautiful." *Sea History* 26 (Winter 1982).

_____. "USS *Texas*: The Ship and the Myth." *Sea History* 31 (Spring 1984).

Sakamaki, Kazuo. *I Attacked Pearl Harbor.* New York: Association Press, 1949.

Saville, Allison, *Ship's Data: The Gazela Primeiro.* Annapolis, Md.: Leeward Publications, 1978.

Sawyer, L. A., and W. H. Mitchell. *The Liberty Ships.* 2d ed. London: Lloyd's of London Press, 1985.

Scheina, Robert L. *U.S. Coast Guard Cutters and Craft of World War II.* Annapolis, Md.: U.S. Naval Institute Press, 1982.

_____. *U.S. Coast Guard Cutters and Craft, 1946–1990.* Annapolis, Md.: U.S. Naval Institute Press, 1990.

Smith, E. W., ed. *Workaday Schooners.* Camden, Maine: International Marine Publishing, 1975.

Spectre, Peter H. "The *Bowdoin* Project." *WoodenBoat* 47 (July–August 1982).

Stackpole, Renny. "The Saga of the Arctic Schooner *Bowdoin.*" *Sea History* (Summer 1986).

Stanford, Joseph M. *Sea History's Guide to American and Canadian Maritime Museums.* Croton-on-Hudson: Sea History Press, 1990.

Stanford, Peter. "*Elissa*: The Long Sea Career." *Sea History* (Fall 1979).

Stanford, Peter, ed. *The Wavertree: An Ocean Wanderer.* New York: South Street Seaport, 1969.

Sternlicht, Sanford, and Edwin M. Jameson. *U.S.F. Constellation: "Yankee Racehorse."* Cockeysville, Md.: Liberty Publishing Co., 1981.

Sumrall, Robert F., and Thomas F. Walkowaik. *USS Kidd DD 661 Warship's Data.* Missoula, Mont.: Pictorial Histories Publishing Co., 1985.

Tazewell, William L. *Newport News Shipbuilding: The First Century.* Newport News, Va.: Mariner's Museum, 1986.

Thomas, Gordon W. *Fast and Able: Life Stories of Great Gloucester Fishing Vessels.* Gloucester, Mass.: Gloucester 350th Anniversary Celebration, 1973.

Thompson, Frederic L. *Lightships of Cape Cod.* Portland, Maine: Congress Square Press, 1983.

Tree, Christina. "Windjammer Days." *Historic Preservation*, July–August 1990.

Trott, Harlan. *The Schooner That Came Home: The Final Voyage of the C. A. Thayer.* Cambridge, Md.: Cornell Maritime Press, 1958.

U.S. Department of the Navy. *Dictionary of American Naval Fighting Ships.* 8 vols. Washington, D.C.: Government Printing Office, 1959.

U.S. Submarine Veterans of World War II, Manitowoc Chapter. *Manitowoc Submarines.* Manitowoc, Wis.: Manitowoc County Historical Society, 1968.

Way, Frederick, Jr. *Directory of Steam Towboats of the Mississippi River System Past and Present.* Sewickley, Pa.: Steamboat Photo Co., 1947.

———. *Way's Packet Directory; 1848–1983.* Athens, Ohio: Ohio University Press, 1983.

■ ■ ■ ■ ■ ■ ■ ■ ■ ■ ■ ■ ■ ■ ■ ■

INFORMATION SOURCES

The following organizations and agencies can supply information on subjects covered in Great American Ships. In
addition, state historic preservation offices, state and local
historical societies, and many of the individual vessel owners
or caretakers have useful information and illustrations.

American Sail Training
Association
P.O. Box 1459
Newport, RI 02840

The Center for Wooden Boats
1010 Valley Street
Seattle, WA 98109

Destroyer Escort Sailors
Association
P.O. Box 680085
Orlando, FL 32868-0085

Great Lakes Historical Society
480 Main Street
Vermillion, OH 44089

Historic Naval Ships
Association (HINAS)
c/o U.S. Naval Academy
Museum
Annapolis, MD 21402-5034

Institute for Great Lakes
Research
Bowling Green State University
12764 Levis Parkway
Perrysburg, OH 43551

MIT Museum
Hart Nautical Collections
265 Massachusetts Avenue
Cambridge, MA 02139

Mystic Seaport Museum
P.O. Box 6000
Mystic, CT 06355

National Archives
Cartographic and
Architectural Branch
Washington, DC 20408

National Association of
Passenger Vessel Owners
1511 K Street, N.W.
Suite 715
Washington, DC 20005

National Maritime Alliance
c/o National Trust for
Historic Preservation
1785 Massachusetts
Avenue, N.W.
Washington, DC 20036

National Maritime
Historical Society
132 Maple Street
Croton-on-Hudson, NY
10520

National Park Service
U.S. Department of
the Interior:

Historic American
Engineering Record
P.O. Box 37127
Washington, DC 20013-7127

National Maritime Initiative
Division of History
P.O. Box 37127
Washington, DC 20013-7127

National Register of
Historic Places
P.O. Box 37127
Washington, DC 20013-7127

National Maritime Museum
San Francisco Maritime
National Historical Park
Fort Mason, Building 201
San Francisco, CA 94123

Submerged Cultural
Resources Unit
P.O. Box 728
Santa Fe, NM 87501

National Trust for
Historic Preservation
Maritime Office
1785 Massachusetts
Avenue, N.W.
Washington, DC 20036

Naval Historical Center
Ships History Branch
Washington Navy Yard
Building 57
Washington, DC
20374-0571

Peabody Museum of Salem
East India Marine Hall
East India Square
Salem, MA 01970

Philadelphia Maritime
Museum
321 Chestnut Street
Philadelphia, PA 19010

Sea Education Association
P.O. Box 6
Woods Hole, MA 02543

Steamship Historical
Society Collection
University of Baltimore
Library
1420 Maryland Avenue
Baltimore, MD 21201

The Mariners' Museum
100 Museum Drive
Newport News, VA 23606

U.S. Coast Guard
Office of the Historian
2100 2nd Street, S.W.
Washington, DC 20593

U.S. Naval Institute
118 Maryland Avenue
Annapolis, MD 21402

■ ■ ■ ■ ■ ■ ■ ■ ■ ■ ■ ■ ■ ■ ■ ■ ■ ■

PHOTOGRAPHIC SOURCES

Abbreviations used refer to the following:
HABS—Historic American Buildings Survey
HAER—Historic American Engineering Record
JCC—J. Candace Clifford
JPD—James P. Delgado
NMI—National Maritime Initiative

2 all, Robert L. Clifford.   **7** top, JCC; middle and bottom, Robert L. Clifford.   **11** U.S. Naval Institute.   **12** Library of Congress.   **13** both, JCC/NMI.   **16** JCC/NMI. **17** JCC.   **19** top, San Francisco Maritime National Historical Park; bottom, Domino's Inc.   **20–21** Richard K. Anderson, HAER.   **21** JCC/NMI.   **22** Richard Frear/San Francisco Maritime National Historical Park.   **23** Schooner Ernestina Commission.   **24** South Street Seaport Museum. **25** JCC/NMI.   **26** both, JCC/NMI.   **29** San Francisco Maritime National Historical Park.   **33** top, John Ericsson; bottom, Library of Congress.   **34** San Francisco Maritime National Historical Park.   **35** top, JPD/NMI; bottom, Samuel Kitrosser.   **37** San Francisco Maritime National Historical Park.   **38** top, Bill Noonan; bottom, HAER. **39** U.S. Army Corps of Engineers.   **40** Keokuk River Museum.   **42** U.S. Coast Guard Historian's Office. **42–43** Jackson County Parks and Recreation.   **44** JCC/ NMI.   **46** Daniel Lenihan/National Park Service.   **47** JCC/NMI.   **48** Mary Ann Stets/Mystic Seaport Museum. **49** JCC/NMI.   **50** top, JPD/NMI; bottom, both, JCC/ NMI.   **52** Richard Frear/San Francisco Maritime National Historical Park.   **53** Raymond Hartjen/Educational Alternatives.   **54** Columbia River Maritime Museum.   **55** U.S. Naval Institute.   **56** Jet Lowe/HAER.

NEW ENGLAND

58–59 Mary Ann Stets/Mystic Seaport Museum.   **61** JPD/ NMI.   **62** Naval Historical Center.   **63** Claire White-Peterson/Mystic Seaport Museum.   **64** Nancy D'Estang/ Mystic Seaport Museum.   **65** both, Claire White-Peterson/ Mystic Seaport Museum.   **66** both, Claire White-Peterson/ Mystic Seaport Museum.   **67** U.S. Coast Guard.   **69** JPD/ NMI.   **70** Ray Williamson.   **71** top, Ray Williamson; bottom, JCC/NMI.   **73** Alison Kuller.   **75** Maine Historic

Preservation Commission. **76** JPD/NMI. **77** Ken Barnes. **79** top, Schooner J. & E. Riggin; bottom, Daniel Pease. **81** top, Richard Files; bottom left, JCC/NMI; bottom right, Neal Parker. **82** JCC/NMI. **83** JCC/NMI. **84** both, JCC/NMI. **86–87** JCC/NMI. **89** top, USS Massachusetts Memorial Committee; bottom, Floating Drydock Photo. **90** JCC/NMI. **91** JCC/NMI. **92** JPD/NMI. **93** both, JCC/NMI. **94** Cape Ann Historical Society. **95** JPD/NMI. **97** JPD/NMI. **98** Lake Champlain Transportation Company. **99** Shelburne Museum.

MID-ATLANTIC

100–01 JCC/NMI. **102** both, JCC/NMI. **103** JCC/NMI. **104** Naval Historical Center. **105** National Museum of American History. **106** both, JCC/NMI. **107** JCC/NMI. **108** JCC/NMI. **109** JCC/NMI. **110** JCC/NMI. **111** Calvert Marine Museum. **112** top, Paula Johnson/Calvert Marine Museum; bottom left, JCC; bottom right, Holly A. Olden and Laura E. Salarno. **113** top, Chesapeake Bay Maritime Museum; bottom, JCC/NMI. **114** JCC/NMI. **115** JCC/NMI. **116** JCC/NMI. **117** top, U.S. Naval Institute; bottom, David Sharps. **119** Hudson River Maritime Center. **120** Naval Historical Center. **121** both, Paul Ditzel. **122** JCC/NMI. **123** JCC/NMI. **124** Jet Lowe/HAER. **125** South Street Seaport Museum. **126** JCC/NMI. **127** South Street Seaport Museum. **129** JCC/NMI. **130** Gerry Weinstein/South Street Seaport Museum. **131** JPD/NMI. **132** top, Hudson Highlands Cruises and Tours; bottom, Suffolk Marine Museum/Mitch Carucci. **133** top, Suffolk Marine Museum/Richard Milligan; bottom, L. M. Nagle, Jr./Flagship Niagara League. **134** JCC/NMI. **135** top, Philadelphia Ship Preservation Guild; bottom, JCC/NMI. **136** JCC/NMI. **137** JCC/NMI. **138** JCC/NMI.

SOUTH

140–41 JPD/NMI. **142** Robert Holcombe/Confederate Naval Museum. **144** JPD/NMI. **145** top, Patriots Point Development Authority; bottom, JPD/NMI. **146** U.S. Naval Institute. **147** JPD/NMI. **148** JPD/NMI. **150** JPD/NMI. **151** JCC/NMI. **152** JCC/NMI. **153** JCC/NMI.

GULF OF MEXICO

154–55 USS Alabama Battleship Commission. **156** U.S. Army Corps of Engineers. **158** USS Alabama Battleship Commission. **159** Apalachicola Maritime Institute. **160** Paul Weaver/Historic Properties Associated. **161** Louisiana Naval War Memorial Museum.   **162** U.S. Naval Institute.   **163** Delta Queen Steamboat Company.   **165** bottom, JPD/NMI.   **167** JPD/NMI.   **168** Pate Museum of Transportation.   **169** USS Arizona Museum.   **170** U.S. Naval Institute.   **171** JCC/NMI.   **172** Galveston Historical Foundation.   **173** JCC/NMI.   **174** JCC/NMI.   **175** JPD/NMI.

MIDWEST

176–77 Duane Galager/Hazard Corporation.   **179** J. Thomas Dunn/Gateway Riverboat Cruises.   **180** Roger R. Osborne/Dubuque County Historical Society.   **181** top, Keokuk River Museum; bottom, Buffalo Bill Museum.   **183** Jackson County Parks and Recreation.   **184** Jayne C. Henderson.   **185** Lin Caufield Photographers/Belle of Louisville Operating Board.   **186** top, U.S. Coast Guard Historian's Office; bottom, JPD/NMI.   **188** top, JPD/NMI; St. Louis Concessions.   **189** Meriwether Lewis Foundation.   **190** U.S. Naval Institute.

GREAT LAKES

192–93 Stmr. William G. Mather Museum.   **194** Chicago Museum of Science and Industry.   **195** Illinois Steamship Company.   **196** Burton Historical Collection/Detroit Public Library.   **197** JPD/NMI.   **199** JPD/NMI.   **200** top, JPD/NMI; bottom, Naval Historical Center.   **201** U.S. Coast Guard.   **202** JPD/NMI.   **203** top, Lake Michigan Maritime Museum; bottom, Michael Koop/Minnesota Historical Society.   **205** City of Two Harbors.   **206** JPD/NMI.   **207** top, Naval Historical Center; bottom, JPD/NMI.   **208** U.S. Army Corps of Engineers.   **210** JPD/NMI.   **211** City of Cincinnati.   **212** Cleveland Coordinating Committee for Cod.   **214** Kevin Foster/NMI **215** Kevin Foster/NMI.   **217** Kevin Foster/NMI.   **218** James R. Morris/*Troy (Ohio) Daily News.*   **218–19** Manitowoc Maritime Museum.   **221** Larry Murphy/National Park Service.

WEST

222–23 Portland Bureau of Fire/Rescue and Emergency Services.   **224** Bill Hanable.   **226** top, John W. Proctor/San Francisco Maritime National Historical Park; bottom, JPD/NMI.   **227** Nautical Heritage Society.   **228** JPD/NMI.   **229** Port of Oakland.   **230** U.S. Lighthouse Society.   **231** Russell Booth/Association for the Preservation of the Presidential Yacht Potomac.   **232–33** San Francisco Maritime National Historical Park.   **234** top, John W.

Proctor/San Francisco Maritime National Historical Park; bottom, JPD/NMI. **235** Maritime Museum Association of San Diego. **236** Roscoe Smith/San Diego Maritime Society. **237** San Francisco Maritime National Historical Park. **238** San Francisco Maritime National Historical Park. **239** San Francisco Maritime National Historical Park. **241** San Francisco Maritime National Historical Park. **242** top, JCC/NMI; bottom, Richard Frear/San Francisco Maritime National Historical Park. **243** both, San Francisco Maritime National Historical Park; bottom, Richard Frear/San Francisco Maritime National Historical Park. **244** Richard Frear/San Francisco Maritime National Historical Park. **245** San Francisco Maritime National Historical Park. **246** JPD/NMI. **247** JCC/NMI. **248** JPD/NMI. **250** top, Bill Dalquist; bottom, JPD/NMI. **251** Richard Frear/San Francisco Maritime National Historical Park. **253** NMI. **254** top and middle, JPD/NMI; bottom, JCC/NMI. **258** Don Watts/Idaho State Historical Society. **259** Columbia River Maritime Museum. **261** JPD/NMI. **262** John W. Proctor/San Francisco Maritime National Historical Park. **263** JPD/NMI. **264** Northwest Seaport. **265** Jet Lowe/HAER. **266** Phil Nutzhorn/Vessel Zodiac Corporation. **267** Washington Historical Society/Tacoma Fire Department.

268 JPD/NMI. **270–71** HAER. **271** Richard Frear, San Francisco Maritime National Historical Park. **272** JCC/NMI. **273** U.S. Naval Institute. **274** U.S. Naval Institute. **278** top, Presidential Yacht Trust; bottom, JPD/NMI. **279** Laura E. Salarno, HAER. **280–81** Robbyn L. Jackson, HAER. **281** JCC/NMI. **288** Smithsonian Institution **290–91** The Mariners Museum **292–93** Smithsonian Institution **294** The Mariners Museum **296** Smithsonian Institution **312** Smithsonian Institution

INDEX

AUTHORS

James P. Delgado is executive director of the Vancouver Maritime Museum in Vancouver, British Columbia. Before this he served as the maritime historian of the National Park Service in Washington, D.C., where he coordinated the National Maritime Initiative, surveying and documenting most of the ships described in this guide. He also was a historian for the Golden Gate National Recreation Area in San Francisco. The author of 13 books and a contributor to numerous magazines and journals, Delgado was trained as a maritime historian and archeologist at East Carolina University in Greenville, North Carolina.

J. Candace Clifford manages the National Park Service's computerized inventory of maritime resources. Clifford, as staff photographer, recorded many of the ships included here for a 1990 inventory and also for studies leading to nominations as National Historic Landmarks in the National Register. Previously she worked for the publications office of the Advisory Council on Historic Preservation. Clifford majored in history at Hamilton College in Clinton, New York.

In this lithograph of 1874 from William Cullen Bryant's *Picturesque America*, boys fish from a beached catboat, with two scow sloops in the background.